LIBRARY OF HEBREW BIBLE/ OLD TESTAMENT STUDIES

534

Formerly Journal for the Study of the Old Testament Supplement Series

HISTORIOGRAPHY AND IDENTITY (RE)FORMULATION IN SECOND TEMPLE HISTORIOGRAPHICAL LITERATURE

edited by
Louis Jonker

t & t clark

Published by T&T Clark International
A Continuum Imprint
80 Maiden Lane, New York, NY 10038
The Tower Building, 11 York Road, London SE1 7NX

www.continuumbooks.com

Visit the T&T Clark blog at www.tandtclarkblog.com

Library of Congress Cataloging-in-Publication Data
Historiography and identity (re)formulation in Second Temple historiographical literature / edited by Louis Jonker.
        p. cm. — (The library of Hebrew Bible/Old Testament studies ; #534)
    Includes bibliographical references and index.
    ISBN-13: 978-0-567-41062-7 (hardcover : alk. paper)
    1. Bible. O.T. Historical Books—Historiography—Congresses. 2. Jews—History—586 B.C.-70 A.D.—Historiography—Congresses. 3. Jews—Identity—Historiography—Congresses. I. Jonker, Louis C.
    BS1205.6.H5H57 2010
    222'.095—dc22   2010010317

ISBN: 978-0-567-41062-7 (hardback)

Typeset by Pindar NZ, Auckland, New Zealand
Printed in the United States of America by Thomson-Shore, Inc

CONTENTS

List of Contributors   vii
List of Abbreviations   viii
Introduction   xi

PART I: *DELIBERATIONS*
IDENTITIES AND EMPIRE: HISTORIOGRAPHIC QUESTIONS FOR THE
    DEUTERONOMISTIC HISTORY IN THE PERSIAN PERIOD   3
    Jon L. Berquist

THE BOOK OF JUDGES AS A LATE CONSTRUCT   15
    Klaas Spronk

NATIONAL IDENTITY AS COMMENTARY AND AS METACOMMENTARY   29
    Mark G. Brett

COMING TO TERMS WITH EZRA'S MANY IDENTITIES IN EZRA-NEHEMIAH   41
    Mark Leuchter

DAVID'S OFFICIALS ACCORDING TO THE CHRONICLER (1 CHRONICLES 23–27):
    A REFLECTION OF SECOND TEMPLE SELF-CATEGORIZATION?   65
    Louis C. Jonker

OTHERNESS AND HISTORIOGRAPHY IN CHRONICLES   93
    Christine Mitchell

PART II: *RESPONSES*
"IDENTITY (RE)FORMATION AS THE HISTORICAL CIRCUMSTANCES
    REQUIRED"   113
    Raymond F. Person, Jr.

"PERSIAN PERIOD STUDIES HAVE COME OF AGE"   123
    Armin Siedlecki

IDENTITY, POWER, AND THE WORLD OF ANCIENT (BIBLICAL)
    TEXT PRODUCTION   133
    Gerrie Snyman

"CONTINUING THESE CONVERSATIONS"   149
    Jacob L. Wright

Index of Biblical References   169
Index of Authors   172

CONTRIBUTORS

Jon L. Berquist, Executive Editor for Biblical Studies, Westminster John Knox Press, Louisville, Kentucky, USA

Mark G. Brett, Whitley College / Melbourne College of Divinity, Australia

Louis C. Jonker, Department of Old and New Testament, University of Stellenbosch, South Africa

Mark Leuchter, Temple University, USA

Christine Mitchell, St Andrew's College, Saskatoon, Saskatchewan, Canada

Raymond F. Person, Jr., Department of Philosophy and Religion, Ohio Northern University, USA

Armin Siedlecki, Emory University, Atlanta, GA, USA

Gerrie Snyman, Department of Old Testament and Ancient Near Eastern Studies, University of South Africa, South Africa

Klaas Spronk, Department of Old Testament, Protestant Theological University, Kampen, Netherlands

Jacob L. Wright, Emory University, Atlanta, GA, USA (Currently Fellow at the S. Daniel Abraham Center for International and Regional Studies, Tel Aviv University, Israel)

LIST OF ABBREVIATIONS

AB	Anchor Bible
ABD	Anchor Bible Dictionary
ACEBT	Amsterdamse Cahiers voor de Exegese van de Bijbel en zijn Tradities
AOTC	Abingdon Old Testament Commentary
AThANT	Abhandlungen zur Theologie des Alten und Neuen Testaments
BETL	Bibliotheca emphemeridum theologicarum lovaniensium
BHRG	Biblical Hebrew Reference Grammar
Bib	Biblica
BibInt	Biblical Interpretation
BibIntS	Biblical Interpretation Series
BZAW	Beihefte zur Zeitschrift für die alttestamentliche Wissenschaft
CBQ	Catholic Biblical Quarterly
FAT	Forschungen zum Alten Testament
HSM	Harvard Semitic Monographs
HTR	Harvard Theological Review
HUCA	Hebrew Union College Annual
JBL	Journal of Biblical Literature
JHS	Journal of Hebrew Scriptures
JNSL	Journal of Northwest Semitic Languages
JSJ	Journal for the Study of Judaism in the Persian, Hellenistic, and Roman Periods
JSJSup	Journal for the Study of Judaism in the Persian, Hellenistic, and Roman Periods: Supplement Series
JSOT	Journal for the Study of the Old Testament
JSOTSup	Journal for the Study of the Old Testament: Supplement Series
JSS	Journal of Semitic Studies
ICC	International Critical Commentary
LHBOTS	Library of Hebrew Bible / Old Testament Studies

OBO	Orbis Biblicus et Orientalis
OT	Old Testament
OTL	Old Testament Library
SBL	Society of Biblical Literature
SBLDS	Society of Biblical Literature Dissertation Series
SBLSymS	Society of Biblical Literature Symposium Series
SemeiaSt	Semeia Studies
SHANE	Studies in the History of the Ancient Near East
SJOT	Scandinavian Journal of the Old Testament
SOTS	Society of Old Testament Studies
TWAT	Theologisches Wörterbuch zum Alten Testament
VT	Vetus Testamentum
VTSup	Vetus Testamentum: Supplementum
WMANT	Wissenschaftliche Monographien zum Alten und Neuen Testament
ZAW	Zeitschrift für die alttestamentliche Wissenschaft

INTRODUCTION

It is commonly accepted in various disciplines and contexts that history writing often (if not always!) contributes to the process of identity (re)formulation. Contemporary societies of transition are often witness to this fact. Histories are rewritten to continue, adapt, correct, and criticize older traditions from the perspective of the socio-historical circumstances of the present.

The awkward term "identity (re)formulation" used in the title of this book gives expression to the very dynamic character of the process of identity negotiation. No one — not individuals, nor groups of people — start from scratch when negotiating an identity. This process is always in continuity — and in discontinuity — with previous and other formulations of identity. The term "identity negotiation" (also commonly used in this context) would have been another option. It gives expression to the "to and fro" character of the process — always in flux, never-ending. Whichever term is used, this book stands in the constructivist tradition in which an essentialist understanding of identity is opposed.

Using the past in order to find a renewed identity in new (socio-political and socio-religious) circumstances is something also witnessed in Hebrew Bible historiographies. The so-called Deuteronomistic History, as well as the works of Chronicles and Ezra-Nehemiah, is often read from the perspective of a community trying to find a new identity in changed circumstances. New publications and conference sessions of recent years indicate a growing awareness among scholars that investigations into the composition and redaction of these works — although this kind of historical scholarship will always remain essential and important for our understanding of this literature — should be complemented with studies on the pragmatic nature of these writings. Not only the question "How did this literature originate?" should be asked, but also "Why did they originate?" and "What do they do to audiences of reception?"

In the historical books section at the International Meeting 2008 of the Society of Biblical Literature (SBL) in Auckland, a group of Hebrew Bible scholars came together to examine this perspective further. They were invited to attend to any aspect related to the topic of "Historiography and Identity," with illustration from biblical historiographical material. The essays in Part I of this volume go back to those conference presentations.

Thematically, the chapters included in Part I ("Deliberations") can be grouped into three pairs. Two of them (Berquist and Spronk) deal with the Deuteronomistic History, two (Brett and Leuchter) with Ezra-Nehemiah, and another two (Jonker and Mitchell) with Chronicles.

Berquist addresses the question "*how* Old Testament historical books function within the context of the Persian period, whether (or not) those texts were created, assembled, or transmitted during the time of the Persian Empire's influence" (p. 3).[1] He criticized traditional theories about the Deuteronomistic History by indicating that those readings — placing this work in an exilic context — give priority to the institution of monarchy and thereby neglect the books of Joshua and Judges that deal with life without the monarchy. Berquist, therefore, sees this history as a narrative motivated by the interests of the Persian period. He comes to the following conclusion:

> The Deuteronomistic History, as a narrative, is an evolutionary story of state formation, moving from simple forms such as chiefdoms to true states such as the monarchy, and eventually to the post-state realities of imperial domination. However, the Persian period is a time of secondary state formation; that is, the Yehudite community is being formed as a result of imperial expansion, not as the result of internal organization. Thus, the Deuteronomistic History in the Persian period is counterfactual. It cannot serve as a history, but instead operates as a fantasy (or a myth of origins) that engages the reader's imagination about an alternate world detached from the present realities of empire. (p. 11)

Spronk's paper was presented in another session in Auckland and was therefore not originally part of the session on identity. Since his contribution relates well to Berquist's paper, Spronk was also invited to prepare a manuscript for inclusion in this book. In his article, he argues against the traditional hypothesis of a Deuteronomistic History, and indicates that the book of Judges was a later insertion between Joshua and Samuel, composed specifically for the purpose of bridging the gap between these books. He bases his argument mainly on those textual and thematic correspondences that can be observed between Joshua and the beginning of Judges, as well as between the end of Judges and Samuel. He associates this textual development with certain Greek parallels, and therefore dates the composition of Judges relatively late, that is, "[s]omewhere in the early Hellenistic age." Spronk concludes:

---

1 Cross-references within this publication are done by supplying the respective page numbers in brackets. Since the responses refer back to the six articles, this particularly applies to Part II.

It is important to note that there is no direct relation between the Greek parallels and the texts discussed above which were used to connect the book of Judges to the books now surrounding it. This may indicate that on this point the old Israelite tradition was prevalent, whereas in stories not recorded or referred to in the older Israelite literature, the writers felt free to tell them according to the fashion of their time. (p. 27)

Brett argues that there is good evidence in ancient Israelite texts to show that various notions of ethnic and national identity — in something like their modern senses — were proposed and debated in historiographical materials. He examines textual evidence mainly from Ezra-Nehemiah, along with selected scholarly commentaries that have illuminated the ancient debates — notably David Goodblatt's *Elements of Ancient Jewish Nationalism* (2006). However, drawing in particular from Charles Taylor's recent work, *A Secular Age* (2007), he suggests that scholarly discussion of identity discourse becomes anachronistic in important respects if the function of the primary literature is understood to be constructing "an identity" in something like a modern sense.

Leuchter investigates the many identities that Ezra shows in Ezra-Nehemiah. He describes Ezra as follows: "Ezra . . . seems to emerge as a study in contradiction, an elusive shapeshifter who alternately seems to champion disparate agendas and typologies" (p. 43). Leuchter considers three alternative identities of Ezra: (i) As a Zadokite; (ii) As a Deuteronomistic Levite; and (iii) As a Persian Imperial Emissary. He comes to the following conclusion:

The Persian period . . . was a time of dramatic cultural and social realignment among those groups who claimed to share in the legacy of ancient Israel . . . This created a crucible for reifying older cultural and kinship-based standards of identity . . . The Persian paradigm brought an end to this. For all of its outward tolerance and permissiveness, Persia created an even greater challenge, for the descendants of ancient Israel were no longer forced to identify themselves in contradistinction to the imperial power but, rather, as part of it, while still maintaining some grip on their once-independent native heritage. The Ezra that emerges in the chapters of Ezra-Nehemiah reflects this new and confusing social paradigm. (pp. 60–1)

Jonker investigates the Chronicler's presentation of David's officials in 1 Chronicles 23–27 from the perspective of social identity theory (with special reference to self-categorization theory). He comes to the following conclusion: "Those who constructed (and/or edited) these texts were engaged in discourse about what it means to be a Levite in the generic sense" (p. 88). He further shows that one can trace in the texts what were considered to be the "marks of *inclusion* into the prototype," but that "there are also clear indications that an *intragroup self-categorization* is made" in these texts (p. 89).

Mitchell shows that one of the key themes in most ancient historiographies is the construction of identity. Beginning with Herodotus, who set his histories in the context of the conflict between Greek and Persian, ancient authors usually constructed identity in relation to an "Other." Mitchell argues that it is, however, difficult to see the Other in Chronicles. She is of the opinion that those traditional Chronicles studies that show how "Israel" is constructed in the book, have not fully explored the possibilities for seeing the Other. She therefore explores other possibilities for the Other against whom Israel is constructed in Chronicles.

Part II of this book contains four responses to the six contributions in the first part. Four scholars from diverse backgrounds (all with a keen interest and respected expertise in Second Temple literature) critically engage with various aspects of the scholarship offered by the authors. Person observes that the three blocks of historiographical literature, the Deuteronomic History (as he calls it), Ezra-Nehemia and Chronicles, all reflect new phases in the identity (re)formulation process, prompted by the unique historical circumstances in which they originated. Siedlecki, on his part, values the methodological contribution these studies make toward a more adequate description of the complexity of identity (re)formulation in Second Temple literature. Snyman particularly focuses on the power relations involved in the process of identity (re)formulation and the production of texts. Wright engages critically with all six essays and calls for a continuation of the discussion on many of the views expressed.

The format of this book is somewhat unconventional for the field of biblical studies. It arises from the very lively discussion we had at the Auckland session — something that we wanted to imitate and include in the publication. A few scholars (one was also present at the session) were approached afterward to write responses to the prepared manuscripts of the panelists. This process not only served as peer review for the publication of this academic book, but also engaged critically with the views expressed in the papers. These responses are included in the book, since they draw lines between, criticize, and affirm the arguments advanced in the first part of the book. They also open the way for further scientific engagement with this fascinating topic. It is therefore no coincidence that the book closes with the following words from one of the respondees: "I look forward to continuing these worthwhile conversations in other times and places."

I would like to express my gratitude to Alice Hunt, the convenor of the historical books section at the SBL International Meeting, who allowed us to organize the session at the Auckland conference. I furthermore would like to acknowledge Claudia Camp (who was present at the session), for her enthusiasm to turn this into a book for further scholarly deliberations. The wonderful cooperation of my fellow panelists to prepare their papers and manuscripts on time, as well as of those who were invited to write responses, is much appreciated. The very professional service of T&T Clark, particularly of Katie Gallof, made the publication process a great pleasure.

Lastly, I hereby acknowledge the financial support I received for this project from the Research Committee of the University of Stellenbosch, as well as leave granted by my institution to attend the Auckland session.

LOUIS JONKER
February 2010

PART I

DELIBERATIONS

IDENTITIES AND EMPIRE

HISTORIOGRAPHIC QUESTIONS FOR THE DEUTERONOMISTIC HISTORY IN THE PERSIAN PERIOD

Jon L. Berquist

Introduction

In this paper, I want to raise a series of questions regarding the role of historiography and identity in reading Persian-period literature. For me, the prime question is how Old Testament historical books function within the context of the Persian period, whether (or not) those texts were created, assembled, or transmitted during the time of the Persian Empire's influence. Given those functions, how do we interpret these books? What is the interplay of history as the subject of these texts and history as the context for the texts' writing? How are these books works of historiography, and what are the historiographic tasks in reading them?

In addition to these questions of historiography, I wish to pursue questions of identity. How do Old Testament historical books operate as, or within, practices of identity formation? How does identity construction work in historical texts and historiographical interpretation? And what lingering traces of identity concerns are visible in textual and literary records?

In order to deal with these questions, we must first review some of the chief theories and definitions of the Deuteronomistic History.

Theories of the Deuteronomistic History

According to what may well be the consensus of biblical scholarship, the Deuteronomistic History refers to the books of Joshua, Judges, 1–2 Samuel and 1–2 Kings, as a literary unit produced by the same author as the book of Deuteronomy and for which Deuteronomy functions as a prologue.[1] This approach follows and adapts the insights of Martin Noth.[2] The Deuteronomistic History combined several different sources to tell the story of Israel's leaders and the story unfolds in ways that reflect and echo the insights and moral principles of Deuteronomy's law code. This may have been the work of a single author or compiler, or a tradition building process over time, perhaps through a Deuteronomic school.[3]

In most cases, theories of the Deuteronomistic History focus on the exile as the time when these earlier sources were compiled.[4] The purpose of the compilation was to preserve the history of Judah and to understand why the monarchy failed. The Babylonian exiles who grieved the loss of their homeland developed

1 T. Römer, *The So-Called Deuteronomistic History: A Sociological, Historical and Literary Introduction* (London and New York: T&T Clark, 2005); A. G. Auld, "The Former Prophets (Joshua, Judges, 1–2 Samuel, 1–2 Kings)," in *The Hebrew Bible Today: An Introduction to Critical Issues* (eds. S. L. McKenzie and M. P. Graham; Louisville: Westminster John Knox, 1998), pp. 53–68; S. L. McKenzie, "Deuteronomistic History," *ABD* 2 (1992), 160–8.

2 M. Noth, *Überlieferungsgeschichtliche Studien, Schriften der Königsberger Gelehrten Gesellschaft. Geisteswissenschaftliche Klasse 18* (1943). [English Edition: M. Noth, *The Deuteronomistic History* (JSOTSup 15; Sheffield: JSOT Press, 1981).]

3 R. F. Person, *The Deuteronomic School: History, Social Setting, and Literature* (Studies in Biblical Literature 2; Atlanta: SBL; Leiden: Brill, 2002); A. F. Campbell and M. A. O'Brien, *Unfolding the Deuteronomistic History: Origins, Upgrades, Present Text* (Minneapolis: Fortress, 2000).

4 E.g., G. Hens-Piazza, *1–2 Kings* (Abingdon Old Testament Commentaries; Nashville: Abingdon, 2006), pp. 4–5. Other theories have maintained a "double redaction," i.e., a monarchic edition, perhaps during the time of Josiah, followed by an exilic redaction, to account for the post-Josianic material in 2 Kings; e.g., R. D. Nelson, *The Historical Books* (Interpreting Biblical Texts; Nashville: Abingdon, 1998), p. 68; and idem, *The Double Redaction of the Deuteronomistic History* (JSOTSup 18; Sheffield: JSOT Press, 1981); cf. M. A. O'Brien, *The Deuteronomistic History Hypothesis: A Reassessment* (OBO 92; Göttingen: Vandenhoeck & Ruprecht, 1989), who holds for a Josianic writing, an exilic edition, and a minor Persian-period redaction. Because both the exilic-composition theory and the double-redaction theory posit an exilic edition that is formative of the Deuteronomistic History's outlook, I restrict my conversation to the theories of an exilic redaction (whether that exilic redaction would be the first or last version of the text). The mentioned scholars agree that there was an exilic redaction that produced the text as it now stands. For a more nuanced treatment of the Josianic and exilic redactional theories as well as current scholarship that adapts and problematizes both approaches, see T. Römer (ed.), *The Future of the Deuteronomistic History* (BETL 147; Leuven: Leuven University Press, 2000). B. Becking, *From David to Gedaliah: The Book of Kings as Story and History* (OBO 228; Fribourg: Academic Press; Göttingen: Vandenhoeck & Ruprecht, 2007), deals with the possibility of a Hellenistic book of Kings before returning to a more consensus position, yet still with more nuance between story and history than many interpreters have brought to the narrative.

this historical understanding to explain why they lost the land — because of the people's rejection of Torah.[5] The history also sets a foundation for an expectation of restoration. God had originally wanted the people to possess the land and thus God gave proper instructions for a way of life that would allow the people to maintain that possession. Were the people to regain their land, they might be able to follow the law better and keep their control of Judah if given a second chance. The readers of the Deuteronomistic History would know what to do differently if they were allowed to return to Jerusalem.

I would argue that such readings of the Deuteronomistic History take priority on the institution of the monarchy. The kingdom becomes the high point of the story, so that the readers (as scholars imagine them) would naturally want to have the monarchy back again. Likewise, this approach highlights the role of the temple; both because of the story's focus on the construction of the temple and because the temple provided the solution that the Israelites had not understood the first time. Through proper temple worship (or more precisely, through the avoidance of improper worship), the people could retain the land and the monarchy. This also provides a theodicy, by arguing that the destruction of Judah and the disenfranchisement of Jerusalem were not God's fault, but rather the result of insufficient human obedience. The layered theological richness of this interpretation of the Deuteronomistic History may well account for some of the popularity of this scholarly approach to the literature.

Thus, theories of the Deuteronomistic History tend to concentrate on the monarchy and temple, described within the context of exilic longing for these lost institutions and setting the stage for their restoration to come. An inherent messianism lies behind these readings, rooted in the longing for the monarchy and a desire for a monarchy without human failings.

I would argue that this reading and construction of a Deuteronomistic History gives insufficient attention to Joshua and Judges, which become mere prologue to the monarchy and also neglects the ending of the story of 2 Kings in the last chapters. When one reads *all* of the Deuteronomistic History from Joshua to 2 Kings, one sees that much of the narrative is given over to life without the monarchy (usually described as a life that is lacking). Furthermore, the scholarly construction of a Deuteronomistic History is too future-oriented, being overly invested in the longing for a new temple and a new monarchy. This future longing is essential to the understanding of the text (in the theory of the Deuteronomistic History), but

5 R. G. Kratz, *The Composition of the Narrative Books of the Old Testament* (trans. J. Bowden; London: T&T Clark, 2005), pp. 156–7, understands a redactional process of integrating either blocks or strata, but in either case the prime principle for this redaction was the law and specifically the first commandment. As such, the Deuteronomistic History would have grown during the exile following 560 BCE; ibid., pp. 181–3, 206–7, 318.

it is not in the text itself; this longing exists in the minds of the interpreters and in their scholarly reconstructions of the minds of the imagined early (or original) readers. If the primary redactional activity behind the Deuteronomistic History took place within Israel's Babylonian exile, then the restoration of a monarchy (or a colonial state that substitutes for the monarchy) would be in the author's/editor's future as well.

The Deuteronomistic History in the Persian Period

Instead of considering the Deuteronomistic History as a narrative motivated by exilic (or earlier) interests, I wish to focus on the Persian period (538–333 BCE).[6] I do not mean to argue that there were no texts or traditions similar to Deuteronomy, Joshua, Judges, Samuel, or Kings prior to 538 BCE, or that the texts of those books were created without concern for historical believability. However, within the Persian period, this compilation of literature functions not as a historical reminiscence that asks questions of "who were we?" or "how can we restore the prior glories?" but instead operates as a construction of identity, asking the question, "who are the Yehudites?" for the postexilic community. Thus, I argue for a shift away from the exilic images of self-justification as a motivation for the writing of the Deuteronomistic History. Instead, the postexilic motives would have to do with discovering where the Yehudites fit into an imperial culture dominated by Persia.[7]

However the Deuteronomistic History functions as a record or reflection of history, these books also participate in the history of the time of their creation. Usual theories of the writing of the Deuteronomistic History require an exilic community of scribes reflecting on the failings of past monarchic history in the light of theological interpretation. Not only did this community undertake this contemplation, they also wrote it and preserved the writings over a period of time. While I find it likely that persons in the exile may well have been thinking in these ways, I think it is improbable that such an exilic community wrote the text of Deuteronomy through 2 Kings. The literary skills required for such a document, represented in our extant literature as six separate books, would have included

6 Römer, *So-Called Deuteronomistic History*, pp. 165–83, offers an excellent introduction to the Deuteronomistic History in its entirety. His treatment is especially to be commended for including a section on the editing of the Deuteronomistic History in the Persian period, thus refusing to collapse the exilic redaction and the final redaction into a single entity.

7 See J. L. Berquist, *Judaism in Persia's Shadow: A Social and Historical Approach* (Minneapolis: Fortress, 1995; Eugene: Wipf & Stock, 2006); and idem, "Constructions of Identity in Postcolonial Yehud," in *Judah and the Judeans in the Persian Period* (eds. O. Lipschits and M. Oeming; Winona Lake: Eisenbrauns, 2006), pp. 53–66.

more physical resources than the exilic community possessed, in order to write and preserve such a sizeable corpus, and to transmit such a literary complex as a unit throughout the time of exile and beyond.

Instead, it seems more feasible that this large body of literature was a production of the Persian period.[8] During the rule of the Persian Empire, the capacity for writing and the infrastructure to support the preservation of texts was significant, reflecting certain imperial priorities related to record keeping and other written documentation as part of the imperial ideology and bureaucratic process. This suggests that the Persian imperial scribes may well have been the authors of the Deuteronomistic History. The Persian Empire possessed and deployed the means of authorship and archival preservation, whereas an exilic Jewish community in Babylonia probably did not have access to such resources.

The Persian Empire would have had several possible motives for sponsoring the writing of the Deuteronomistic History, besides a strictly archival interest. Let me suggest three literary themes of the Deuteronomistic History in particular, all of which would fit Persian imperial strategies. First, the Deuteronomistic History explains why the Yehudites do not have self-governance. The reason is that their state lost in military conflict against Babylonia. Not only was this a military defeat, but it was also the fault of Judah's own political leaders, and even God supported the end of the Judean state. Second, the Deuteronomistic History shows why Jerusalem is the appropriate center for self-identity and regional administration. Numerous other capitals, families, shrines, and regions of Israel and Judah have some legitimate historical claim on leadership roles, but none of them were, in the end, the religious centers that the Judeans themselves chose, that turned out well for the people, or that God supported. Only Jerusalem could function as the community's political, legal, financial, religious, and civic center. Third, almost none of Israel's or Judah's leaders served the people well, with a few noteworthy exceptions mostly limited to the more distant past. More than that, the governments of Israel and Judah were, for the most part, unsavory and unhelpful. The Deuteronomistic History depicts Yehudites as having a history of poor self-governance, and can argue within an imperial context that they should not be allowed self-governance, perhaps even for their own protection and self-interest.

Thus, the Deuteronomistic History serves an imperial function, presenting a story in which the Yehudites are not capable of self-governance. They lost their claim on independent control of the land rightly (according to their own religion as well as their own historiography), and they are better off without self-control.

---

8 J. L. Berquist, "Scribes, Archives, and the Cultural Poetics of Yehud," (paper presented at New Historicism and Biblical Studies Consultation, SBL annual meeting, Boston, 1999).

Note that the Deuteronomistic History itself does not focus on the key ideas of "exilic identity," such as emotional attachment to the land or the need to worship in only one place. These are not factors that are emphasized at the end of the Deuteronomistic History's story. Instead, the story ends in 2 Kings with a horrific series of failed rulers who have jeopardized the entire people of the land (2 Kgs 23:26–25:26) and an evil former king who needs to eat at the emperor's table (2 Kgs 24:9; 25:27-30).[9] The Deuteronomistic History does not end in longing for restoration, and there remains no sense that a renewed monarchy could do any better.

This imperial function for the Deuteronomistic History accords with known patterns of Persian rule. The empire used writing for archival means, to store within central locations, the documentation of their rule and its legitimacy. Such documents could have been archived within imperial palaces and capital cities within Persia, but vernacular accounts would almost certainly have been stored within local shrines and other administrative outposts. As archives, these are not meant to be texts that are read; they are meant to be preserved, untouched.[10]

If this is the case, then the Deuteronomistic History constructs identity in an imperial context. That is, the text forms the reader's Persian identity as part of the imperial power. If so, then neither the Yehudites nor the exiles are the Deuteronomistic History's intended audience. If scribes or other Yehudites were to read these texts, the reading would become a part of their transfer of allegiance to the empire. They would read it as part of becoming Persian vassals, owing a debt to their rightful rulers and beginning to see themselves as parts of the empire rather than as members of a separate people.

Of course, this assertion contradicts much of what has been said about the Deuteronomistic History, and especially about its role in exilic identity formation. One can no longer posit, on the basis of the Deuteronomistic History, the presence of an exilic community that longs for restoration and strives to keep itself together while being an ethnic minority in Babylonia.

---

9   I take this ending as a legitimate part of the Deuteronomistic History and, indeed, as one of its key points. Römer, *So-Called Deuteronomistic History*, p. 177, considers it to be a late, Persian-period addition to the story.

10   J. L. Berquist, "The Politics of Canon in Persian Yehud," (paper presented at Social-scientific Study of the Second Temple Period section, SBL annual meeting, Denver, 2001); and D. C. Polaski, "What Mean These Stones? Inscriptions, Textuality and Power in Persia and Yehud," in *Approaching Yehud: New Approaches to the Study of the Persian Period.* (SemeiaSt 50; ed. J. L. Berquist; Atlanta: SBL, 2007), pp. 37–48.

Identity after Empire

However, the literature known as the Deuteronomistic History survived the Persian Empire. In a new context, the literature took on another life, and with it, another ideology and another set of meanings.

At some point, the archival copy or copies of the Deuteronomistic History stored in the Second Jerusalem Temple caught the interest of scribes. The text found a new readership. These scribes occupied a strange social space as bureaucrats within the Persian Empire's far-flung administrative apparatus while simultaneously living as members of a local Yehudite community.[11] This hybrid identity gave them access to texts such as the Deuteronomistic History while giving them a different reading position.[12] This ambivalent relationship to empire within a semi-autonomous colony, as expressed in hybridized identity, begins a postcolonial life of the text.

First of all, these scribes begin to read the Deuteronomistic History as a text, rather than an archive. In this reading, they change the function of the text. Through reading, they create the text as a narrative, instead of an object. When they read as postcolonial peoples, they begin to discover a history that they claim as their own. This claiming-as-their-own is not necessarily a historical reality or an ethnic reality; it is a matter of identity.

In this reading, the scribes discover a past, a time before the empire. Although they live at empire's geographic edge and in the approach of the Persian Empire's chronological end, they first experience the end of the empire through reading about the time before the empire. The text of the Deuteronomistic History, in this sense, resists empire; the text imagines a world without the empire. In particular, the text celebrates heroes of the past, for whom the reader can yearn. These characters such as David, Solomon, Josiah, and others are then seen as persons who resisted empire or ran their own politics.

In terms of genre, therefore, these Persian-period scribes are reading the Deuteronomistic History not so much as historiography. That is, they would not read it as a record of the past, and they would not read to understand what happened. The text presents its own logic of what happened (bad worship resulted in political catastrophe, which God solved through empire), but the reading position has changed. No longer is the reader one who is becoming imperial; these readers living at the edge of empire are becoming postcolonial.

If so, then the scribes are not reading these books as either history or historiography, nor the Deuteronomistic History as historical fiction. By "historical

---

11   J. L. Berquist, "Wisdom and Scribes in Persian Yehud," (paper presented at Literature and History of the Persian Period section, SBL annual meeting, Nashville, 2000).

12   Berquist, "Constructions of Identity."

fiction," I mean a genre that presents a compelling narrative set in the midst of plausible facts about the past, as the readers would have known those facts.[13] The success of the Deuteronomistic History as literature for these scribes is not based upon plausibility. Instead, they are reading for the power of the text to create an alternative world. These postexilic readers interpret the Deuteronomistic History as a story about how life could be like in consciously counterfactual contexts, that is, the context of life without empire. Such life is not depicted as desirable within the Deuteronomistic History; the pre-imperial life of judges and monarchs is nasty and brutish and ultimately ineffectual in building lasting identity or society. Tribalism and monarchy alike repeatedly fail to bring peace, prosperity, solidarity, or faith. But the power of the text comes alive in this reading that imagines a counterfactual world. In terms of genre, this is neither historiography nor historical fiction; the genre is fantasy. In fantasy, the reader imagines a world that is obviously different from the present experience. Fantasies are important texts for the construction of identity; in fact, they are still genres thought most suitable for childhood and adolescence, when identity formation is pertinent.

These Persian-period scribes read the Deuteronomistic History as an escape from their imperial, bureaucratized existence. They imagine a different world. They long for independence, even though the text shows self-reliance to be miserable. In their reading, they repress the daily experience of empire, and yet at the same time, they are reproducing empire, both in the sense that they are consuming an imperial text and in that they return to their lives as imperial bureaucrats.

These scribes are not alone. I would suggest that biblical scholarship, festooned in its critical objectivity, has read the Deuteronomistic History as fantasy — but as a peculiar kind of fantasy named history. In such reading, scholars have told the stories of ancient kings, at times even in romantic ways. Scholars have recognized the powerful narrativity of these stories, interpreting them as stories of rise, establishment, and authorization for a monarchy. Repeatedly through the history of interpretation, the Deuteronomistic History has become legitimation for the rise of new monarchies. Scholars read the Deuteronomistic History, and become imperial themselves.

Yet the text itself continues to resist this imperialist reading, or at least the text

---

13 R. Boer, *Novel Histories: The Fiction of Biblical Criticism* (Sheffield: Sheffield Academic Press, 1997; repr. Atlanta: SBL, 2006), has argued that Noth creates the Deuteronomistic History as though it were a historical novel. My own reading of Noth parallels Boer's reading significantly, although I choose a different "reading as though" while Boer pursues a metacommentary (or a meta-metacommentary) into fiction. Becking's distinction between story and history reflects some of the same distinction I wish to draw between reading as historical fiction and reading as historiography.

persists in offering grist for alternative readings. The Deuteronomistic History can be read as a recounting or documentation of how all conquests fail, how genocides destroy the aggressors as well as the victims, how monarchies (and all governments) dwindle and consume themselves.

In the present as in the ancient past, the text itself does not produce identity. Instead, the reading of the text offers conflicting opportunities for identity, imperial or postcolonial. The work of historiography is necessarily a work of identity formation, and through that newly formed identity, one reads the historiography differently.

Toward a New Understanding of the Deuteronomistic History

The Deuteronomistic History, as a narrative, is an evolutionary story of state formation, moving from simple forms such as chiefdoms to true states such as the monarchy, and eventually to the post-state realities of imperial domination. However, the Persian period is a time of secondary state formation; that is, the Yehudite community is being formed as a result of imperial expansion, not as the result of internal organization.[14] Thus, the Deuteronomistic History in the Persian period is counterfactual. It cannot serve as a history, but instead operates as a fantasy (or a myth of origins) that engages the reader's imagination about an alternate world detached from the present realities of empire. The Deuteronomistic History obscures the formation of colonial Yehud by claiming that Israel was a failed state. As such, the text distracts the Persian-period reader from the realities of the empire, while at the same time reinforcing the presumed reality of empire.

Still, the Deuteronomistic History resists empire by imagining an alternative world in which smaller communities (monarchies, clans, or villages) can live independently. In these acts of imagination the seeds of resistance can be found.

The scholarly move to read the Deuteronomistic History as an exilic text is likewise a fantasy, or else a misreading of the text by displacing the history into a different context, obscuring the empire by imagining the story in a time of exile and imagining exile as a time without government instead of as a time of empire. Most theories of the Deuteronomistic History also emphasize a theological component, that is, a condemnation of wrong Israelite worship that resulted in political demise, whereas the story concerns itself more with the impossibility of human governance.

Perhaps the failings of the Deuteronomistic History theory (or, put otherwise, the ways in which these theories succeed as misreadings of the text) lie in the choices of boundaries for the text. Instead of reading Joshua-Judges-Samuel-Kings

---

14 Berquist, *Judaism in Persia's Shadow*, p. 245.

as individual books or as a unit, the theory of the Deuteronomistic History fuses this text with a prior agenda and a subsequent context. The prior agenda is that of Deuteronomy, but perhaps the theory reads the covenantal and moral parts of Deuteronomy with greater attention than it accounts for the anti-monarchic statements within Deuteronomy. The subsequent context is that of exilic longing for restoration, a scholarly commonplace that has no grounding. Within this longing is a messianism, a desire for a next step in the story that the story itself does not provide. Caught between Deuteronomy's Moses and an awaited messiah, scholarship has turned these historiographies into a Deuteronomistic History of its own making, a misreading of imperial archives and postcolonial fantasy.

Yet this misreading is not a new one. Not long after the Persian-period books of the Deuteronomistic History, the Chronicler wrote again, expanding the context to stories, earlier than Moses. Ben Sira later fuses this grand Primary History with the prophets, subsumed in a wisdom text. Subsequent changes of context include Old Testament theologies, the story of the Bible from Genesis to Revelation, creeds and canonical readings. This history of misreading is a fine history indeed.

Theoretical Considerations for Historiography and the Formation of Identity

A single text produces multiple identities, depending upon the readers. Reading for history (i.e., what happened to others) and reading for identity (i.e., who am I and what is possible in my world) are two different but related strategies of reading. In most cases, each strategy justifies itself in terms of the other, or at least in unstated assumptions about the other.

Thus, the historiographical effects of these texts and the identity formation processes are both ancient and modern. In this reality, two implications should be noted. One has to do with the scholarly distinction between emic and etic, that is, between the descriptions of an ancient society in terms modern scholars would recognize over against the descriptions that native members of that ancient society would recognize. Such a distinction, while still heuristically and pedagogically beneficial, may not be sustainable, because both ancients and moderns are involved in identity construction as they reflect on the same texts and imagine historical contexts for them. A second implication has to do with the maximalist–minimalist debates still ongoing as the chief expression of current scholarly interest in historiography. To some extent, these parallel discourses are inevitable results of the ways historiography and identity are interrelated.

A single text reflects multiple possible genres, depending upon the reading strategy. In a postmodern sense, no text contains unambiguous clues as to how it should be read. Instead, interpretive communities have habits of reading that claim genre recognition as a basis for producing certain readings of texts, but these readings are not objective or incontrovertible. It may be more helpful to think of these genres as *uses* of the text, and thus to think of imperial or decolonizing uses of the Deuteronomistic History. This will combine the need to examine historiography and the move to find identity (both ancient and modern) in the act of our reading.

THE BOOK OF JUDGES AS A LATE CONSTRUCT

Klaas Spronk

Introduction

The exegesis of the book of Judges may have been dominated too long by the discussion about the Deuteronomistic History. When in the middle of the twentieth century, Martin Noth presented his theory about the books from Deuteronomy to Kings as the work of one author — describing the conquest and loss of the promised land, using different sources, but arranging and framing them from a clear view on the reasons of the downfall of Israel and Judah — this theory was welcomed as a brilliant new insight, which was much more compelling than the many contradictory attempts to find traces of the sources that seem to have been used in the Pentateuch.[1] After the initial success, however, came the refinement of the theory leading to the "unsettling wide array of conflicting options that encourage scepticism of past attempts to sort out discrete redactional layers in the Dtr history."[2] The many detailed analyses can no longer be held together in one coherent view. The Deuteronomist(s) who was or were held responsible for large parts of the historical books of the Old Testament became "elusive."[3] The situation with regard to the book of Judges is well illustrated by the recent

---

1 R. Kratz, *Die Komposition der erzählenden Bücher des Alten Testaments: Grundwissen der Bibelkritik* (Göttingen: Vandenhoeck & Ruprecht, 2000), p. 219. H. J. Kraus, *Geschichte der historisch-kritischen Erforschung des Alten Testaments* (2. Überarbeitete und erweiterte Auflage; Neukirchen-Vluyn: Neukirchener Verlag, 1969), pp. 458–9, wrote: "Diese Erklärung zum Werk des Deuteronomisten hat eine beschämende Lücke in der alttestamentlichen Wissenschaft geschlossen."

2 S. A. Meier, "Review of Raymond F. Person Jr., *The Deuteronomic School: History, Social Setting, and Literature* Atlanta: Society of Biblical Literature, 2002," *JBL* 122 (2003), 160–5 (160).

3 Cf. *Those Elusive Deuteronomists: The Phenomenon of Pan-Deuteronomism* (eds.

publication of two monographs in the classic tradition of redaction-critical studies but with totally different conclusions. In the first, Philippe Guillaume challenges Noth's theory about a Deuteronomistic writer/redactor and presents a new reconstruction of the growth of text.[4] In the second, Andreas Scherer, who calls Guillaume's ideas "ebenso verblüffend wie befremdlich,"[5] presents his own conclusions as a confirmation of Noth's view, although he finds a "polyphony of Deuteronomistic voices." Scherer also notes a new trend in the historical critical approach to the problem of the relation between the Pentateuch and the Former Prophets: a farewell to the theory of the Deuteronomists and a return of the idea of a Hexateuch which was so popular in the period before Martin Noth. Scherer does not agree with this trend, but he is even more critical with regard to those who want to escape the problems by limiting themselves to a synchronic analysis of the Masoretic text as it is transmitted to us. In his view this leads to simplification, not leaving room for the different voices of the different layers of the text. What is usually presented as respect for the text as a unity results in a limited view on the text based on the framework the exegete imposes onto it:

> Der Wunsch, den Texten möglichst hohen Respekt zu zollen, führt so, wenn auch ungewollt, zu einem Resultat, das auf das Gegenteil hinausläuft. Statt Exegese zu betreiben, die dem Facettenreichtum der mehrstufige entstandenen Texte Rechnung trägt, wird, bedingt durch den Zwang, alles auf ein und derselben Ebene zu betrachten, Eisegese kultiviert.[6]

The synchronic analysis of the book of Judges usually leads to beautiful results: clear structures around interesting themes. But other synchronic studies lead to other structures and other central themes — just as almost every redaction critic nowadays seems to have his or her own Deuteronomist.[7]

An interesting and promising new approach is suggested in Graeme Auld's

---

L. S. Schearing and S. L. McKenzie; JSOTSup 268; Sheffield: Sheffield Academic Press, 1999).

4 P. Guillaume, *Waiting for Josiah: The Judges* (JSOTSup 385; London: T&T Clark, 2004).

5 A. Scherer, *Überlieferungen von Religion und Krieg: Exegetische und religionsgeschichtliche Untersuchungen zu Richter 3–8 und verwandten Texten* (WMANT 105; Neukirchen-Vluyn: Neukirchener Verlag, 2005), p. 9.

6 Ibid., p. 18.

7 See also the discussion between G. Andersson, *The Book and Its Narratives: A Critical Examination of Some Synchronic Studies of the Book of Judges* (Örebro: Universitetsbibliotheket, 2001) and G. Wong, "Narratives and Their Contexts: A Critique of Greger Andersson with Respect to Narrative Autonomy," *SJOT* 20 (2006), 216–30; with the response again by Andersson, "A Narratologist's Critical Reflections on Synchronic Studies of the Bible: A Response to Gregory T. K. Wong," *SJOT* 21 (2007), 261–74.

theory about the "Book of Two Houses" (that is: the house of David and the house of the God of Israel built there by Solomon) as "the root-work that supports the whole tree of Genesis–Kings."[8] This "Book of Two Houses" would have received a first introduction in the stories about Samuel, and afterward the story of Moses to the Judges would have been added in anticipation of the "two houses," that is, it was written with the books of Samuel and Kings in mind and many of its stories appear to contain "pre-playing elements of the royal story."[9]

In the present article, I will elaborate on this idea, starting with a study of the way in which the book of Judges is connected to the book Joshua. Can the combination of correspondences to and differences with the book of Joshua be explained from the suggested point of view? Is it possible to relate the way that the book of Judges is connected to the book of Joshua, to the way the first-mentioned is connected to the books of Samuel and Kings? If so, it may be possible to support the idea of the book of Judges as a late construct, the work of a writer who connected the older history of Israel, contained in the books of Genesis to Joshua, with the newer history of its kings. This can perhaps be explained within the framework of Karel van der Toorn's theory about the Hebrew Bible as a product of scribal culture. He compares the production of the history of Israel with the work of Berossus in Babylon and Manetho in Egypt, collecting and editing older material in an effort to publish and preserve a national literature.[10] It would explain both the presence of such an extent of heterogeneous material in the book, as well as the many homogeneous elements that in the eyes of so many scholars point in the direction of a coherent literary piece of art. The late date of the book in its present form would also explain why the reader who comes from the book of Joshua is hardly prepared for this follow-up and why there are hardly any references in the books coming after the book of Judges to the persons and events as they are described there. For instance, from the reference in 1 Sam. 12:8-11, where a retrospective is given — starting with Jakob and

8 G. Auld, *Samuel at the Threshold: Selected Works of Graeme Auld* (SOTS Monographs; Aldershot: Ashgate, 2004), p. 24.

9 G. Auld, "The Deuteronomist between History and Theology," in *Congress Volume Oslo 1998* (VTSup 80; eds. A. Lemaire and M. Sæbø; Leiden: Brill, 2000), pp. 353–67 (355); also his "Samuel and Genesis: Some Questions of John Van Seter's 'Yahwist'," in *Rethinking the Foundations. Essays in Honour of John Van Seters* (eds. S. L. McKenzie *et al.*; BZAW 294; Berlin: De Gruyter, 2000), pp. 23–32 (24–5). Similar conclusions about the Judges as "protokings" are found with M. Z. Brettler, "The Book of Judges: Literature as Politics," *JBL* 108 (1989), 395–418 (407) and P. J. van Midden, "A Hidden Message? Judges as Foreword to the Book of Kings," in *Unless Some One Guide Me . . . Festschrift for Karel A. Deurloo* (eds. J. W. Dyk *et al.*; ACEBT Suppl 2; Maastricht: Shaker Publishing), pp. 77–86.

10 K. van der Toorn, *Scribal Culture and the Making of the Hebrew Bible* (Cambridge: Harvard University Press, 2007), p. 259.

ending with Samuel — one gets the impression that the scribe was familiar with that period, but he only mentions a selection from what is recorded in the book of Judges. Some important Judges, like Othniel, Ehud, Deborah, and Samson, are left out. Gideon is mentioned by his other name, Jerubbaal, and the name of Barak is replaced by the otherwise unknown Bedan. The fact that Samson is missing is all the more remarkable because in the survey of 1 Samuel 12 the Philistines are mentioned among the enemies of Israel. The only one of the saviors named here who can be held responsible for the reported liberation from the Philistines is Samuel. It seems that the author of these words was not familiar with the stories of Samson as we know them as part of the history of Israel. This apparent omission in the canonical text was also noticed by the ancient scribes and some of them felt obliged to correct the text by replacing in 1 Sam. 12:11, the name of Samuel by that of Samson (as can be found in some manuscripts of the Septuagint and in the Peshitta). The Hebrew text — as the most problematic — has to be regarded here as representing the older stadium of the text. Apparently, most of the stories of the Judges were known, as can also be derived from the reference to the death of Abimelek mentioned in 2 Sam. 11:22, but the information may have been taken from other sources than the book of Judges.

If the book of Judges in its present form can be regarded as a late construct, this would also give a plausible explanation for the fact that the ancient Greek version of the end of the book of Joshua offers a different account of the continuation of the history of Israel compared to the way it is told in the book of Judges. In the final lines, which have no equivalent in Hebrew, reference is made to the ark. In this way it is related to the book of Samuel, because the ark is not mentioned in the book of Judges. It is also stated that, the Israelites worshipped other gods and that the Lord therefore delivered them into the hands of Eglon, king of Moab. This suggests that the introductory chapters of Judges were not known to the translator, because in the book of Judges the reference to this king is found in 3:12. Did the book of Judges receive its present form after the Greek translation of the book of Joshua was made?

The Connection to the Book of Joshua

The discussion about the relation between the final chapters of Joshua and the beginning of Judges is complicated.[11] Scholars nowadays usually speak, following the title of an article by Erhard Blum, of a "compositional knot."[12]

---

11 Cf. the summary by E. Noort, *Das Buch Josua: Forschungsgeschichte und Problemfelder* (Erträge der Forschung 292; Darmstadt: Wissenschaftliche Buchgesellschaft, 1998), pp. 198–205.

12 E. Blum, "Der kompositionelle Knoten am Übergang von Josua zu Richter: Ein

Many see it as their task to unravel it. The recent monograph by Mareike Rake on this subject has not made things easier.[13] According to her, in most of the cases of parallel texts in the book of Joshua and the first chapters of Judges, the text in Joshua is dependent upon those in Judges 1. She is also of the opinion, contrary to the outcomes of many other redaction-critical studies,[14] that the report of Joshua's death in Judg. 2:7-9 should be dated earlier than the version in Joshua 24. The problem with this way of reconstructing the growth of the text as a process of numerous editorial activities, is that one can never be certain on the basis of the transmitted text that one text is older or more original than the other. One always has to reckon with the possibility, as is admitted by Rake, that in a next stage the older text may have been re-edited on the basis of the later text. Without new evidence there will never come an end to this discussion. One can, however, also look at the problem of the relation between the books of Joshua and Judges from the angle of the book of Judges as a late construct.

There can be no doubt about it that in its present form, the book of Judges is presented as a sequel to the book of Joshua. This is already indicated by its beginning. Just like the book of Joshua it starts with the reference of the death of the primary figure in the preceding book: "It happened after the death of Joshua/ Moses." According to critical scholars things become problematic, however, when one notes the — sometimes contradictory — repetitions in the first two chapters. Taking a closer look it can be noted that the quotations contain positive information about Judah, taken from Josh. 15:13-14 (cf. Judg. 1:20), 15-19 (cf. Judg. 1:11-15), and negative information about the other tribes, taken from Josh. 15:63 (cf. Judg. 1:21, with the Benjaminites instead of the Judahites), 16:10 (cf. Judg. 1:29), and 17:11-13 (cf. Judg. 1:27-28). To this is added new information, distributed in a similar way and therefore the dichotomy is deepened: a positive stance toward Judah and a negative one toward the other tribes. There are no compelling reasons to assume that in these parallels Judges is not dependent on Joshua. It is far more likely that we have to see the first chapters of the book of Judges as a kind of recapitulation of the book of Joshua.[15] The story is

---

Entflechtungsvorschlag," in *Deuteronomy and Deuteronomic Literature: Festschrift C. H. W. Brekelmans* (BETL 133; eds. M. Vervenne and J. Lust; Leiden: Brill, 1997), pp. 181–212.

13 M. Rake, *"Juda wird aufsteigen!": Untersuchungen zum ersten Kapitel des Richterbuches* (BZAW 367; Berlin: De Gruyter, 2006).

14 Cf., among others, E. Noort, "Josua 24, 28–31, Richter 2, 6–9 und das Josuagrab: Gedanken zu einem Straßenbild," in *Biblische Welten: Festschrift für Martin Metzger zu seinem 65. Geburtstag* (OBO 123; ed. W. Zwickel; Göttingen: Vandenhoeck & Ruprecht, 1993), pp. 109–30, 113–15; H. N. Rösel, "Lässt sich eine nomistische Redaktion im Buch Josua feststellen," *ZAW* 119 (2007), 184–9.

15 This interpretation can be compared to the way in which S. Frolov explains the repetition in his article "Joshua's Double Demise (Josh. xxiv 28–31; Judg. ii 6–9): Making

retold from a new perspective. The character of this new perspective is indicated at the beginning. Just as Joshua took over from Moses, now Judah takes over from Joshua. Judah is presented as appointed by YHWH (1:2). Judah proves to be competent for this task, because, just like Joshua, it is able to deal with the kings from Canaan (1:5-8; cf. Joshua 10). Exactly where Judges 1 differs from Joshua, it concerns the obvious attempt to put Judah in a more favorable light than it appears in the text of Joshua. This is what has happened in 1:21, where — compared with the parallel in Josh. 15:63 — the name of the Judahites is replaced by the name of the Benjaminites as the ones who must be blamed for not driving out the Jebusites from Jerusalem.[16] In 1:8 it is told that the Judahites conquered Jerusalem. Because there is no reference in 1:8 of the Jebusites, we can assume that in the eyes of the author it does not contradict 1:21. Conquering and burning a city is one thing; definitively driving away the inhabitants is something else. The same distinction is made in v. 18-19: Judah subdued Gazah, Ashkelon and Ekron, but at the same time it is remarked that it was not able to supplant the inhabitants of the Philistine coast, which is nothing else than the region of the mentioned cities.[17] What is more important, however, is that in this way — by combining 1:8 and 1:21 — not only the negative picture of Judah in Josh. 15:63 could be corrected, but it also left room for the later report of David taking the city of Jerusalem and making it his capital (2 Sam. 5:6-12). Note that in the story of David the Jebusites are explicitly mentioned: "the king and his men went to Jerusalem unto the Jebusites, the inhabitants of the land." This underlines the parallel with Judg. 1:8, 21.

With regard to the tribes, Judges 1 has the same order as Joshua 14–19, except for Simeon and Benjamin. In the list according to the book of Joshua the tribe of Simeon is mentioned in the middle, after Benjamin. In Judg. 1:3 Simeon has moved to the beginning and is closely related to Judah. The probable reason for this is that already in the book of Joshua, the tribes of Judah and Simeon are closely related. According to Josh. 19:19 Simeon's heritage was surrounded by the land that was given to Judah. So it seems to be only logical that when Judah goes, Simeon follows. The position of Simeon as second in the line of tribes also has a parallel in 1 Chronicles 4, where Simeon is mentioned after Judah and before Reuben. The fact that Benjamin is mentioned earlier in Judges 1 — compared with the list in Joshua — can be related to the place that this tribe takes

---

Sense of a Repetition," *VT* 58 (2008), 315–23, but he restricts his theory to Judg. 1:27–2:5 as a re-evaluation of Joshua 14–24.

16 Cf. J. C. de Vos, *Das Los Judas: Über Entstehung und Ziele der Landbeschreibung in Josua 15* (VTSup 95; Leiden: Brill, 2003), pp. 166–7.

17 Cf. B. Halpern, *The First Historians: The Hebrew Bible and History* (San Francisco: Harper & Row, 1988), p. 136.

in the rest of the book of Judges. In ch. 20–21, it plays a prominent part in the battle between the tribes. In this battle, it is again Judah who goes first. This is indicated in 20:18 where precisely the same question and the same answer by YHWH is indicated compared with 1:2.

The story of the messenger in Bochim, the following reports of Joshua releasing the people, of the people serving YHWH during the life of Joshua, of Joshua's death, and finally, of the next generation forgetting YHWH (2:1-10), can be read together[18] and be regarded as a deliberate reaction to the book of Joshua as well. The connection is made by the reference to Gilgal in 2:1. This reminds of the passing through the river Jordan and the 12 stones placed there as a memory of what YHWH had done for his people (Josh. 4:19-20). When the messenger is said to have come from Gilgal, this is more than topographical information. In Judges 2 the messenger of YHWH repeats what Joshua had spoken according to Joshua 24, referring to YHWH's acts on behalf of his people in the past and to Israel's obligations within the covenant with YHWH. The resolute answer of the people in Josh. 24:24 is in glaring contrast with the outcome as established in Judg. 2:2. They have not acted according to their solemn words. The repetition of the report of Joshua releasing the people and of Joshua's death and burial, already described in Josh. 24:28-31, can be explained as a means to emphasize the change in reaction of the people. In Josh. 24:31, the positive attitude of the people is mentioned after the death of Joshua; in Judg. 2:7 it is mentioned before the death of Joshua, whereas after his death the covenant is soon forgotten. So the emphasis is on the reaction of the people. From this point of view the repeated message of Joshua's death can be explained as a consequence of the recapitulation of the whole book of Joshua as an introduction to the book of Judges. It may seem to be illogical, but it is functional.

The Connection to the Books of Samuel

Keeping the results in mind, the analysis of the way the book of Judges is related to the previous book, we shall now look at the way it is related to the following book, namely Samuel. On some points they correspond; the book of Judges is connected to the previous book of Joshua with reference to the missing leader ("After the death of Joshua"), the final chapters emphasize repeatedly the fact that Israel did not have a king. The repeated phrase "in these days there was no king in Israel" (17:6; 18:1; 19:1) is generally acknowledged as a pro-monarchical refrain, which uses the horrible stories in the last chapters of the book of Judges

18 Cf. ibid., p. 137 and A. van der Kooij, "'And I Also Said': A New Interpretation of Judges II 3," *VT* 45 (1995), 294–306 (305–6), for the opinion that Judg. 1:1–3:6 is a coherent introduction to the era of the judges.

as arguments in favor of the appointment of a king with the power to bring peace and justice.

Apart from this correspondence, there are a number of topographical correspondences between the books of Judges and Samuel. The story of the outrage in Gibea foreshadows the controversy between Saul and David, because it takes place in towns related to these future kings. The travelers, coming from a very hospitable Bethlehem — David's place of birth — wrongly pass by the later city of David, Jebus (19:10-12, with the hardly accidental remark that this is Jerusalem), to get into trouble in Gibea, the later home town of Saul. To this can be added that Rama is also mentioned in 19:13. Within the story there is no clear reason for this. It seems that this remark had the intention of relating this story to a coming event, namely the appearance of Samuel who was born in Rama (1 Sam. 1:19; 2:11). The mentioning of Shiloh in 18:31; 21:12, 19, and 21 has a counterpart in 1 Samuel 1, where it is mentioned as the place of the temple. Within this framework it is also possible to assume that the location Mizpa — as the place of the gathering of the tribes for the battle against the Benjaminites (20:1, 3; 21:1, 5, 8) — is somehow related to the fact that in the same place the Israelites, guided by Samuel, defeated the Philistines (1 Sam. 7:5-14). These topographical connections between the book of Judges and the next book have their counterparts in the repetition of city names from the book of Joshua in Judges 1. Additionally, the story of YHWH's messenger in Bochim is also related to the story of the entrance into the land by means of the reference to a city, namely Gilgal.

Apart from these topographical correspondences, there is a clear correspondence between the extraordinary behavior of a man cutting his dead wife into twelve pieces sending them to all the tribes of Israel (Judg. 19:29) and Saul's way of convoking the Israelites by sending them the pieces of his oxen (1 Sam. 11:7). Furthermore, since the information provided in Judges 19 about the man is most uncommon, one may assume that this narrative was modeled on the Saul story.

Another interesting correspondence between the books of Samuel and the book of Judges is the use of the phrase שאל באלהים. Within the stories of Saul and David this way of asking the will of God can be regarded as a "Leitmotiv."[19] The downfall of Saul is connected with it, as becomes clear in the story of his attempt to make contact with the spirit of the dead Samuel, when it is no longer possible for him to make contact with YHWH (1 Sam. 28:6, 16). The rise to power of David, on the other hand, is related to his successful attempts to get divine advice. Good examples of this can be found in 1 Sam. 22:10, 13 and especially 2 Sam. 2:1 (David asks YHWH: "Shall I go up?"). The way it is described there has its closest parallel within the Old Testament in the scene in Judg. 18:5-6,

---

19 H.-F. Fuhs, "שאל *šā'al* [ask]," *TWAT* VII (Stuttgart: Kohlhammer, 1993), 910–26 (921).

where the oracle is also given to people on their way.[20] In the book of Judges the expression returns in the repetition of the question addressed to God who shall go up first (1:1, 20:18). This is an indication that the attested deliberate references to the next book in the final chapters of Judges are part of the overall design of the book. A closer look at the story of Samson will confirm this.

There are many parallels between 1 Samuel 1 and Judges 13. Both stories begin by presenting the problem of a barren woman. The texts also introduce the respective husbands with exactly the same words: "And there was a certain man of Zorah, of the family of the Danites, and his name was Manoah" (Judg. 13:2); "And there was a certain man of Ramathaim-Zophim, of the hill-country of Ephraim and his name was Elkanah" (1 Sam. 1:1). The introduction of a story with ויהי איש אחד מן may seem to be very common, but it is not. Within the Old Testament we only find it in these two places.[21] In both stories the woman eventually gives birth to a son who was promised by God under the condition of keeping to a number of prescriptions. In Judges 13 the messenger of YHWH orders the unnamed woman: She is not allowed to drink wine or strong drink or eat something unclean and no razor shall come upon the head of her son, because he shall be a Nazirite for life. In 1 Sam. 1:11 Hannah makes a vow herself: "I will give him unto YHWH all the days of his life, and there shall no razor come upon his head." Afterward she has to explain to the priest that she was not drunk when she uttered the words.

The best way to explain these parallels is that the author of the Samson story was familiar with the story of the birth of Samuel.[22] The correspondences in the form and content can hardly be coincidental or ascribed to a common pattern of miraculous birth stories. When one compares the two narratives, one notices a number of elements that seem to have been added in Judges 13. The story is made more miraculous with a messenger of YHWH replacing the priest. The element of abstinence from strong drink is also more natural in the story of Hannah. Naming the son a Nazirite in Judges 13 can also be regarded as a later, exaggerating, and in fact incorrect interpretation of the given prescriptions. The motivation for relating Samson to Samuel can be found in the words of the messenger of YHWH: "the child shall be a Nazirite of God from the womb. And he shall begin to deliver Israel out of the hand of the Philistines" (Judg. 13:5). When

20 Ibid., 920.
21 It is used without אחד also in Gen. 39:2; Judg. 17:1; 19:1; 1 Sam. 9:1; 2 Sam. 21:20; and 1 Chron. 20:6. See on the discussion about the repetition of this expression as an argument in redaction critical studies M. Leuchter, "'Now There Was a [Certain] Man': Compositional Chronology in Judges — 1 Samuel," *CBQ* 69 (2007), 429–39.
22 Cf. R. Bartelmus, *Heroentum in Israel und seiner Umwelt* (AThANT 65; Zürich: Theologischer Verlag, 1979), pp. 85–6.

the woman repeats these words to her husband she changes the reference of the deliverance from the Philistines to a reference to Samson's death: "the child shall be a Nazirite of God from the womb to the day of his death" (13:7). This can be seen as a reference to the later battles against the Philistines by Samuel, Saul, and David. During his lifetime Samson was not able to defeat these enemies. It was only under the reign of King David that the Philistines were defeated definitively.

Another reference to the reign of King David can be found in the story of Samson carrying the gates of the Philistine city of Gazah to the mountain opposite of Hebron (16:3), which is the place where David is crowned as king (2 Sam. 2:3-4) after having served the Philistines.[23]

All this can be interpreted as indications that in its present form the stories about Samson were meant as an introduction to the history as recounted in the books of Samuel. Once the reader is put on this track he may notice more common elements: Samson being driven by the spirit of YHWH like King Saul; Samson inventing a riddle and in this way showing himself to be wise like Solomon; Samson getting involved with foreign women, which recalls the risky marriage policy of King Solomon and of King Ahab; Samson bound and blinded like the last king of Judah, Zedekiah.

One can therefore note a correspondence between the end of the book of Judges and the books of Samuel which has much in common with the correspondence between the beginning of Judges and the book of Joshua. As was remarked above the function of the priest in the story of the birth of Samuel is taken over in the parallel story about the birth of Samson by the messenger of YHWH. In a similar way, the role of Joshua in the story of the making of the covenant in Joshua 24 is now taken up in the story about the broken covenant in Judges 2 by a messenger of YHWH. The writer/editor of the book of Judges shows an inclination toward the supernatural.

The Greek Connection

Now that it has become clear that the book of Judges was composed with both the books of Joshua and Samuel in mind — and therefore has to be dated relatively late — it is all the more interesting to review other evidence pointing in this direction, namely the often noticed Greek parallels. A survey of the history of research in this matter may give some indication about the texts involved and how these texts relate to those discussed above as connecting points with earlier Israelite literature.

A first parallel with Greek texts and ideas can be found with regard to cutting off a prisoner's thumbs (1:6). It has also been reported by Aelian that the

---

23 I owe this reference to Claudia Camp.

Athenians decided that "every one of the Æginetæ should have his thumb cut off from his right hand, so that he might for ever after be disabled from holding a spear, yet might handle an oar" (*Various Histories*, bk 2, ch. 9).[24]

Bernd Diebner makes some interesting remarks about Sisera, Jael, their names and their interaction.[25] The non-Semitic name Sisera can be related to Greek σισύρα, which means "cloak made of goatskin." In ancient Greek literature, since Herodotus, this is used to indicate a barbarian: σισυροφόρος, "one who is wearing a goatskin." The name of Jael is easier to translate: "mountain goat." Because of this meaning the attention is drawn to an interesting parallel from Greek mythology, namely of the god Zeus as a newborn child hiding from the deadly threat of Kronos and being fed by the goddess Amaltheia with the milk of a goat. This is all the more interesting because according to Judg. 4:19 Sisera asks for water, but Jael gives him milk to drink and then she covers him with a blanket. Although this indicates that she concealed him, it might also remind of the covering of a child. All the possible associations that become apparent against the Greek background give extra drama to the story.

Gideon's army of only 300 soldiers (7:6) can be associated with the small group of brave soldiers of the Spartan king Leonidas with which he fought the mighty Persian army in Thermopylae (Herodotus 7.205.2). Herodotus also mentions a battle between Sparta and Argos of 300 selected men on each side (1.82).[26]

The fable of Jotham (9:8-15), with the trees talking to each other, has many parallels, like the Akkadian story of the quarrel between the tamarisk and the palm-tree, each claiming superiority over the other. A similar text is found in an Aramaic text from the fifth century BCE found in Egypt, containing a discussion between a pomegrate-tree and a bramble.[27] The connection with the Greek fables of Aesopus is therefore not unique. Many commentaries refer to Aesopus' fables mentioning the fir-tree and the bramble, or the pomegranate, apple-tree, and the bramble, quarelling about who is the best.[28]

---

24 Cf. G. F. Moore, *Judges* (ICC; Edinburgh: T&T Clark, 1895), p. 17.

25 B.-J. Diebner, "Wann sang Deborah ihr Lied? Überlegungen zu zwei der ältesten Texte des TNK (Ri 4 und 5)," *ACEBT* 14 (1995), 106–30.

26 Cf. J. P. Brown, *Israel and Hellas, Volume II* (BZAW 276; Berlin: De Gruyter, 2000), p. 84.

27 Cf. T. H. Gaster, *Myth, Legend, and Custom in the Old Testament: A Comparative Study with Chapters from Sir James G. Frazer's Folklore in the Old Testament* (New York: Harper & Row, 1969), pp. 423–7.

28 The very close parallel found by C. Briffard, "Gammes sur l'acte de traduire," *Foi et Vie* 101 (2002), 12–18 is based on a misunderstanding. We are dealing here with the work of a Jewish or Christian editor of the fables of Aesopus. Especially the unexpected reference to the cedars of the Libanon points in this direction. This would also not be the only example of fables from other times and places being attributed to Aesopus (cf. J. F. Priest, "The Dog in the Manger: In Quest of a Fable," *Classical Journal* 81 (1985), 49–58).

The story of the sacrifice of Jephthah's daughter (11:29-40) has many parallels in Greek literature. Comparable stories also refer to vows made to the gods,
with fatal consequences for a daughter or a son.[29] According to some scholars this
is no more than a universal motive.[30] According to Baumgartner, however, the
correspondence between the Greek stories and the story of Jephthah's daughter
"ist zu auffällig, um zufällig zu sein."[31] The story in Judges 11 shares a number
of details with the way Euripides at the end of the fifth century BCE described
the fate of Iphigeneia: the father is experiencing a military crisis; both Jephthah
and Agamemnon have ambivalent feelings, feeling sorry for themselves and in
a way blaming their daughter; in both stories the daughter can be regarded as the
real hero, accepting her fate and encouraging her father to keep to his vow; both
stories end with the indication that the memory of the girl shall be kept alive. All
this makes it very likely that this story — which is uncommon within the biblical
context — was for some reason borrowed from Greek tradition.

With reference to the possible connections between the biblical Samson and
Greek Herakles, the correspondence of so many shared elements makes it highly
likely that one was influenced by the other, with the more dominant and wide-
spread Greek culture as the giving partner. In both stories, a god is involved in the
conception of the coming hero; both heroes defeated lions; both stories contain
episodes with bees and foxes; both heroes lost their beloved to another man; both
fought against armies; both are related to wells of water; both worked as slaves;
both remove gates and pillars; both lose their life through a woman.[32]

One final correspondence mentioned in commentaries on the book of Judges
is the rape of the virgins, as narrated in ch. 21. This is often compared with
the Roman legend of the Sabine women, mentioned in the works of Livy and
Plutarch.[33] According to Soggin a better parallel can be found in the Greek story
of the Messenians abducting the girls from Laconia during the celebration of a
festival of Artemis.[34] This also has a setting in the cult, but a major difference is

29 Cf. Gaster, *Myth*, p. 430 and J. G. Frazer, *Apollodorus* (Cambridge: Harvard, 1921),
pp. 394–404.
30 Cf. B. Becking, "Iphigeneia in Gilead: Over het verstaan van Richteren 11:29–40,"
Kerk en Theologie 41 (1990), 192–205 (202).
31 W. Baumgartner, "Israelitisch-Griechische Sagenbeziehungen," in *Zum Alten
Testament und seiner Umwelt* (Leiden: Brill, 1959), pp. 147–78 (153); cf. T. Römer, "Why
Would the Deuteronomists Tell about the Sacrifice of Jephthah's Daughter?" *JSOT* 77
(1998), 27–38.
32 Cf. the survey by C. Nauerth, "Simsons Taten: Motivgeschichtliche Überlegungen,"
Dielheimer Blätter 21 (1985), 94–120.
33 Cf. R. Gnuse, "Abducted Wives: A Hellenistic Narrative in Judges 21?" *SJOT* 22
(2008), 228–40.
34 J. A. Soggin, *Judges: A Commentary* (OTL; London: SCM Press, 1981), p. 304; cf.
Gaster, *Myths*, p. 445.

that in the Greek story the girls were ransomed back to their families. This parallel is thus limited to just one common aspect and is therefore not so convincing like the parallels between the stories of Jephthah and Samson which depend on several aspects.

Conclusion

It is important to note that there is no direct relation between the Greek parallels and the texts discussed above which were used to connect the book of Judges to the books now surrounding it. This may indicate that on this point the old Israelite tradition was prevalent, whereas in stories not recorded or referred to in the older Israelite literature, the writers felt free to tell them according to the fashion of their time.

The Greek evidence discussed above may be evaluated in the light of Van der Toorn's theory about a Hellenistic background for the origin of the Bible.[35] Somewhere in the early Hellenistic age the Jewish scribes wanted to offer an authoritative version of the history of Israel, stretching from creation to the restoration after the Babylonian exile. Our analysis of the book of Judges indicates that these scribes already had the book of Joshua at their disposal, followed by the stories of the kings beginning in Samuel. The book of Judges was produced to fill the gap in between. A number of traditional stories were used as a basis and to this, new material was added. The scribes started their version of the history — connecting the period of Joshua with that of Samuel — with a recapitulation of the book of Joshua, beginning it in the same way as the book of Joshua: "And it happened after the death of . . ." At the other end of the book they connected it with the book of Samuel by a number of proleptic signals. Read within the present context — between the story of the good leader Joshua succeeded by the equally successful tribe of Judah and the references to the failing king — the stories of the Judges contain serious warnings against bad leadership. The fable of Jotham indicates that it is not always the best who becomes king. The story of Jephthah's daughter reminds us of the fact that kings may think that they can negotiate with the gods, like Agamemnon did, much to the disadvantage of those close to him. Looking at Samson one should realize that people having power can use this arbitrarily. On the other hand, mighty men like Sisera and Samson, can also become weak as a child, giving in to the temptation of being treated like a child by a woman who exposes his vulnerability. It is a view on power and the powerful that can also be found in Qohelet with his warnings against the foolish (4:13) and childish king (10:17), just as Qohelet warns against an impulsive vow,

---

35 See note 10.

like the one by Jephthah.[36] This agreement with Qohelet is another indication for the relatively late date of the book of Judges in its present form. Within this framework it is also interesting that the positive attitude concerning Judah, the tribe of David, corresponds to the perspective taken by the Chronicler. When we also take into account the more formal parallel in 1 Chronicles 4 with regard to the place of Simeon as the tribe mentioned after Judah, just as in Judges 1, it becomes tempting to assume that these books stem from the same period.

36 Cf. Römer, "Why Would the Deuteronomists," 38.

NATIONAL IDENTITY AS COMMENTARY
AND AS METACOMMENTARY

Mark G. Brett

Introduction

David Goodblatt's work *Elements of Ancient Jewish Nationalism* (2006) is a significant recent contribution to the debate about whether nationalism can be said to exist in the ancient world. Goodblatt joins a chorus of biblical scholars who have rejected a dominant view in the humanities — classically expressed by Benedict Anderson — that nationalism is an inherently modern phenomenon and that its arrival in the West is associated in particular with the invention of the printing press, the decline of divinely authorized dynasties, and the rise of capitalism.[1] A number of biblical scholars have argued to the contrary that national identity, in something like a modern sense, can be found in ancient Israel. Some historians, like Goodblatt, have developed their argument in relation to Hellenistic times, while others have found evidence of nationalism in earlier periods.[2]

In this paper I will in effect attempt to split the difference between Goodblatt and Anderson by arguing that a number of the analogies between modern nationalism and Israelite nationalism may be well founded, but attempts to construe

---

1 B. Anderson, *Imagined Communities: Reflections on the Origin and Spread of Nationalism* (2nd edn; London: Verso, 1991); cf. A. Hastings, *The Construction of Nationhood: Ethnicity, Religion and Nationalism* (Cambridge: Cambridge University Press, 1997), who emphasizes the spread of literacy rather than print capitalism as such.

2 See, e.g., D. Mendels, *The Rise and Fall of Jewish Nationalism* (New York: Doubleday, 1992); S. Grosby, *Biblical Ideas of Nationality: Ancient and Modern* (Winona Lake: Eisenbrauns, 2002); A. Roshwald, *The Endurance of Nationalism* (Cambridge: Cambridge University Press, 2006); M. G. Brett, "Nationalism and the Hebrew Bible," in *The Bible in Ethics* (eds. J. W. Rogerson, M. Davies, and M. D. Carroll; Sheffield: JSOT Press, 1995), pp. 136–63.

these analogies as essentially matters of social identity and need to be carefully qualified. While the concept of identity may appear to be more neutral and readily available as a tool for historical comparison, some "metacommentary" is necessary if we are to avoid the threat of anachronism. That is, we need to take a closer look at what biblical commentators are *not* saying about ostensibly neutral notions of identity, and reflect on some "perspicuous contrasts" between the world of the commentator and the world of the text.[3] As Charles Taylor has suggested,

> It will almost always be the case that the adequate language in which we can understand another society is not our language of understanding, or theirs, but rather what one could call a language of perspicuous contrast.[4]

The Making of National Identities

After a lengthy survey of definitions — both of nationality and of ethnicity — Goodblatt defines national identity as "a belief in a common descent and shared culture available for mass political mobilization." He notes that the salient indicators of a "shared culture" may shift over time. Moreover, the *factual content* of shared beliefs about kinship or culture is less important than a readiness to *act* on the basis of those shared beliefs. Thus, Goodblatt clarifies that by "nationalism" he means "the invocation of national identity as the basis for mass mobilization and action."[5]

While I have a number of reservations about this definition, it does provide Goodblatt with a workable conceptual tool for undertaking a fruitful historical investigation into the usage of terms such as "Israel," "Judah," and "Zion" in the Second Temple period. Mindful of the distinction between commentary and metacommentary in this context, I would say that Goodblatt provides an

---

3 See the classic essay by F. Jameson, "Metacommentary (1971)," in Jameson, *The Ideology of Theory: Essays 1971–1986* (London: Routledge, 1988), pp. 3–16. Here I am deliberately blending the concept of metacommentary — a reflexive analysis of commentators' worldviews — with Charles Taylor's argument for making explicit the "perspicuous contrasts" between the culture of a text and the culture of an interpreter; see C. Taylor "Understanding and Ethnocentricity," in Taylor, *Philosophy and the Human Sciences* (Cambridge: Cambridge University Press, 1985), pp. 116–33; cf. D. J. A. Clines, "Metacommentating Amos," in Clines, *Interested Parties: The Ideology of Writers and Readers of the Hebrew Bible* (Sheffield: Sheffield Academic Press, 1995), pp. 76–93.

4 Taylor, "Understanding and Ethnocentricity," 125.

5 D. M. Goodblatt, *Elements of Ancient Jewish Nationalism* (Cambridge: Cambridge University Press, 2006), pp. 26–7.

illuminating *commentary* on the vocabulary of national identity in a manner that explicitly seeks to avoid the charge of anachronism. But in developing his argument, he goes further than mere commentary to ask how this nationalism was "constructed," emphasizing in particular that the public reading of scripture and priestly leadership would have assisted in fomenting a nationalist consciousness:

> Widespread and regular public recitation of biblical texts would explain how ideas of common descent and shared culture could reach a mass audience. This, I submit, is certainly what was going on by the Hellenistic period. And it may have already been the case, albeit in a more limited way, under the domination of the Achaemenids.[6]

He reaches this conclusion after reviewing the evidence for public reading of scripture in the Persian period and deciding that it is weaker than the evidence from Hellenistic times. Along the way, he acknowledges in particular the work of Theodore Mullen and Philip Davies in identifying the potential contribution of biblical texts to the creation of social identity.[7]

Goodblatt ends up conflating ethnic and national identity, but we will leave that problem to one side for the time being. His linking of national consciousness to a mass audience is lent plausibility, I would suggest, in part because Benedict Anderson laid the foundations of this conceptual link, and he laid those foundations in a way that is occluded in Goodblatt's discussion. Anderson famously defined nationalism as an imagined political community — "imagined as sovereign because the concept was born in an age in which Enlightenment and Revolution were destroying the legitimacy of the divinely-ordained, hierarchical dynastic realm."[8] It is the egalitarian impulse that is most characteristic of modern nationalism. Particular expressions of national identity might highlight a range of component elements in various ways — common territory, language, statehood, shared traditions, history, or kinship — but in themselves such factors would not distinguish *national* identity from other kinds of social identity. The specificity of nationalism derives from the idea of an essentially "horizontal" community

---

6 Goodblatt, *Elements*, p. 48.

7 See Goodblatt, *Elements*, pp. 30–1, referring to E. T. Mullen, *Narrative History and Ethnic Boundaries: The Deuteronomistic History and the Creation of Israelite National Identity* (Atlanta: Scholars Press, 1993); E. T. Mullen, *Ethnic Myths and Pentateuchal Foundations: A New Approach to the Formation of the Pentateuch* (Atlanta: Scholars Press, 1997); P. R. Davies, *In Search of Ancient Israel* (Sheffield: Sheffield Academic Press, 1992), pp. 114, 117–18. For a review of studies that see biblical texts as "identity-forming" see J. C. Miller, "Ethnicity and the Hebrew Bible: Problems and Prospects," *Currents in Biblical Research* 6/2 (2008), 170–213.

8 Anderson, *Imagined Communities*, pp. 15–16.

who is the bearer of sovereignty and the basis of collective action. The people are seen as larger than clan or tribal units and as fundamentally homogeneous in that they are perceived as only "superficially divided by the lines of status, class, locality, and in some cases even ethnicity."[9]

Thus, for example, with the stirrings of English nationalism in the sixteenth century, Bishop John Poynet was able to assert that "the country and the commonwealth are a degree above the king" and by implication that popular sovereignty had displaced the sovereignty of the monarch.[10] It is no accident that English nationalism in this period was partly modeled on Deuteronomy, a biblical book that established a remarkably modern-looking division of powers which limited the sovereignty of Judah's king and established the priority of national "brotherhood" over the loyalties of clan solidarities.[11] It is precisely this imagined solidarity that allows us to suggest that an analogy between modern nationalism and the Deuteronomic social vision is not entirely anachronistic.

Sixteenth-century England was not, however, the first context within which the interpretation of Deuteronomy was drawn into a political experiment that could in this regard be characterized as ethnic nationalism. Consider, for example, Tamara Eskenazi's recent proposal that:

> Ezra-Nehemiah, like some writers in Periclean Athens, is concerned with a form of citizenship rights. The preoccupation with so-called mixed marriage in both communities is a product of new social structures that emerge in both societies, with Deuteronomy as the newly defining framework, even polity, for EN and Judah.[12]

9 L. Greenfeld, *Nationalism: Five Roads to Modernity* (Cambridge: Harvard University Press, 1992), p. 3.

10 See W. S. Hudson, *John Poynet: Advocate of Limited Monarchy* (Chicago: University of Chicago Press, 1942), p. 61.

11 See, e.g., B. Halpern, *The Constitution of the Monarchy in Israel* (Missoula: Scholars, 1980), pp. 234–5; idem, "Jerusalem and the Lineages in the Seventh Century BCE," in *Law and Ideology in Monarchic Israel* (eds. B. Halpern and D. W. Hobson; Sheffield: Sheffield Academic Press, 1991), pp. 11–7; Frank Crüsemann, *Die Tora: Theologie und Sozialgeschichte des alttestamentlichen Gesetzes* (Munich: Kaiser, 1992), pp. 235–322, who with conscious reflection on modern analogies regards Deuteronomy as a constitution with a vision of "Theokratie als Demokratie", pp. 273 and 287; E. Otto, "Human Rights: The Influence of the Hebrew Bible," *JNSL* 25 (1999), 1–14; B. Levinson, "The First Constitution: Rethinking the Origins of Rule of Law and Separation of Powers in Light of Deuteronomy," *Cardozo Law Review* 27 (2006), 1853–88.

12 T. C. Eskenazi, "The Missions of Ezra and Nehemiah," in *Judah and the Judeans in the Persian Period* (eds. O. Lipschits and M. Oeming; Winona Lake: Eisenbrauns, 2006), p. 509. Aristotle claims that "on account of the large number of citizens it was decided on

Arguing against the view that Ezra-Nehemiah is supporting priestly and aristocratic elites and directly promoting Persian imperial interests, Eskenazi understands Ezra-Nehemiah to be posing a challenge to elite groups and promoting a more egalitarian solidarity of Judeans based on ethnic affinities, rather than on hierarchy. One thinks, for example, of the critique of the nobles in Nehemiah 5 in the name of "brotherhood." Eskenazi suggests that throughout Ezra-Nehemiah the public symbolism of the Torah "demystifies" the priests by vesting authority in sacred texts rather than in priestly families. Accordingly, Ezra 8:15-19, 24-30 empowers Levites to serve alongside priests, a vision that is more in tune with Deuteronomy's way of seeing the cult than with the hierarchical picture of the restoration in Ezekiel 40–48, which has the Levites as a second cultic class below the Zadokite priests.

While it is quite clear that there is no straight line between this particular egalitarian impulse in Ezra-Nehemiah and modern visions of political equality, it is equally important to bear in mind that modern nationalisms have habitually veiled their histories of suppression and that these modern histories have only been uncovered gradually, layer by layer. Under the veils of modern egalitarian ideology one would now have to recognize the stories of slavery, women's suffrage, the rights of ethnic minorities and indigenous people. This point is made by Charles Taylor in his book *A Secular Age* (2007), but in the present moment we would only have to note the ongoing debates about the *UN Declaration on the Rights of Indigenous Peoples* (2007) to realize that the modern story of equality still has some unwritten chapters.

To put the focus back on the Persian period once again, I find Eskenazi's argument both compelling and elusively incomplete. The discourse of the "holy seed" (*zera' haqqodesh*) in Ezra 9:1-2 does not appear in priestly texts, but the phrase "holy people" does appear in Deut. 7:6, and indeed, *'am kadosh* appears in the context of a prohibition of mixed marriage. Yet even when Deuteronomy excludes the prior inhabitants of Canaan purely on ethnic grounds (along with the neighboring Ammonites and Moabites in Deut. 23:3-4), Deuteronomic legislation nowhere places an absolute ban on intermarriage. Indeed, Deut. 23:7-8 specifically opens the community to Egyptians — "for you were a stranger in their land" — while Ezra 9:1 explicitly *prohibits* marriage to Egyptians. Ezra-Nehemiah has hardened the opposition to foreign women beyond anything that we find in previous laws, and this while promoting the public symbolism of the Torah.

The image of the "holy seed" would appear to fit admirably within an imagined Deuteronomic community marked predominately by horizontal solidarity rather

the proposal of Pericles that a man should not be a member of the citizen body unless both his parents were Athenians" (*Athenaion Politeia*, 26.3).

than by clan factions or priestly hierarchies. And while such a vision would conflict with Zadokite supremacy, it is actually not far removed from the vision of the Holiness Code, which, for example in Leviticus 19, promotes a lay vision of holiness beyond the confines of the temple and the priesthood. In other words, Ezra's "egalitarian" impulse in the discourse of the "holy seed" would appear to be shared, at first blush, with both the Holiness Code and with Deuteronomy.[13]

Although Ezra is represented as a priest, his idea of ethnocentric holiness does not conform to what we know about the purity system in Leviticus and Numbers. The problem is exemplified in Nehemiah 8 where there is an intriguing representation of the public reading of scripture. Ezra reads the law in "the seventh month," and he initiates the Festival of Booths on the "second day" of the month, conspicuously overlooking the Day of Atonement, or Day of Purgation. This is a crucial oversight since this ritual was designed precisely to purify the whole community, ostensibly Ezra's concern. According to priestly legislation, the Festival of Booths begins on the *fifteenth* day of this month, and the Day of Atonement is held on the *tenth* (Lev. 23:26-44; Num. 29:7-38). While many attempts have been made to get round this difficulty, it seems to me that there are essentially two options: either the priestly calendar of festivals had not yet stabilized, or the authors of Ezra-Nehemiah had reservations about it.

Why would they have had reservations? In the account of the Day of Atonement in Leviticus 16, we find a text which would have been inconvenient for an ethnocentric interpretation of priestly tradition: "This shall be a statute for you forever: In the seventh month, on the tenth day of the month, you shall deny yourselves and do no work, neither the native-born *nor the stranger (ger) who resides among you.* For on this day atonement shall be made for you, to cleanse you from all your sins. You shall be clean before Yhwh" (Lev. 16:29-30).[14] This and other examples illustrate that, contrary to Ezra-Nehemiah's view, there is nothing inherently defiling about strangers in priestly theology.

Jacob Milgrom maintains that Leviticus has no general prohibition on intermarriage and that Ezra 9 is an exercise in "halakhic midrash," i.e., legal

---

13 For a more detailed discussion of the following argument, see M. G. Brett, *Decolonizing God: The Bible in the Tides of Empire* (Sheffield: Sheffield Phoenix Press, 2008), pp. 112–31; cf. M. Leuchter, "Coming to Terms with Ezra's Many Identities in Ezra-Nehemiah," in this volume.

14 In Israel Knohl's complex account of the "Day of Atonement" texts, he argues that the Priestly tradition has been enhanced in its consciousness of the *gerim* by the "Holiness School." See I. Knohl, *The Sanctuary of Silence* (Minneapolis: Fortress, 1995), pp. 27–8; cf. also pp. 53 and 93. Eskenazi observes that instead of the usual terminology for marriage, Ezra-Nehemiah repeatedly uses the *Hiphil* of יָשׁב "cause to dwell" ("The Missions of Ezra and Nehemiah," 520-521) a word choice that seems to fall in the same semantic field as "reside," גֵּר in Lev. 16:29.

imagination.[15] Lev. 21:14 *does* stipulate that priests must marry only Israelites, and this can be regarded as the "exception which proves the rule": "if priests were to be distinguished in this way with a higher grade of holiness, then the general population were free to marry strangers."[16] Among the lengthy regulations on sexuality in Leviticus, nothing is said about the laity marrying foreigners. The concern expressed in Neh. 13:28 about the intermarriage of a priest would be perfectly defensible in terms derived from the Holiness Code, without needing to conclude that lay intermarriage inevitably compromised the integrity or the solidarity of the "holy seed."

In short, the ethnic or "nativist" purity[17] imagined by Ezra seems to promote one model of horizontal solidarity at the expense of other models that could have been derived from Deuteronomy or from the Holiness Code. The Persian period seems therefore to provide evidence of competing models of horizontal solidarity.

Nationalisms and Sovereignties

It might be suggested that even if the "nativist" politics of Ezra-Nehemiah can be interpreted as proposing a "horizontal" or egalitarian ethnic nationalism, the advocacy of such a view in a colonial province on the edge of the Persian Empire could hardly fit the modern criterion of popular sovereignty.

In response to this objection, I want to make two historical points about the

---

15 J. Milgrom, *Leviticus 17–22* (New York: Doubleday, 2000), pp. 1584–6. See further S. Olyan, *Rites and Rank: Hierarchy in Biblical Representations of Cult* (Princeton: Princeton University Press, 2000), pp. 63–102; C. Hayes, *Gentile Impurities and Jewish Identities: Intermarriage and Conversion from the Bible to the Talmud* (Oxford: Oxford University Press, 2002), pp. 19–44. K. Sparks, *Ethnicity and Identity in Ancient Israel* (Winona Lake: Eisenbrauns, 1998), pp. 295 and 318, has suggested that Ezra 6:19-21 allows for the possibility of "proselyte" women, but it is more likely that this text simply distinguishes between returning exiles and other Judeans (presumably non-exiles) who had "separated themselves from unclean practices." Ezra-Nehemiah never mentions *gerim*, and unlike the Priestly legislation, never clarifies the possibility that foreigners might not commit abominations.

16 J. Joosten, *People and Land in the Holiness Code* (Leiden: Brill, 1996), p. 85. Milgrom, *Leviticus 17–22*, p. 1820 curiously resists Joosten's conclusion without sufficient argument. On pp. 1805–6, Milgrom indicates that the prohibition of intermarriage in Lev. 21:14 applies only to the high priest, and not even to Zadokite priests in general (as it does in Ezek. 44:22). Cf. Hayes, *Gentile Impurities*, pp. 27–8 and 230 n. 31.

17 Nehemiah's administration has also been interpreted in terms of a nativist cultural revitalization by D. Tollefson and H. G. M. Williamson in "Nehemiah as Cultural Revitalization: An Anthropological Perspective," *JSOT* 56 (1992), 41–68. See my reference to "primordial nativism" in M. G. Brett, "Interpreting Ethnicity: Method, Hermeneutics, Ethics," in *Ethnicity and the Bible* (ed. M. G. Brett; Leiden: Brill, 1996), p. 13, and the further argument in M. G. Brett, *Decolonizing God*, pp. 112–31.

complexity of claims to sovereignty. First, to reflect on our Antipodean context for a moment, the sovereignty of modern Australia was and is divided. When, for example, the colony of Victoria first took steps in the 1880s to exclude Chinese immigrants from Hong Kong — even when they carried British identity papers — this began a complex legal separation from British sovereignty that continues today, without Victoria becoming a republic or severing all legal ties with Britain.[18] The federation of the colonies in 1901 similarly represented a reformulation of Australian sovereignty without requiring the formation of an entirely separate republic. Moreover, the First Nations still assert their own sovereignty in the face of legal claims that the tides of colonial history have overwhelmed it.

Turning to the ancient sources, it might be thought that Maccabean nationalism evidences a much stronger assertion of sovereignty than what we find in the Persian period. But Steve Weitzman has offered an important perspective on this contrast in his response to David Goodblatt's work. Weitzman argues that it may be less anachronistic to understand the Maccabean revolt as an attempt to secure a higher level of recognition from the Seleucid king, who had the power to grant a limited range of sovereign powers within the empire:

> One mark of status in the age of Seleucid rule was the right to declare one's city and temple "sacred and inviolable" — immune or protected from external interference like temple robbery or the removal of those seeking asylum in the temple.[19]

Weitzman suggests that one of the earliest accounts of the revolt can be read in this way, noting that the speech in 2 Macc 3:12 has the high priest using the highly significant phrase "sanctity and inviolability" that appears in the coinage of this period. In other words, the revolt need not be seen in terms of a quest for absolute political independence but as a mobilization of national identity when foreign rule represented a particular threat to Jewish faith and practice.

Earlier expressions of Israelite national identity may be viewed in a similar way, beginning perhaps with Deuteronomy's response to the threat posed by Assyrian imperial power.[20] In *Decolonizing God*, I have proposed that during the Persian period Ezra-Nehemiah's understanding of ethnic iden-

---

18 M. Lake, "White Australia as the Declaration of Australian Sovereignty: An Investigation of the Gendered and Racial Subjectivities of the Self-Governing Male Subject," (paper read at New Worlds, New Sovereignties conference, University of Melbourne, 6–9 June 2008).

19 S. Weitzman, "On the Relevance of Ancient Jewish Nationalism," (paper presented at International SBL, Vienna, July 2008); see K. Rigsby, *Asylia: Territorial Inviolability in the Hellenistic World* (Berkeley: University of California Press, 1996).

20 See the discussion in Brett, "Nationalism and the Hebrew Bible"; idem, *Decolonizing*

tity may be fruitfully compared with modern anti-colonial movements that have promoted a "nativist" agenda — that is, an *overt* program of reinstating "indigenous cultural tradition" which is presented as unsullied and uniquely "authentic."[21] Recent studies have described a range of examples where nativism has functioned as an oppositional discourse in the formation of postcolonial states. Arising as critiques of the West, these examples demonstrate ironically that national identities were produced within territorial borders defined by the colonial powers, rather than by pre-colonial cultures, and within these borders native elites produced fictive unities between the present and the past. An interpretation of the Persian period that is mindful of this modern nativist dynamic would have much closer affinities with Daniel Smith-Christopher's work on the "hidden transcripts" of resistance in Ezra-Nehemiah than with John Kessler's rather disquieting neglect of the nativist dimension when he proposes an analogy between the *golah* returnees and modern colonialist "Charter Groups."[22] But whether or not it is justified to make these parallels between Ezra-Nehemiah and ethnic nationalism, there is another problem of anachronism that belongs particularly to constructivist accounts of ethnic identity.

Identity and Anachronism

The preceding discussion illustrates that national identity in ancient Israel was a matter of historically extended argument and debate. But it does not follow that Israelite nationality was formed as a social identity in something like a modern sense. The key difference that needs to be recognized is, in Charles Taylor's vocabulary, the difference between a "porous" self in the enchanted worlds of antiquity and a "buffered" self in the disenchanted worlds of modern Western culture. A porous self is vulnerable to the spiritual world "as immediate reality, like stones rivers and mountains," whereas the modern self is buffered and more self-reflexive — not immediately impinged on by gods and demons, and also

---

God, ch. 5, drawing in particular on E. Otto, *Das Deuteronomium: Politische Theologie und Rechtsreform in Juda und Assyrien* (Berlin: De Gruyter, 1999).

21 See the introductory discussion in M. Boroujerdi, *Iranian Intellectuals and the West: The Tormented Triumph of Nativism* (Syracuse: Syracuse University Press, 1996), pp. 1–19; cf. D. Conversi, "Conceptualizing Nationalism," in *Ethnonationalism in the ContemporaryWorld* (ed. D. Conversi; London: Routledge, 2002), p. 10; M. Goswami, *Producing India: From Colonial Economy to National Space* (Chicago: Chicago University Press, 2004), pp. 10, 283–5.

22 e.g., D. Smith-Christopher, *A Biblical Theology of Exile* (Minneapolis: Fortress, 2002), pp. 22–3, 37–45; J. Kessler, "Persia's Loyal Yahwists: Power, Identity and Ethnicity in Achaemenid Yehud," in *Judah and the Judeans in the Persian Period* (eds. O. Lipschits and M. Oeming; Winona Lake: Eisenbrauns, 2006), pp. 91–121.

empowered to see religious construals precisely as construals, as *options* that may be adopted or rejected by an authentic self without thereby falling into the hands of malevolent spiritual powers.[23]

Taylor's detailed historical narrative in *A Secular Age* illustrates how up until relatively modern times disbelief in gods or spirits was extremely difficult to conceive of, whereas it is now a commonplace in Western cultures to see belief in God as "a failure of reason, or a culpable self-indulgence."[24] The burden of Taylor's narrative, however, is not to rehearse a conventionally Whiggish plot about the triumph of science,[25] but rather to explain how the characteristic inability of earlier societies to imagine themselves outside of a particular embeddedness (in clans and tribes or sacred structures) was turned within a few modern centuries into a matter of choosing an identity. In the unfolding of this complex story, modern nationalism plays a key role that historically relied upon the disenchanting mission of Protestantism, with its emphasis on the personal — rather than ritual — connection with God.

It will of course be necessary to simplify the most salient aspects of Taylor's argument, but it goes roughly like this: The Protestant abolition of the enchanted cosmos was an unintended consequence of attacks on Catholic practices of the sacred, especially those embodied in the power of priestly hierarchies and the privileged vocations. Belief in the priesthood of all believers sanctified ordinary life and promoted an egalitarian impulse that was first enacted as resistance to the rule of Rome and then secularised into the horizontal solidarities of modern nationalism and economic exchange, as opposed to the hierarchical structures that in pre-modern societies had been directly embedded in metaphysical reality.[26] To risk a summary statement of the obvious, our modern secular nationalisms generally lack religious foundations in the sense of an underlying Great Chain of Being that sanctions dynasties or priestly jurisdiction. Our legal systems are overtly human constructions, rather than laws which have been maintained "since

---

23   C. Taylor, *A Secular Age* (Cambridge: Belknap, 2007), pp. 12, 3–39; cf. S. Tambiah, *Magic, Science, Religion and the Scope of Rationality* (Cambridge: Cambridge University Press, 1990), p. 134; S. Wilson, *The Magical Universe* (London: Humbledon & London, 2000), p. xvii.

24   Taylor, *A Secular Age*, p. 591. Biblical scholars have on occasion promoted the idea that particular texts in the Hebrew Bible can be characterized as "secular," e.g., proverbs, customary laws, and even the entire book of Esther. But, as in the case of medieval carnivalesque genres, such texts do not in themselves provide a comprehensive grasp on the worldview of their authors.

25   Taylor points out that the autonomization of nature is found already in Aquinas and in providential Deism, without implying atheism. Cf. ibid., pp. 91, 221–69, 336.

26   Ibid., pp. 77, 95, 104, 146, 155, 179.

time out of mind" or which derive from a sacred founding moment in the "time of origins."

The consequences of the changes wrought by modernity are spelled out by Taylor in a way that has direct relevance for our discussion of ancient historiography. Pre-modern sacred traditions were generally *not seen as facilitators of social identity*, largely because questions of identity — in something like a modern sense — only become conceivable under conditions of "social disembeddedness." The "porous" self sits too deeply in the metaphysical conditions of identity to make any sense of the modern formulation of our questions.[27] Hence, Taylor concludes, for example, that for a pre-modern tribe,

> The abolition of the law would mean the abolition of the subject of common action, because the law defines the tribe as an entity . . . a tribe can only resume its life on the understanding that the law, although perhaps interrupted in its efficacy by foreign conquest, is still in force.[28]

As I suggested earlier, there is good reason to think that already in the seventh century BCE, under the pressure exerted by the Assyrian empire, Judah's Deuteronomic theologians reinterpreted earlier legal traditions in a manner that established the priority of national "brotherhood" above the obligations of clans and tribes, at the same time establishing a division of powers that decentered the role of Judah's king. To that extent, an analogy with modern nationalism is justified. The Deuteronomic innovations were linked with Moses, rather than with Josiah, apparently because the earlier foundations of Mosaic authority provided the law with a more secure grounding in metaphysical reality than what may have been derived from kingship (an unusual view in the ancient Near East). Nevertheless, measured against the disenchantments of modernity, the degree of "disembedding" in seventh-century Judah or sixth-century Babylon was extremely limited.[29] It is highly doubtful that the Deuteronomic theologians imagined that they were in the business of forging a national "identity" in something like a modern sense. A similar qualification would apply to the Second Temple historiography that was influenced by Deuteronomy.

It might be conceded, at this point in the argument, that a tour through Taylor's narrative about modernity may be an unnecessary exercise in metacommentary if

27 Ibid., pp. 149, 192, 208. This argument develops certain aspects of Taylor's earlier influential work, *Sources of the Self: The Making of the Modern Identity* (Cambridge: Harvard University Press, 1989).

28 Taylor, *A Secular Age,* p. 193.

29 See for example, ibid., pp. 154–5. Cf. his argument that the "fragilization" of modern religious identities required the birth of exclusive humanism (pp. 19, 556 and 833 n. 19).

scholars are already completely clear that references to identity formation in the study of ancient religious texts should be seen as explanatory "etic" hypotheses with no immediate connection to the "emic" (including exegetical) questions of how historical agents viewed their own beliefs and actions. But recent biblical scholarship on historiography and identity seems often unclear about this methodological distinction. Much more energy has been devoted, for example, to debates over defining "ethnicity," or in Goodblatt's case to defining "nationalism," than to debating the risks of anachronism inherent in concepts of identity.

Even some of the debates about whether ethnicity should be seen in "primordial" or in "constructivist" terms have not been wholly clear about distinguishing between etic or emic scholarly objectives.[30] The "primordial" approach to ethnicity, associated especially with Clifford Geertz and Edward Shils, could be described in terms that overlap considerably with what Taylor calls the "porous" self: "Congruities of blood, speech, custom, and so on are seen to have an ineffable, and at times overpowering coerciveness in and of themselves."[31]

My hypothesis in relation to Second Temple historiography, then, would be that each new historical challenge evoked revisions of ethnic and national identity, but even when those revisions were fiercely contesting alternative perceptions of reality, the overriding issues for the historical actors themselves would not have been the making of identity as such. As Taylor puts it, "there is a condition of lived experience, where what we might call a construal of the moral/spiritual is lived not as such, but as immediate reality, like stones, rivers and mountains."[32] The ancient revisions of Zion theology and Israelite identity, as revolutionary as they may have been in biblical times, are not likely to have departed from primordial attachments. Modern constructivist identities, whether national or individual, are negotiated on significantly different terms.

30 It is important to note that this distinction turns on the *objectives* of interpretation, not on the avoidance of concepts from an interpreter's own culture. The emic/etic distinction is in this sense a continuum, rather than a sharply defined dichotomy, since if an interpreter is to avoid ethnocentric impositions then emic objectives often require explicit cross-cultural comparisons or "perspicuous contrasts." See Taylor, "Understanding and Ethnocentricity," 87–102; Brett, "Interpreting Ethnicity," 12–13. Cf. J. M. Hall, *Ethnic Identity in Greek Antiquity* (Cambridge: Cambridge University Press, 1997), pp. 18–19.

31 C. Geertz, "The Integrative Revolution: Primordial Sentiments and Civil Politics in the New States," in his influential *The Interpretation of Cultures* (New York: Basic Books, 1973), pp. 259, 255–310; idem, "Primordial Ties (1963)," in *Ethnicity* (eds. J. Hutchinson and A. D. Smith; Oxford: Oxford University Press, 1996), pp. 40–5; cf. E. Shils, "Primordial, Personal, Sacred, and Civil Ties," *British Journal of Sociology* 8 (1957), 130–45.

32 Taylor, *A Secular Age*, p. 12.

COMING TO TERMS WITH EZRA'S MANY
IDENTITIES IN EZRA-NEHEMIAH[1]

Mark Leuchter

For all of its hallmarks of official authenticity, the date, purpose, and scope of Ezra's mission to Yehud remains shrouded in mystery for scholars of Persian-period Judaism. Was he an agent of Artaxerxes I and dispatched in 458 BCE, thereby preceding Nehemiah, or Artaxerxes II and sent in 398 BCE, following Nehemiah's tenure and continuing his policies? Or, as some have suggested, is Ezra fictitious, a literary *topos* simply meant to support the position of Nehemiah as preserved in the Ezra-Nehemiah corpus?[2] The difficulties raised by these questions are compounded by a growing view among scholars that Ezra-Nehemiah developed over a very long period of time, and thus the historical information it contains is obscured by the temporal distance between these ostensible events and

---

1 This paper is the result of the discussion following the presentation of my essay "Ezra's Mission and the Levites of Casiphia," published in *Community Identity in Judean Historiography: Biblical and Comparative Perspectives* (eds. G. N. Knoppers and K. A. Ristau, Winona Lake: Eisenbrauns, 2009), pp. 173–96, and benefits from the insights of my fellow panelists and the other attendants at the historiography section organized by Louis C. Jonker at the 2008 International Meeting for the SBL in Auckland, New Zealand.

2 For the diversity of views regarding these considerations, see D. Rooke, *Zadok's Heirs: The Role and Development of the High Priesthood in Ancient Israel* (Oxford: Oxford University Press, 2000), pp. 153–5; L. S. Fried, "You Shall Appoint Judges: Ezra's Mission and the Rescript of Artaxerxes," in *Persia and Torah: The Theory of Imperial Authorization of the Pentateuch* (SBLSymS; ed. J. W. Watts; Atlanta: Scholars Press, 2001), pp. 63–89; J. Schaper, "The Temple Treasury Committee in the Time of Nehemiah and Ezra," *VT* 47 (1997), 201; S. M. Olyan, "Purity Ideology in Ezra-Nehemiah as a Tool to Reconstitute the Community," *JSJ* 35 (2004), 14; R. C. Steiner, "The *mbqr* at Qumran, the *episkopos* in the Athenian Empire, and the Meaning of *lbqr'* in Ezra 7:14: On the Relation of Ezra's Mission to the Persian Legal Project," *JBL* 120 (2001), 628–30; J. Blenkinsopp, *Ezra-Nehemiah.* (OTL; Louisville/London: Westminster John Knox, 1988), p. 144.

the formation of the text.[3] Finally, the admixture of agendas and traditions surrounding the figure of Ezra are legion. He is a Zadokite by birth but bears much in common with Levite scribes, and draws from Priestly and Deuteronomistic concepts in equal measure.[4] Did the historical Ezra feel free to combine these two nearly mutually exclusive troves of ideas or do they represent discrete redactional strata?[5] If the former, which ideological stream was more firmly bound to his role as an administrator over the entirety of the province of Ebar-Nehara? And if Ezra was charged with overseeing officials in Ebar-Nehara, why does the record of Ezra's mission only relay his actions in the province of Yehud?[6]

Perhaps, the most pressing question is: why does the text seem to deliberately obscure any clear view of Ezra at every turn? Though we may sense redactional

---

3 J. L. Wright, "A New Model for the Composition of Ezra-Nehemiah," in *Judah and the Judeans in the Persian Period* (eds. O. Lipschits & M. Oeming; Winona Lake: Eisenbrauns, 2006), pp. 346–9. For a different model of redaction but similar conclusions regarding a lengthy time span of this development, see J. Pakkala, *Ezra the Scribe: The Development of Ezra 7-10 and Nehemia 8* (BZAW 347; Berlin: De Gruyter, 2004), pp. 291–9.

4 See Blenkinsopp, *Ezra-Nehemiah*, pp. 152–7. Alice Hunt notes that there is no overt mention of a Zadokite priesthood in Ezra-Nehemiah (*Missing Priests: The Zadokites in Tradition and History* [LHBOTS 452; London: Continuum, 2006], pp. 98–104), only Aaronides. Hunt's thorough study requires a more detailed reply than can be provided here; for the time being, I will tentatively suggest that the appeal to Aaron may be an attempt to amplify the antiquity and sacral hegemony of the Zadokite priestly line, especially considering the likelihood of competing groups contending for religious authority, as James W. Watts has recently discussed (*Ritual and Rhetoric in Leviticus: From Sacrifice to Scripture* [New York: Cambridge University Press, 2007]; Watts, "The Torah as the Rhetoric of Priesthood," in *The Pentateuch as Torah: New Models for Understanding Its Promulgation and Acceptance* [eds. G. N. Knoppers and B. M. Levinson, Winona Lake: Eisenbrauns, 2007], pp. 319–31). First Esdras takes this one step further by arranging cultic materials from a variety of sources for the purposes of creating a document with a decidedly priestly focus over against the more balanced Zadokite priest-Levite scribe content of Ezra-Nehemiah. For this view, see Wright, *Rebuilding Identity: The Nehemiah Memoir and Its Earliest Readers* (BZAW 348; Berlin: De Gruyter, 2004), pp. 39, 322–4, and his discussion on 1 Esdras in his forthcoming commentary on Ezra-Nehemiah; see also below with respect to Neh. 8:13–18. In general, Ezra-Nehemiah fits within the parameters of literature that was indeed part of the Zadokite curriculum of the fifth–fourth centuries BCE; see G. Boccaccini, *Roots of Rabbinic Judaism: An Intellectual History from Ezekiel to Daniel* (Grand Rapids: Eerdmans, 2002), pp. 49–72 (especially 71); though the history of the text of Ezra-Nehemiah is, as Boccaccini notes, complicated by the variants and extrabiblical sources.

5 Wright, e.g., sees the temple concerns of Ezra 7–8 as indicating a pro-priestly redactional strata (*Rebuilding Identity*, pp. 338–9).

6 Williamson's view here is that Ezra was empowered to oversee the Jewish communities throughout Ebar-Nehara (*Ezra, Nehemiah*, pp. 103–5), which is reasonable considering the historical context in which these communities developed (Leuchter, "Ezra's Mission").

layers and tensions within the Nehemiah material,[7] the picture of Nehemiah is fairly consistent with what we might expect of a non-Zadokite Jewish governor of Yehud in the mid-fifth century BCE.[8] The successive redactors of the Nehemiah materials seem to follow some basic genotype in their presentation of Nehemiah's interests, actions, and affiliations.[9] Ezra, by contrast, seems to emerge as a study in contradiction, an elusive shapeshifter who alternately seems to champion disparate agendas and typologies. This may be, as some commentators have suggested, a result of desperate times resulting in desperate measures; there is much to recommend this view. The historical Ezra's (exegetical) combining of long-held mutually exclusive biases might have been a way of removing ancient Israelite law from the realm of the theoretical and making it the foundation for practical solutions to pressing socio-political problems.[10] But this is not revealed in a linear or lucid fashion, as there are no narratorial cues to let the reader know that Ezra does this. And despite the common scholarly view that Ezra possessed and utilized a fairly mature form of the Pentateuch (based primarily on the implications of Nehemiah 8),[11] the account of Ezra's authority and activity in Ezra 7–10 makes only brief allusions to the Pentateuch's Priestly and Deuteronomic traditions, stopping far short of any overt indication that a complete Pentateuch was indeed in his hand.[12]

---

7 Wright, *Rebuilding Identity*, passim.

8 Fried, "The Rescript of Artaxerxes," 85–8; H. G. M. Williamson, *Studies in Persian Period History and Historiography*. (FAT 38; Tübingen: Mohr-Siebeck, 2004), pp. 60–3.

9 Williamson's reconstruction of Nehemiah's personal political and religious interests from the materials in the Nehemiah Memoir is instructive; see his *Studies in Persian Period History and Historiography*, pp. 271–6. So also his observations regarding commonalities between the depiction of Nehemiah and extra-Biblical evidence concerning other Persian governors.

10 While Deuteronomy contains elements pointing to an intended practical application, both the Covenant Code (Exodus 21–23) and the Holiness Code (Leviticus 17–26) are examples of ideological literature not geared for implementation but intellectual/polemical discourse. See B. M. Levinson, "The Manumission of Hermeneutics: The Slave Laws of the Pentateuch as a Challenge to Pentateuchal Theory," in *Congress Volume 2004* (VTSup 109; ed. Andre Lemaire; Leiden: Brill, 2006), p. 323; J. R. Stackert, *Rewriting the Torah: Literary Revision in Deuteronomy and the Holiness Legislation* (Ph.D. diss, Brandeis University, 2006), pp. 218–19; B. Wells, "What is Biblical Law? A Look at Pentateuchal Rules and Near Eastern Practice," *CBQ* 70 (2008), 223–43; M. Leuchter, "The Manumission Laws in Leviticus and Deuteronomy: The Jeremiah Connection," *JBL* 127 (2008), 635–53.

11 W. M. Schniedewind, *How The Bible Became A Book: The Textualization of Ancient Israel* (New York: Cambridge University Press, 2004), pp. 183–4; Williamson, *Ezra, Nehemiah*, p. 283.

12 Ezra may have known the Priestly (P) and Deuteronomic (D) writings, as well as other textual collections, but with the exception of Nehemiah 8 (see below), none of the references to Ezra's fluency with these law codes identify them as part of a single Pentateuch.

There can be little doubt that the redactors responsible for shaping Ezra-Nehemiah were highly literate, well versed in native Israelite tradition as much as they were fluent with the common Persian culture of political and administrative discourse.[13] The literary clarity with which Nehemiah is presented contrasts so sharply with the ambiguity surrounding Ezra that the latter cannot be seen as a mere accident or the inadvertent result of successive redactions. Rather, the redactors have seen fit to create a character who casts a variety of shadows but whose actual likeness remains elusive.[14] By examining these shadows, we may be able to obtain some image of the individual or individuals — i.e., the redactors behind the text as much as Ezra himself — responsible for their contours.

Ezra as a Zadokite

Though very likely the result of a secondary accretion,[15] the genealogical information in Ezra 7:1-5 clearly identifies Ezra as a member of the Zadokite priesthood. The genealogy itself is widely recognized to be inaccurate and historically unreliable in its details, as it traces an unbroken priestly line all the way back to the origin of the priesthood itself through unlikely avenues. Nevertheless, such an illustrious list of ancestors makes it highly likely that Ezra was perceived by ancient audiences to have been a prominent Zadokite.[16] No redactor or author would be so bold as to ignore long-standing prohibitions against ascribing priestly status to individuals who did not possess the proper lineage roots (e.g., 1 Kgs 12:31), and throughout Ezra-Nehemiah, Ezra is indeed regarded and regularly referred to as a priest.[17] As in many genealogies, however, the list of ancestors

---

See P. Mandel, "The Origins of Midrash in the Second Temple Period," in *Current Trends in the Study of Midrash* (JSJSup 106; ed. C. Bakhos; Leiden: Brill, 2006), p. 24.

13 For the administrative fluency of Israelite scribes in a Persian context, see D. S. Vanderhooft, "New Evidence Pertaining to the Transition from Neo-Babylonian to Achaemenid Administration in Palestine," in *Yahwism after the Exile: Perspectives on Israelite Religion in the Persian Era* (eds. R. Albertz and B. Becking; Assen: Van Gorcum, 2003), p. 234.

14 I do not wish to suggest here that such redactional strata are not behind the relative obscurity of Ezra, only that the principal redactors of Ezra-Nehemiah saw fit to leave Ezra deliberately ambiguous as a hermeneutical statement in its own right. Following G. N. Knoppers' observations concerning the Chronicler's work (*I Chronicles 10–29*. [AB; New York: Doubleday, 2004], p. 789), I suggest below that this literary characteristic is an important indication of cultural/social circumstances in the redactors' times.

15 Pakkala, *Ezra the Scribe*, p. 24 n. 7, with further sources listed there.

16 *Pace* Pakkala, *Ezra the Scribe*, pp. 24–25.

17 I do not disagree with Pakkala's view (*Ezra the Scribe*, p. 25) that the references to Ezra's priestly status are often muted with respect to priestly function. However, as I note in the ensuing discussion, these are not secondary accretions but rather seem to be inherent to

and its relative length serve rhetorical purposes, and the fact that several notable chief Zadokite priests are missing from this list is a red flag to the reader that the genealogical information has been shaped with a specific agenda. In Ezra's case, the genealogy ties him to three central priestly figures: Seraiah (the last chief priest of pre-exilic Judah),[18] Zadok, and of course Aaron. Here, as elsewhere in Ezra-Nehemiah, lists of ancestors bind a specific group or individual to an authoritative community or subcommunal collective. In Ezra's case, the list serves a mediating purpose. Ezra's origination among the Jews of Mesopotamia grants him esteem associated with the Golah community that legitimizes his place in the politics of Yehud,[19] but the genealogical information in Ezra 7:1-5 also makes clear that Golah origins do not diminish his fitness for leadership among the priestly hierarchy in Yehud. It may well be the case that the Zadokite priestly leadership in Yehud that had been in place before Ezra viewed his mission as an unwelcomed challenge to their own socio-religious authority; the list of ancestors constitutes an argument against this view, identifying Ezra as one of their own.[20]

The list, however, plays with the form and sequence of ancestors in order to make this point. The anachronistic placement of Zadok's name in the genealogy has suggested to some commentators that this is not a reference to the same Zadok who founded the priestly line in Jerusalem in the tenth century BCE.[21] However, we must not rule out the possibility, even the likelihood, that the sequence here serves a symbolic purpose in the service of an ideological agenda related to the memory of the re-orchestration of priestly lineage hierarchies either during Ezra's lifetime or similar dynamics reflecting the theo-political world of the redactors.[22] Moving the reference to Zadok closer in sequence to Ezra may reflect a time

---

the memory and characterization of Ezra when read in tandem with other priestly flourishes in Ezra-Nehemiah.

18 I use the term "chief priest" following Rooke's conclusion that the office of "High Priest" significantly post-dates the fifth century BCE (*Zadok's Heirs*, p. 218).

19 See P. R. Bedford, "Diaspora: Homeland Relations in Ezra-Nehemiah," *VT* 52 (2002), 152–65.

20 This strategy of creating or highlighting "insider" status through the introduction to a biblical personality finds an antecedent in Jeremiah 1, where Jeremiah is presented as a good member of the northern Shilonite sacral tradition despite his role as an emissary of the Josianic court. See Leuchter, *Josiah's Reform and Jeremiah's Scroll: Historical Calamity and Prophetic Response* (Sheffield Phoenix Press, 2006), pp. 70–86. The form of discourse is different in Ezra 7:1-5 (using an ancestor list exclusively) but the concerns are the same, since Ezra represents an outsider royal presence sent to a smaller region and its priestly leadership.

21 See, among others, S. Japhet, *I & II Chronicles*. (OTL; Louisville/London: Westminster John Knox, 1993), p. 151; Pakkala, *Ezra the Scribe*, p. 25.

22 Similar genealogical flourishes characterize the superscription of Zephaniah; see below. Genealogical adjustments are also deployed extensively by the Chronicler for socio-political purposes; see Y. Levin, "Who Was The Chronicler's Audience? A Hint from

when other Zadokite priestly families vied for dominance in Yehudite religious politics, and the rhetorical implications of a closer (albeit contrived) genealogical connection to Zadok in Ezra 7:2 would weigh in Ezra's favor. In any event, the reason for the connection to Zadok is obvious: it officially declares Ezra to be of the "ruling" priestly house long associated with the temple,[23] one which had been restored to socio-political prominence earlier in the period of restoration. The extensive tracing of the line to Zadok also opens the door to its extension back to Aaron, the purpose of which is related to the ritual re-enactment of the Exodus and Wilderness wandering.[24] This bestows upon Ezra's mission a dimension transcending its administrative purpose, perhaps serving as an argument against other Zadokites in powerful positions in Jerusalem who questioned Ezra's authority.

The crucial element in this genealogy, however, is the mention of Seraiah. Most scholars have noted that identifying Ezra as Seraiah's son is a giveaway of the genealogy's artifice, as the stretch of time between Seraiah's lifetime in the early sixth century and Ezra's in the mid-fifth (or, according to some, early fourth) prohibits a father–son relationship.[25] There can be no reasonable argument against this view, of course, but we must pause before reading the text as a simple attempt to pass off a fictitious relationship as historically accurate. Other genealogies seem to "skip" generations in order to establish the affiliation of the individual in question with an ancestral line — for example, the genealogical details regarding Jonathan b. Gershom b. Moses in Judg. 18:30.[26] Here, a figure current in tenth-century lore is associated with the foundation of a twelfth-century shrine and an even earlier Mushite priestly line in order to validate the sanctuary's place in the reform cult of Jeroboam.[27] Whoever the actual Jonathan may have been, he is remembered in tradition as a Mushite, and thus the author of Judges 18 links him closely to Moses (via Gershom). A similar logic may underlie Ezra's

his Genealogies," *JBL* 122 (2003), 229–45; idem, "From Lists to History: Chronological Aspects of the Chronicler's Genealogies," *JBL* 123 (2004), 601–36.

23   As opposed to Aaronides more generally; see Boccaccini, *Roots of Rabbinic Judaism,* pp. 61–8.

24   Leuchter, "Ezra's Mission." See also K. Koch, "Ezra and the Origins of Judaism," *JSS* 19 (1974), 184–5; Williamson, *Ezra, Nehemiah,* p. 93.

25   E.g., Pakkala, *Ezra the Scribe,* p. 24. On the possibility of Ezra's mission as occurring in 398 BCE, see above. The traditional dating to 458 BCE, however, is more likely, as will be discussed in the conclusion to the present study.

26   Well known is the secondary nature of the נ in the name מִישֶׁה in Judg. 18:30, leaving the original name מֹשֶה.

27   B. Halpern, "Levitic Participation in the Reform Cult of Jeroboam I," *JBL* 75 (1976), 36–7. It is obviously impossible to ascertain an accurate date for the lifespan of Moses, but a time preceding the mid-twelfth century seems likely. See L. E. Stager, "Forging an Identity: The Emergence of Ancient Israel," in *The Oxford History of the Biblical World* (ed. M. D. Coogan; New York: Oxford University Press, 1998), p. 107.

identification as the "son" of Seraiah: he may not be Seraiah's biological son, but the genealogical information suggests that he is of Seraiah's family line. The identification of Ezra with this particular line makes abundantly clear that he is not simply a Zadokite, but of the very family that could lay claim to the chief priesthood in the Jerusalem Temple.

We must bear in mind that while the list of names in Ezra 7:1-5 contains genealogical details, it is not actually a genealogy but a dramatically extended patronym. Extended patronyms are usually deployed to highlight the significance of a character in history. First Sam. 1:1 contains an extended patronym for Elqanah, Samuel's father, in order to clarify that Samuel comes from a long line of sacral figures, and 1 Sam. 9:1 does the same with respect to proving that Israel's first king, Saul, is a good member of the hinterland clan culture.[28] Extended patronyms in the book of Jeremiah highlight the importance of individuals within the drama of the twilight years of monarchic Judah,[29] and the prophet Zephaniah's unusually long patronym carries relevant ethno-cultural overtones as well as a link to the reign of Hezekiah (Zeph. 1:1). Ezra's extended patronym follows this pattern, and its sheer scope makes a strong statement regarding Ezra's role in the nation's history. The connection to Aaron (the foundation of the cult), Zadok (the foundation of the monarchy), and Seraiah (the destruction of the temple) suggests that Ezra's mission represents another pivotal, formative moment in Israel's religion on par with these other root experiences. In each case, the lineage details in question relate to the chief cultic functionary at the time; while Ezra could not have functioned as part of a cultically active priesthood while living in Babylon, the rhetorical force of his genealogical details strongly suggest that he was fit for the job, and sets the stage for his mission to Yehud to fall into a cultic category.[30]

---

28 Leuchter, *Josiah's Reform and Jeremiah's Scroll*, pp. 21–30; idem, "Samuel, Saul and the Deuteronomistic Categories of History," in *From Babel to Babylon: Essays in Honor of Brian Peckham* (ed. J. Rilett-Wood *et al.*, LHBOTS 455; T&T Clark, 2006), pp. 101–9.

29 For an examination of this phenomenon within the Jeremiah tradition, for example, see D. A. Glatt-Gilad, "The Personal Names in Jeremiah as a Source for the History of the Period," *Hebrew Studies* 41 (2000), 31–45.

30 B. J. Schwartz notes a similar issue with respect to Ezekiel, insofar as exilic circumstances prohibited cultic activity ("A Priest Out of Place: Reconsidering Ezekiel's Role in the History of the Israelite Priesthood," *Ezekiel's Hierarchical World: Wrestling with a Tiered Reality* [SBLSymS; eds. S. L. Cook and C. L. Patton; Atlanta: SBL, 2004], p. 65). I disagree with Schwartz's view, however, that Ezekiel's prophetic activity and status were not strongly connected to his self concept as a priest. The vehicle of prophecy itself became the expression of priestly status in the absence of cultic activity; see M. A. Sweeney, "Ezekiel: Zadokite Priest and Visionary Prophet of the Exile," *SBL 2000 Seminar Papers* (Atlanta: SBL, 2000), pp. 728–51. There is good evidence that the Zadokites in exile (and later, living in the eastern Diaspora) developed an intellectual and literary curriculum to compensate for

We can also glean a degree of evidence regarding Ezra's Zadokite/priestly status beyond his genealogical details. While scholarly skepticism regarding the authenticity of the Artaxerxes Rescript is justified, that it is a midrashic-type work of Jewish scribal origin ensures that the cultic/juridical authority granted Ezra within the Rescript derives not from imperial mandates but from native Jewish ones.[31] The memory of Ezra among the Jewish redactors of Ezra-Nehemiah is one of a legitimate priest. Here, it is highly significant that Ezra is granted two primary duties: to appoint "judges and magistrates" throughout Ebar-Nahara (Ezra 7:25) and to oversee sacrifices on behalf of Artaxerxes in the Jerusalem Temple (Ezra 7:16-17). The former, while Deuteronomistic in expression,[32] would fall under the jurisdiction of the chief priest in the Persian period; the latter clearly presupposes Ezra's fitness to enter the temple and conduct rituals therein, and there is no opposition to this view anywhere in Ezra-Nehemiah. Considering the synthesis achieved in the Rescript with respect to the rest of Ezra-Nehemiah — for the former appears to have been composed with an eye to a much larger work[33] — it seems that the late author/redactor inherited a work with a reading tradition affixed to it that quite readily identified Ezra as capable, even poised, to assume major priestly responsibilities.

And yet, Ezra does not do any of this. We hear nothing of him assuming the role of chief priest.[34] We have no record of his ritual activity or an account of his conducting of sacrifices. We do not learn anything about the outcome of his mission as a supervisor over the juridical offices Ebar-Nehara.[35] We do not even

---

their separation from the Jerusalem temple cult (Leuchter, "The Jeremiah Connection"), thus picking up on Ezekiel's choice to engage alternate forms of discourse in order to support and reinforce Zadokite priestly centrality. Priesthood in exile may not have revolved around a sacrificial cult but, instead, around an intellectual discourse, and this same circumstance would have characterized an educated priest such as Ezra. For further connections between Ezekiel and Ezra, see Koch, "Ezra and the Origins of Judaism," 195. With these antecedents in place, it is entirely likely that Ezra was enculturated with these ideas and was identified as a potent Zadokite priest capable of taking of taking up an active ministry in Jerusalem.

31 A. C. Hagedorn, "Local Law in an Imperial Context: The Role of Torah in the (Imagined) Persian Period," in *The Pentateuch as Torah: New Models for Understanding it Promulgation and Acceptance* (eds. G. N. Knoppers and B. M. Levinson; Winona Lake: Eisenbrauns, 2007), pp. 69–71; L. L. Grabbe, "The Law of Moses in the Ezra Tradition: More Virtual than Real?" *Persia and Torah*, pp. 93–4.

32 See the discussion later in this essay.

33 Hagedorn, "Local Law."

34 *Pace* K. Koch, "Ezra and Meremoth: Remarks on the History of the High Priesthood," in *Sha'arei Talmon: Studies on the Bible, Qumran and the Ancient Near East Presented to Shemaryahu Talmon* (eds. M. Fishbane and E. Tov; Winona Lake: Eisenbrauns, 1992), pp. 105–10; idem, "Ezra and the Origins of Judaism," 190.

35 Comparative evidence, however, is suggestive. See Fried, "Rescript of Artaxerxes," 67–84 (though her conclusion regarding the strictly secular nature of Ezra's role in appointing

learn anything about the duration of his position in Yehud; unlike Nehemiah, there is no account of him leaving office and returning to the eastern Diaspora. The content of Nehemiah 8 notwithstanding,[36] Ezra dissolves into the ether within the expanse of Ezra-Nehemiah, a very strange phenomenon considering the extensive details surrounding him in Ezra 7–10 that builds up such enormous priestly anticipation and then, inexplicably, comes to a full stop. What appears to be a developing triumphant proclamation of Zadokite authority shifts gears entirely and focuses on the lay-Levite leadership of Nehemiah's tenure, often with a critical eye on the Jerusalem priesthood. The argument that Ezra and Nehemiah were originally two independent works only secondarily joined at a late point in time may account for some of the problems arising from what we might term a *clerus interruptus*.[37] However, another possibility arises, and this is that the sudden halt of Zadokite characteristics regarding Ezra's role and legacy within Ezra-Nehemiah is the result of conscious, rhetorical design, and meant to be a component part of a composite whole. We must therefore consider the other major sacerdotal discourse within the book that flavors Ezra's literary character, namely, that of the Deuteronomistic Levite tradition.

Ezra as a Deuteronomistic Levite

Before identifying the passages in Ezra 7–10 that characterize Ezra in Levitical terms, a word is in order with respect to defining the phrase "Deuteronomistic

---

satrapal judges [88–9] is open to question); Steiner, "The *mbqr* at Qumran, the *episkopos* in the Athenian Empire, and the meaning of *lbqr'* in Ezra 7:14: On the Relation of Ezra's Mission to the Persian Legal Project," *JBL* 120 (2001), 623–46.

36 With J. L. Wright ("Writing the Restoration: Compositional Agenda and the Role of Ezra in Nehemiah 8," in M. Leuchter [ed.], "Scribes Before and After 587 B.C.E.: A Conversation," *JHS* 7 [2007], Article 10, 25–9 [http://www.arts.ualberta.ca/JHS/Articles/article_71.pdf]), I view Nehemiah 8 as a late addition to Ezra-Nehemiah that was composed for its current literary context. Pakkala proposes a somewhat different view, seeing Nehemiah 8 as a late development of an early account that was originally part of an Ezra memoir (*Ezra the Scribe*, pp. 136–79). As David Kraemer notes, however, the Ezra of Nehemiah 8 is dramatically different than the Ezra of Ezra 7–10 ("On the Relationship of the Books of Ezra and Nehemiah," *JSOT* 59 (1993), 80–3). Pakkala's view is still possible (though attempts to restore an early versiuon, but in light of Kraemer's observations, it is evident that a late redactor's manipulation of an early extant Ezra tradition yielded an entirely different type of narrative and thematic thrust). The resulting text is thus designed to fit into the larger structure of Nehemiah 8–10 and serves as a keystone to the Nehemiah corpus in general (Leuchter, "Ezra's Mission").

37 For an argument regarding the original independence of the Ezra and Nehemiah corpora, see J. C. VanderKam, "EN or Ezra and Nehemiah?" in *Priests, Prophets and Scribes: Essays on the Formation and Heritage of Second Temple Judaism in Honour of Joseph Blenkinsopp* (JSOTSup 149; eds. E. Ulrich *et al.*, Sheffield: Sheffield Academic Press), pp. 55–75.

Levite." Joachim Schaper has argued for a distinction between types of Levites in the Second Temple literature,[38] and a similar distinction should be made with respect to texts referring to earlier Levite groups and ideas. The animosity between the Deuteronomistic engineers of the Jeremiah tradition and the priests of Anatoth, for example, reveal tensions between this Levite group and the Deuteronomistic establishment.[39] And yet Deuteronomy repeatedly emphasizes the place and authority of Levites throughout both the hinterland and the central sanctuary and judiciary.[40] Whether or not this reflects a late-seventh-century dynamic or derives from an exilic context is immaterial for our present concerns.[41] What it attests to is Levite divisiveness in a period preceding that of Ezra or the shapers of Ezra-Nehemiah, and one that likely persisted into the fifth century. A natural point of division would also characterize Levite culture during the Neo-Babylonian period, as many Levites would have been deported to Mesopotamia while others remained displaced in the homeland.[42] Here, a significant shift in Levitical responsibility can be discerned. The liturgical works deriving from the Levites of the homeland groups emphasize despoiled cultic institutions and in fact create a sort of cult-of-desolation, with the community defining itself through their relationship to the remains of Jerusalem and other major sites in Judah ruined by the Babylonian forces.[43] By contrast, the exilic redaction of

---

38 J. Schaper, *Priester und Leviten im achämenidischen Juda* (Tübingen: Mohr Siebeck, 2000), pp. 294–5.

39 Leuchter, *Josiah's Reform and Jeremiah' Scroll*, 97–100, with respect to the implications of Jer. 11:18-23. Even if this text and the notices regarding the men of Anatoth are not directly attributable to the prophet, they suggest a culture of opposition between the Levites of the rural territories (such as the region in Benjamin where Anatoth was located) and the urban culture of Jerusalem standing behind the production of the major texts influenced by Deuteronomy.

40 M. Leuchter, "'The Levite In Your Gates': The Deuteronomic Redefinition of Levitical Authority," *JBL* 126 (2007), 417–36; idem, "Why is the Song of Moses in the Book of Deuteronomy?" *VT* 57 (2007), 295–317. See also K. Van der Toorn, *Scribal Culture and the Making of the Hebrew Bible* (Cambridge: Harvard University Press, 2007), pp. 93, 95–6 (though he is less certain about ascribing literary responsibilities to Levites in the pre-Persian period).

41 Many scholars still advocate a late pre-exilic context for this material. See Leuchter, "The Levite In Your Gates"; B. M. Levinson, *Deuteronomy and the Hermeneutics of Legal Innovation* (New York: Oxford University Press, 1997), pp. 98–143; M. A. Sweeney, *King Josiah of Judah: The Lost Messiah of Israel* (New York: Oxford University Press, 2001), pp. 159–69.

42 For Levites remaining in Judah, see P. D. Hanson, *The Dawn of Apocalyptic: The Historical and Sociological Roots of Jewish Apocalyptic Eschatology* (Philadelphia: Fortress Press, 1979), p. 227; Schaper, *Priester und Leviten*, p. 163.

43 The most thorough examination of these texts is that of J. Middlemas, *The Troubles of Templeless Judah* (Oxford: Oxford University Press, 2005). That these texts derive from

Deuteronomy and Jeremiah — both works heavily steeped in Levitical thought — emphasize the transcendence of identity from the strictures of life bound to the homeland, employing sophisticated methods of literary exegesis as a means of devotion in and of itself and empowering Levites to command sacral authority through the production and teaching of sacred literary traditions.[44]

Indeed, Levites who were taken into captivity would have advocated the Deuteronomistic tradition as it developed among the exilic community since it established a basis for their ongoing authority independent from sacred sites in the homeland.[45] Considering the paucity of Levites in Ezra's delegation to Yehud (Ezra 8:15), it would seem likely that many Levites enjoyed a high degree of authority and influence in the eastern Diaspora and were reluctant to leave that behind; the Deuteronomistic tradition must have been firmly entrenched in this world, providing scribal/exegetical means for communal identity to be adjusted with the unfolding of time.[46] With the shift to Persian hegemony, the literary skills of these Levites would have provided them with the opportunity to secure imperial administrative positions over/within the communities living in Babylon and Persia proper.[47] This was not inconsistent with the original role mandated for Levites within Deuteronomy, which conceived of Levites as local exegetical/scribal agents of the Josianic establishment.[48] Thus, the Deuteronomistic Levite tradition would have led many a Levite to become well versed in the rhetoric, policies, and praxes of the Persian Empire not only as a matter of utilitarian expedience but also, as a pseudo-sacral responsibility concomitant with the earlier words of Jeremiah to seek the welfare of the host culture (Jer. 29:7).

In short, the Deuteronomistic Levite tradition had blossomed in the eastern Diaspora as a distinct theological/intellectual institution. This must be viewed in sharp contradistinction to the developing Priestly tradition of the Zadokite priesthood, which does not exhibit any overt conciliatory tendencies regarding foreign dominators. In the Priestly tradition, holiness derives not from interaction with imperial powers but is isolated within the community and the priesthood at

Levite authors is indicated by their formalistic similarity to other liturgical works in the Psalter and elsewhere regarded as the work of Levite composers. The Psalter in general is the result of Levitical shaping during the Second Temple period; see M. S. Smith, "The Levitical Redaction of the Psalter," *ZAW* 103 (1991), 258–63.

44 Leuchter, *Polemics of Exile*, 182–4; idem, "The Temple Sermon and the Term מקום in the Jeremianic Corpus," *JSOT* 30/1 (2005), 93–109.

45 Leuchter, "The Levite In Your Gates," 433–5.

46 This is evident with respect to the account of the courting of the Levites of Casiphia; see below.

47 Vanderhooft, "New Evidence," 234.

48 Leuchter, "The Levite In Your Gates," 419–25.

its apex.[49] While there is no doubt that the Zadokites of Jerusalem accepted the authority of their Persian patrons, they enjoyed relative autonomy over Jewish life in Yehud. This must have included dominion over the role of Levites who returned during the restoration period of the late sixth-century who took up duties in the temple following its completion in 516 BCE. The Deuteronomistic Levite tradition yielded a different sort of Levite, one whose responsibilities were pedagogical, social/administrative, and scribal in nature rather than simply part of the Zadokite pecking order in Jerusalem.[50] The Levites of Casiphia, whom Ezra apparently recruited to his service in his delegation to Yehud, stand out as examples of this very breed of Diaspora Levite. Both they and their locale are identified in Deuteronomistic terms, and their recruitment to his delegation points to their administrative abilities as equally important as their sacral heritage.[51] If Levites already stationed in the Jerusalem Temple had sacerdotal duties, those recruited by Ezra would have functioned differently, and the imperial nature of Ezra's appointment would be well served by a staff ready to support imperial-administrative measures.

While we have seen that a strong thematic undercurrent binds Ezra to the Zadokite priesthood, it is impossible to overlook the similarities evident between the characterization of Ezra within Ezra-Nehemiah and the Deuteronomistic Levite tradition. However dramatic the buildup in Ezra 7:1-5 to the mention of Aaron, the text trumps even this in the very next verse by the emphasis on his role as a "skilled scribe" devoted to exegesis of YHWH's Torah (v. 6).[52] That Ezra's scribal interests and abilities are stressed in this manner suggests that it was uncommon for a Zadokite to carry these qualifications. It is beyond doubt that a Zadokite elite in either Yehud or the eastern Diaspora would have possessed a high degree of education and literacy, but if Zadokites were typically regarded as authoritative scribal exegetes of YHWH's Torah, would the author behind Ezra 7:6 have gone to such lengths as to spell out Ezra's geographical

---

49 Boccaccini, *Roots of Rabbinic Judaism*, pp. 49–72; Watts, *Ritual and Rhetoric*, pp. 142–72.

50 Van der Toorn also notes this feature of Second Temple Levitical behavior (*Scribal Culture*, pp. 92–6). Though van der Toorn views this as a postexilic phenomenon, the impulse not only for scribalism but for engagement with the general public and administration of social conduct is woven into the preexilic core layers of Deuteronomy itself; see M. Weinfeld, *The Place of the Law in the Religion of Ancient Israel* (VTSup; Leiden: Brill, 2004), pp. 84–90.

51 Leuchter, "Ezra's Mission."

52 Here, the *Wiederaufnahme* created by the עזרא הוא from the editor who added the genealogical details (similarly Pakkala, *Ezra the Scribe*, p. 24) creates additional sociological depth. It should be read not simply as the repetitive resumption of the name "Ezra" but, perhaps, closer to "[yet], this very same Ezra who came up from Babylon was a skilled scribe . . ."

origin ("[he] came up from Babylon") and exegetical predilections in this way? The likely answer is "no." First, the Zadokite priesthood was firmly entrenched in Jerusalem by the mid-fifth century; the reference to Ezra's Babylonian origin automatically places him in a somewhat distinct cateogory. Furthermore, the P legislation in Leviticus which delineates the right and responsibility of a Zadokite priest to teach and interpret the law makes no mention of the scribal process.[53] Rather, it intimates an *oral* setting wherein priestly instruction is to take place. Ezekiel, a forerunner to Ezra in that he too is a Zadokite living in Mesopotamia, also takes it upon himself to teach the law through the vehicle of prophecy, and he too limits the degree to which scribal processes factor into his rhetoric.[54] That Ezra is so closely associated with the chief priestly Zadokite line and then is immediately set in a category so distinct from all that we know of Zadokite modes of learning and teaching strongly indicates that a redactor has deliberately attempted to move Ezra from the Zadokite spotlight and cast him in the colors of a Deuteronomistic Levite.

The parallels between the characterization of Ezra in Ezra 7–10 and subsequent episodes in the book of Nehemiah involving Levites also warrant a closer look. The rebuilding of the Jerusalem wall and the establishment of its gates provide for the Levites under Nehemiah a place to re-engage older Deuteronomistic modes of socio-religious administration, and in a manner that expands authority beyond the confines of the temple.[55] In a similar vein, Ezra is charged in the Rescript to establish "judges and magistrates" throughout all of Ebar-Nehara

53   W. M. Schniedewind, "The Textualization of Torah in the Deuteronomistic Tradition," in *Das Deuteronomium zwischen Pentateuch und deuteronomistischem Geschichstwerk* (eds. E. Otto and R. Achenbach; Vandenhoeck & Ruprecht, 2004), pp. 153–4.

54   Especially telling in this regard is Ezek. 2:8–3:3[4], where the scribal process narrated in Jeremiah 36 (especially vv. 1-4, 17-18) is completely reversed: the written scroll goes *into* the prophet's mouth and the divine word is spoken, not written and read aloud. For the orality of Zadokite teaching, see also Schwartz, "A Priest Out of Place," 68. Ezekiel's activity takes place during a transitional period with respect to orality and literacy in priestly/prophetic discourse. See J. Schaper, "Exilic and Post-Exilic Prophecy and the Orality/Literacy Problem," *VT* 55 (2005), 332–9.

55   The Nehemiah Memoir makes repeated reference to the rebuilding of the gates in the construction of Jerusalem's wall (Neh. 1:3; 2:3, 8, 13, 17; 6:1; 7:3; 11:19; 12:25, 30; 13:19, 22). Considering Nehemiah's empowerment of Levites and the earlier Deuteronomic emphasis on Levitical authority in the gate (Leuchter, "The Levite In Your Gates," 419–25), we may conclude that the emphasis on the rebuilding of the gates is related to the administrative role of Levites during Nehemiah's tenure as governor, bringing "out" a Levitical responsibility that had previously been confined to the temple (Schaper, "Temple Treasury," 200–6). This is consistent with Williamson's evaluation of Nehemiah's personal religious and political agenda regarding the authority of the temple faculty (*Studies in Persian Period History and Historiography*, pp. 274–5).

(Ezra 7:25), even further beyond the temple complex. It is no coincidence that this charge utilizes the Aramaic equivalent of the Deuteronomic mandate charging Levites with juridical authority (Deut. 16:18-20). Of course, one of the outstanding events in the narrative of Ezra's mission is his separation of Israelite men from "foreign" women via the proclamation of a mass divorce, something that also surfaces in Nehemiah 13 following the demarcation of the legitimate community in Nehemiah 8–10. The centerpiece of this unit is the Levitical prayer in Nehemiah 9, one that finds an antecedent in Ezra's similar prayer in Ezra 9.[56] Both prayers engage in a recitation of sacred history, both sideline the relevance of the temple, and both petition YHWH through the invocation of earlier scripture.[57] One is left with the unavoidable impression that the redactors of Ezra-Nehemiah have positioned Ezra not only to anticipate the features of the Nehemiah Memoir, but indeed to bestow upon the Levites therein a special authoritative status by establishing a strong "Zadokite" precedent.

The famous episode of Ezra's reading of the Torah in Nehemiah 8 is the final link in this chain. Scholars are divided over the provenance and historicity of this episode, but regardless of the time at which it entered Ezra-Nehemiah, it bestows upon Ezra the qualities of a Deuteronomistic Levite and invokes earlier historiographic episodes that relate to this tradition. Ezra calls the people together in a manner similar to Josiah and deploys Levites throughout the assembly to teach the people the "sense" of the text he reads aloud.[58] Just as in Deuteronomy, Levites are responsible for teaching the text and translating it into digestible terms. In the same episode, Ezra is described as a priest when retrieving the Torah for the assembly (v. 2), but he is expressly identified as a scribe when reading from it and overseeing its dissemination by his Levite agents (v. 4).[59] Like the shift from Zadokite genealogy to personal scribal mandate in Ezra 7:1-6, this distinction makes clear that scribal exegesis and teaching of the sort we encounter in Neh. 8:1-

---

56 Leuchter, "Ezra's Mission."

57 The non-mention of the temple in Nehemiah 9, especially, has generated a tremendous diversity of scholarly opinion regarding its provenance. See G. A. Rendsburg, "The Northern Origins of Nehemiah 9," *Bib* 72 (1991), 365–6; Williamson, *Studies in Persian Period History and Historiography*, p. 292; M. J. Boda, *Praying The Tradition: The Origin and Use of Tradition in Nehemiah 9* (BZAW 277; Berlin: De Gruyter, 1999), pp. 189–95. See also Kraemer, "On the Relationship," 79, who notes that Nehemiah 9 is the first example of the *Heilsgeschichte* that invokes Sinai, which carries implications regarding the significance of the temple in the culture of the authors of the prayer and the redactors who incorporated it into Ezra-Nehemiah.

58 The similarity to Josiah's covenant ceremony in 2 Kgs 23:1-3 is discussed by M. Duggan, *The Covenant Renewal in Ezra-Nehemiah (Neh 7:72b–10:40). An Exegetical, Literary, and Theological Study* (SBLDS 164; Atlanta: Society of Biblical Literature, 2001), p. 122.

59 Kraemer, "On the Relationship," 80–3.

12 is an entirely different typological category than Zadokite priestly behavior. Whereas the Holiness Code and Ezekiel subordinate the Levites to the activities and authority of "higher" priestly offices (Numbers 16–18; Ezek. 44:10-13), Neh. 8:1-12 makes Ezra's priestly behavior a subset of his larger scribal duties. This too is entirely consistent with Deuteronomy and its understanding of priest-hood (where *all* priests are Levites), and strongly reflects the influence of the Deuteronomistic Levite tradition in the characterization not only of Ezra but of the communal standard he appears to establish.

Perhaps, the most significant clue in this regard is the "discovery" of the new law narrated in vv. 13-18.[60] Here, a text regarding the festival of Sukkot is consulted and a new ordinance is declared as arising from the consultation (v. 15), though as all commentators have observed, the Pentateuch does not contain this ordinance.[61] This is often regarded as a parade example of scriptural exegesis already at work within the Hebrew Bible, and rightly so considering the unsubtle manner in which the narrator equates an obviously late and secondary interpretation with an established textual tradition, i.e., the Sukkot legislation in Lev. 23:34-43,[62] part of the Holiness Code (H). What is often overlooked, how-ever, is the rhetorical effect of having this specific legislation subjected to the Deuteronomistic Levitical type of exegesis. Holiness Code is a Zadokite work that pulls no punches in polemicizing against the Deuteronomic legislation for the sake of supplanting it, and is a major chapter in an ongoing rivalry between Deuteronomistic and Zadokite ideological camps.[63] The H authors, living and working in exile in Babylon, appropriated the methods of lemmatic exegesis earlier employed by the Deuteronomists as a way of superseding them as the undisputed theological-intellectual elite of their time and place.[64]

Nehemiah 8:13-18 challenges that claim. By subjecting Lev. 23:34-43 to a Deuteronomistic Levitical method of exegesis under the auspices of Ezra the scribe, the redactors declare that H can be abstracted from a context that

---

60 The substance of the discussion here regarding Neh. 8:13-18 is the result of a con-versation with my colleague Mark Brett following the SBL historiography session from which the present volume of essays emerges. I am grateful to him for his valuable insights regarding the use of the Holiness Code in this passage.

61 For a variety of comments concerning this exegetical development of the Leviticus 23 text, see Williamson, *Persian Period History and Historiography*, pp. 237–9; R. J. L. Milgrom, *Leviticus: A Book of Rituals and Ethics* (Minneapolis: Fortress Press, 2004), p. 283 (Milgrom attempts to reconcile the Nehemiah 8/Leviticus 23 material); Pakkala views Neh. 8:13-18 as based on a version of the Leviticus 23 legislation earlier than the version now found in the Pentateuch (*Ezra the Scribe*, p. 164).

62 See especially Fishbane, *BibInt*, pp. 109–12.

63 Leuchter, "The Jeremiah Connection."

64 Ibid.

empowers the Zadokite priesthood and with the very tradition its exilic authors sought to marginalize. The passage is very clear, too, that the entire cultic faculty of the temple deferred to this approach to actualizing the law (vv. 13, 17), and it is only after this exegetical tradition is enacted that the Levitical prayer of Nehemiah 9 is recited. In the context of chs 8–10, Neh. 8:13-18 declares that entrance into the sacral community (demarcated finally in Nehemiah 10) is not only a matter of identifying with the prayer chanted by the Levites in Nehemiah 9 but also requires a recognition that the Deuteronomistic Levite tradition of scribal exegesis is the authentic vehicle for adhering to the law, regardless of the compositional origins or polemical intent of the law in question.[65] As a Zadokite, Ezra would have been empowered to teach the collections of Zadokite laws, but in this case, he does so as a scribe of the Deuteronomistic Levite tradition. That this, exegetical event takes place during the Sukkot festival also recalls Deut. 31:9-13 wherein the Levites themselves are charged with publicly reading the law entrusted to them every seventh year during the Sukkot festival,[66] likely in relation to regular redactional expansion/updates of the written lawcode housed in the central sanctuary.[67] By making H the centerpiece of this process of expansion, Neh. 8:13-18 subordinates Zadokite legal texts to scribal processes and teachings situated beyond the traditional social ranks of the Zadokite priesthood.[68]

It is highly significant that despite the reintroduction of Ezra in Nehemiah 8, he makes no further appearance as the book of Nehemiah continues. But the fact that Ezra 9 anticipates the Levites' prayer in Nehemiah 9 makes up for Ezra's

---

65 Within this hermeneutical matrix, however, is undoubtedly an historical tradition regarding the observance of the Sukkot festival implemented in either the time of Ezra or Nehemiah, for the selection of Lev. 23:34-43 would otherwise be a pedestrian text to subject to this literary treatment. Insofar as Nehemiah 8 is patterned upon Josiah's covenant ceremony in 2 Kgs 23:1-3 (Duggan, *Covenant Renewal*, p. 122), one would imagine that the Passover legislation would be a more suitable source for this rhetorical flourish, given the prominence of the Passover in Josiah's regnal account.

66 See similarly Fishbane, *Biblical Interpretation*, pp. 112–13.

67 A seven-year interval between public proclamations of the "official" law code would allow for the processes of legal expansion legislated in Deut. 17:8-13 to yield enough new laws to warrant a redaction of the master copy of the written corpus; see Leuchter, *Josiah's Reform and Jeremiah's Scroll*, pp. 33–8. Its public proclamation would then provide a basis for regional Levite scribe-magistrates to subsequently implement those laws on a village by village basis (Deut. 16:18-20), thereby explaining how the entire nation would be privy to individual legal disputes brought before the central sanctuary (Deut. 17:13).

68 That these verses are not found in the 1 Esdras parallel text further suggests that they have been deliberately excised by a partisan redactor/editor for the purposes of emphasizing the ritual dimensions of reading the Torah over against the exegesis inherent to the Levite-scribal tradition.

absence by implying that the Levites uttering the prayer are entrusted with Ezra's scribal authority. This recalls the passing of the torch from Moses to the Levites in Deuteronomy (Deut. 31:9-13, 25-26) as well as the continuity of tradition from prophet to scribe throughout the book of Jeremiah (cf. especially Jeremiah 45).[69] In each case, the teaching and methodology identified with each personality outlasts and outshines the personality itself. Ezra thus joins two other important figures in Biblical tradition strongly associated with the Deuteronomistic Levite tradition, leaving behind a method of scribal exegesis and communal teaching that could continue to contend against Zadokite claims to exclusive socio-religious hegemony.

We therefore encounter an ambivalent Ezra within the literary world of Ezra-Nehemiah. He is undoubtedly presented as a Zadokite priest, but he is also undoubtedly presented as a Deuteronomistic Levite scribe. Why have both theological camps attempted to claim Ezra as their respective champion? In Israelite religion, different sacral groups typically rally behind different and fairly polarized symbolic figures: Moses and Aaron, Abiathar and Zadok, Jeremiah and Ezekiel, etc. One could easily imagine this same pattern extending to Ezra and Nehemiah, since Ezra is a Zadokite and the layman Nehemiah supports pro-Levite policies,[70] but this is not the case. While Nehemiah is a cornerstone of Ezra-Nehemiah, the character of Ezra remains the keystone to the rhetorical shape of the entire corpus. In considering the presentation of Ezra as an imperial emissary, we may understand why the otherwise familiar pattern is broken.

Ezra as a Persian Imperial Emissary

The one constant underlying the varying shades coloring Ezra is his status as an official representative of the Persian royal court. Unfortunately, the extant literary material does not provide us with a tremendous degree of detail regarding the specifics of his mission, but the memory of Ezra serving in an official capacity is not subject to the same apparent contradictions as his Zadokite or Deuteronomistic Levite status. The Rescript in Ezra 7, while late and midrashic, contains certain authentic elements that suggest an original official charge underlying the

---

69 As mentioned above, the scribes in Jeremiah 26–45 are presented as Levites (Leuchter, *Polemics of Exile*, pp. 105–7), and thus the parallel to Deut. 31:25-26 is even more pronounced.

70 Kraemer suggests that the Ezra material derived from priestly authors while the Nehemiah material was a lay composition ("On the Nature," 92); and it is with the laity that Levites traditional had greater interaction both in Zadokite and non-Zadokite sources (ergo the interaction with regional populations in Deut. 16:18-20; see also Stackert, *Rewriting the Torah*, p. 277, for the P/H/Ezek texts).

current form of the text.[71] The mission that Ezra is charged with is consistent with Persian diplomatic and administrative praxes in the mid-fifth century BCE, as is the selection and dispatching of a member of a regional priesthood as an agent of the royal court.[72] Finally, there are strong indications that the documents in Ezra 4–6 are primarily drawn from authentic administrative archives dating from the time of Nehemiah;[73] their placement in the Ezra half of Ezra-Nehemiah reinforces Ezra's role as set within a Persian administrative context.[74] Indeed, the placement of Ezra 4–6 directly before the introduction to Ezra in Ezra 7 points to Ezra's mission as part of a larger imperial enterprise beginning much earlier and in need of an "inside man" to realign Yehudite affairs with the administrative order within the larger satrap of Ebar-Nehara.[75]

Significant in this regard is the regular allusion to Ebar-Nahara as a sort of sacred space, the broad region wherein Artaxerxes allows Ezra to carry out the practical, political wisdom of "the God of Heaven" — not a deity exclusively concerned with Yehud or Jerusalem as the locus of sanctity. Ezra-Nehemiah persistently sets the political actions of Yehud within the context of the larger

71 Fried, "Rescript of Artaxerxes," 88; Steiner, "Persian Legal Project," 636–8.

72 Steiner, "Persian Legal Project," 628–38.

73 For a thorough consideration of these texts, see R. C. Steiner, "Bishlam's Archival Search Report in Nehemiah's Archive: Multiple Introductions and Reverse Chronological Order as Clues to the Origin of the Aramaic Letters in Ezra 4–6," *JBL* 125 (2006), 641–85. Steiner makes a compelling case for the documents in Ezra 4–6 as largely authentic administrative records drawn from a library of materials collected during Nehemiah's tenure. Nevertheless, there is evidence that these texts have been subjected to secondary redactional shaping (Williamson, *Studies in Persian Period History and Historiography*, pp. 257–69).

74 This would account for VanderKam's observations regarding the lack of such documents in the Nehemiah material ("Ezra and Nehemiah"), and further supports the view that the Ezra account was constructed to anticipate the Nehemiah Memoir (Wright, "A New Model," 342–5; Leuchter, "Ezra's Mission," though Wright and I have different views regarding the sequence and agenda of redactional materials in Ezra 7–10). It also suggests that the Nehemiah Memoir possessed substantially greater literary integrity than the Ezra materials and originated at a time closer to the historical Nehemiah (though Wright is doubtlessly correct that many elements in Nehemiah point to Hellenistic-era accretions; see his "A New Model," 345–9), lest it, too, would require similar "official" documentation to legitimize its contents and ideological agenda.

75 Here we encounter the hermeneutical significance of the literary sequence, a stylistic device I have discussed elsewhere (Leuchter, "Song of Moses," 308–10). This is of course only part of the reason for the flow of content from Ezra [1–3] 4–6 and the ensuing material in Ezra-Nehemiah, which conforms to a historicizing pattern meant to model older traditions of leadership. See S. Japhet, "Periodization Between History and Ideology II: Chronology and Ideology in Ezra-Nehemiah," in *Judah and Judeans in the Persian Period* (eds. O. Lipschits and M. Oeming; Winona Lake: Eisenbrauns, 2006), pp. 502–5.

satrapy.[76] The Jewish commonwealth does not stand alone; its subgroups and their leaders are all part of a much larger, much more ornate and intricate network that empowers them into being. Ezra's hegemony over all of Ebar-Nehara (Ezra 7:21) must be understood against this worldview. However specific his actions may be with respect to Jewish life in Yehud, they are not strictly Jewish acts of strictly Jewish interest but are subsumed within the cogs of a much grander international machine.[77] The imperial emphasis with respect to Ezra and his direct charge from Artaxerxes carries rhetorical significance for the way one reads the Nehemiah Memoir and thus regards the extent and character of Nehemiah's own authority as governor of Yehud. The Ezra material was redacted with an eye to the Nehemiah Memoir, allowing Nehemiah to appear to carry forward Ezra's actions and policies in good form.[78] The challenges to Nehemiah's power by forces within Yehud and elsewhere are therefore not simply a matter of Jewish vs. non-Jewish strife but constitute challenges to the Persian throne that stood directly behind Ezra.[79] This strategy would be effective in reifying policies in line with Nehemiah's agenda during periods of political uncertainty within the province of Ebar-Nehara in relation to Yehud, and thus the specifics regarding Ezra's administrative role are obscured by the literary agenda of the redactors of later periods. It strains credulity, however, to imagine that the redactors' choice to utilize Ezra in this way was not rooted in a well-known public memory of his actual status as a Persian royal emissary, carrying with him a considerable degree of authority that may have focused on life in Yehud but which also tied into responsibilities throughout the larger satrapy.[80]

---

76 T. B. Dozeman, "Geography and History in Herotodus and in Ezra-Nehemiah," *JBL* 122 (2003), 457–64.

77 This rhetorical consideration may go to addressing the perennial difficulty regarding Ezra's ostensible role over all Ebar-Nehara, which some have taken to be a charge unrelated to Jewish matters (Fried, "Rescript of Artaxerxes", 85–8) while others have considered to relate to Jewish communities in the satrapy outside of Yehud but possessing religious connections to it (Williamson, *Ezra, Nehemiah*, pp. 103–5). There are good reasons to see the historical Ezra as charged with actually engaging the Jewish communities of Ebar-Nehara (see Leuchter, "Ezra's Mission"), but within the literary context of Ezra-Nehemiah, the satrapal reference carries significant implications for the provincial politics of Yehud. See the ensuing discussion.

78 Wright, "A New Model"; Leuchter, "Ezra's Mission."

79 A case in point is the characterization of Sanballat in relation to Nehemiah, insofar as the Nehemiah Memoir goes to great lengths to excommunicate Sanballat from any claims to "insider" status and thus the ability to challenge Nehemiah's own policies. See G. N. Knoppers, "Nehemiah and Sanballat: The Enemy Without or Within?" in *Judah and the Judeans in the Fourth Century B.C.E.* (eds. G. N. Knoppers, O. Lipschits, and R. Albertz; Winona Lake: Eisenbrauns, 2006), pp. 305–31.

80 That Ezra's historical mission did possess a Yehud-centered concern is supported by

This understanding of the manner in which Ezra's administrative role is used to support Nehemiah's policies carries a significant implication: that Ezra indeed preceded Nehemiah, and that his mission to Ebar-Nehara and Yehud should be dated to the seventh year of Artaxerxes I (458 BCE). If Ezra had not been active before Nehemiah, it is unlikely that the redactors of Ezra-Nehemiah would have produced a corpus that presents Nehemiah carrying out on the provincial level what Artaxerxes had empowered Ezra to do throughout all of Ebar-Nehara. But even this is a matter of rhetorical spin. The historical Ezra may have preceded Nehemiah, but the literary Ezra — the only Ezra we are able to directly encounter — was constructed only after (or, at the earliest, during) Nehemiah's tenure. In sum, Ezra-Nehemiah confirms that Ezra was a royal administrative emissary that both Zadokite priests and Deuteronomistic Levite scribes saw as a suitable vehicle to advance their respective traditions. Though the specifics of this administrative characteristic remain elusive, neither group is presented as independent of his official imperial status.

Conclusion

The Persian period, even more so than the Neo-Babylonian period, was a time of dramatic cultural and social realignment among those groups who claimed to share in the legacy of ancient Israel. Exile and subjugation under Babylon obviously posed major challenges to older traditions and presuppositions, but this spurred a retreat of sorts into those older traditions, forcing an ideological circling of the wagons, so to speak. Lines were drawn between disparate socio-religious groups and polemical stances were taken.[81] This created a crucible for reifying older cultural and kinship-based standards of identity, regardless of whether or not they were capable of carrying on in any practical sense under the conditions of exile or forced migration.[82] The Persian paradigm brought an end to this. For all of its outward tolerance and permissiveness, Persia created an even greater challenge, for the descendants of ancient Israel were no longer forced to identify themselves in contradistinction to the imperial power but, rather, as part of it, while still maintaining some grip on their once-independent native heritage. The

a comparison with similar socio-political matters in contemporaneous Greek culture. See T. C. Eskenazi, "The Missions of Ezra and Nehemiah," in *Judah and Judeans in the Persian Period*, pp. 524–6, but Williamson's view regarding Ezra's authority over the Jewish communities of Ebar-Nehara is compelling as well (*Ezra, Nehemiah*, pp. 103–5).

81 Hence the exilic redaction of both H and D, in mutual exclusion to each other; see Levinson, "Manumission of Hermeneutics"; Leuchter, *Polemics of Exile*, pp. 161–5 (re: "Deuteronomistic" redaction in Jeremiah over against Zadokite tradition, pp. 180–4).

82 This is especially the case with H, at least with respect to the manumission legislation (as per Levinson, "Manumission of Hermeneutics," 316–22).

Ezra that emerges in the chapters of Ezra-Nehemiah reflects this new and confusing social paradigm. The fluidity with which his genealogical list is structured is a powerful indication that in the Persian period, fixed patterns of lineage hierarchy were open to reinterpretation as communal collectives were in the process of reformulation in the shadow of the imperial power.[83] Moreover, both the traditions that favor his Zadokite status and those that highlight his Deuteronomistic Levite scribal role do so in genetic conjunction with the Persian imperial miasma; within Ezra-Nehemiah, there is no indication that either tradition conceives of itself as independently potent. This is the result of a new worldview that no longer understood Israel as a nation among other nations, but as a people within a pluralistic environment that could only achieve social definition in relation to the whole.[84]

A function of this new national understanding is a sense of transformation within the discreet theological streams undergirding Ezra-Nehemiah. We may identify Zadokite and Deuteronomistic Levite rhetoric throughout the Ezra material, but they do not contradict each other so much as complement each other in the final form of the work. Regardless of the points at which these disparate traditions entered Ezra-Nehemiah or the original social context in which they were fostered before being set to text, the redactors of Ezra-Nehemiah presupposed the compatibility of these ideologies and social identities in creating the literary Ezra. In previous epochs it would be inconceivable to present a historical figure as equally conversant with and supportive of such mutually exclusive sacral ideologies. Yet the combination of Zadokite and Deuteronomistic Levite values, methods, and claims to social authority is precisely what makes the Ezra of Ezra-Nehemiah such an important and effective character. It is he who sets the bar for what subsequent individuals and factions would have to accept in order to legitimately lay claim to being Israelite, and it is difficult to imagine that this was purely a literary invention. Even if various passages within Ezra-Nehemiah are laden with theological and political agenda, they suggest that there were indeed members of the Zadokite ranks who adopted attitudes consistent with the Deuteronomistic Levite tradition.[85] Likewise, the texts in Ezra-Nehemiah that advance the aforementioned perspective do not forsake

---

83   See similarly Fishbane, *BibInt*, p. 265, though he views this process of redefinition as beginning with the exile.

84   See also Hagedorn, "Local Law," 76, who notes that the formation of the Pentateuch is a direct result of this grappling with Persian cultural imperialism, though the Pentateuch itself is not the result of an imperial authorization.

85   A precedent for this is found in the amalgam of figures making up the seventh-century Deuteronomistic movement, which may have been heavily influenced by northern Levitical ideology (as per M. Weinfeld, *Deuteronomy 1–11* [AB; New York: Doubleday, 1991], pp. 44–60) but which appears to have rallied numerous individuals to its folds. See

the significance of the temple, its ritual function, and its sacerdotal faculty, but highlight its essential position in the administration not only of Yehud but of Ebar-Nehara.[86]

In essence, a new standard of social identity emerges in Ezra-Nehemiah, one that transcends older divisions between "Levites" (Deuteronomic or otherwise) and "Zadokites" as the end-all of individual or group ideology. The covenantal community of Nehemiah 10 is defined en masse by the symbolic dimensions of Ezra throughout the corpus, accepting the compatibility of Zadokite *and* Levite leadership and the sanctity of both priestly/temple-based authority and Levite/ scribal administration. This combination was perhaps a necessary measure to reify the Yehudite community and its parent group in the eastern Diaspora against other social collectives in Yehud who could lay claim to authentic Israelite heritage and who fostered religious traditions that left little room for the former's system of thought.[87] Those scholars who see Nehemiah 10 as attesting to a precursor to Jewish sectarianism of the later Second Temple period are therefore justified in this view, since this text identifies a single group as viable in both imperial and theological terms.[88]

Nevertheless, there must be antecedents still to this group. The redactors of Ezra-Nehemiah create the model of a proto-sect in Nehemiah 10, but this indicates the character of the redactors themselves and their own ideological platform. Just as Deuteronomy reflects the work of a group that wished to eclipse older social divisions defined by praxis and belief, so too does Ezra-Nehemiah testify to the development of a movement in the Persian period that sought to redefine social hierarchies and standards of communal affiliation, and one that clearly persisted into the Hellenistic era as well.[89] That this movement viewed Ezra as a symbolic spokesperson suggests that the historical Ezra was among those who — to one degree or another — saw the benefit in dissolving the barriers that long separated Zadokites and Levites in response to the needs of a new historical reality and its challenges to Jewish identity in and beyond Yehud. We cannot

---

P. Dutcher-Walls, "The Social Location of the Deuteronomists: A Sociological Study of Factional Politics in Late Pre-Exilic Judah," *JSOT* 52 (1991), 77–94.

86   This same ethic emerges in full form in the Chronicler's work, as the latter is heavily concerned with the scribal/administrative duties of Levites (see Leuchter, "The Levite In Your Gates," 433 n. 64) but incorporates them into the institution of the temple and its faculty.

87   Bedford, "Diaspora."

88   A. Sivertsev, "Sects and Households: Social Structure of the Proto-Sectarian Movement of Nehemiah 10 and the Dead Sea Sect," *CBQ* 67 (2005), 61–4.

89   H. Mantel traces the later Pharisaic and Sadducaic sects to the time of Ezra as well ("Dichotomy of Judaism in the Second Temple Period," *HUCA* 44 [1973], 55–87), though his evaluation is based on reading Ezra-Nehemiah as a generally accurate historical source.

know what measures the historical Ezra actually took to act on this impulse, but the redactors of Ezra-Nehemiah have rewarded him for his foresight by creating a character of immense hermeneutical potency that channeled their own vision of Persian-period Judaism into an accessible form and an enduring context.[90]

---

90   That the final link in the revelatory chain in Avot 1.1 is the "Great Assembly" (traditionally understood as founded by Ezra) points to the persistent concept of Ezra as the fountainhead of the Pharisaic sectarian tradition that ultimately developed into Rabbinic Judaism. See Leuchter, *Polemics of Exile*, pp. 190–4.

DAVID'S OFFICIALS ACCORDING TO THE CHRONICLER (1 CHRONICLES 23–27)

A REFLECTION OF SECOND TEMPLE SELF-CATEGORIZATION?

Louis C. Jonker

Introduction[1]

In the recently published *New History of South Africa,* the editors, Hermann Giliomee and Bernard Mbenga, introduce their work (after a short summary of the main factors that influenced South African history) with a note on historiography. They state the following:

> As historians of South African history, we are fully conscious of our apartheid past in which gross racial injustices were committed. We are also aware of the distorted historiography of the past. *We have set out to redress past distortions and biases.* This multi-authored book draws on the perspectives of different 'schools' of historians, while also incorporating the most recent scholarship on South African history. We tried to synthesise the material and to make it accessible to both the academic and the general reader.
>
> *Our goal has been to present our history in all its complexity in a fair and balanced manner. We have striven for objectivity.* Yet it would be foolhardy to deny the persistence of subjectivity [italics added].[2]

Whether the editors and authors of this volume have achieved their goal of

---

1 An earlier version of this paper was discussed at an *Oberseminar* of the Dept. Ancient Studies, University of Stellenbosch. I thank my colleagues for their valuable comments and criticisms, and I hereby acknowledge the assistance of Ms Nadia Marais with the bibliographical research.
2 H. Giliomee and B. Mbenga, *New History of South Africa* (Cape Town: Tafelberg, 2007), p. x.

striving to be as objective as possible in their historiographical endeavor remains a question to be answered elsewhere.[3] The main point to be taken note of here in my own introduction, however, is the very basic notion that no historiography can ever be objective. Although the editors of this volume strive to be so, they have to admit that subjectivity persists. There is always something more to historiography than merely the objective reconstruction of a past reality. Even when one strives "to redress past distortions and biases" (as the editors frankly state their mission in the introduction) one does not do so without any own bias. Revisionist histories are (again!) the products of interaction between socio-historical circumstances and the interests pursued in those circumstances.

The books of Chronicles are no different. Sarah Japhet[4] and many other commentators have convincingly shown that a major force behind the origin of this book was the experience of a gap between the formative traditions of the past and the complex reality experienced by the authors during the late Persian era. According to Knoppers[5]:

> Chronicles was composed not necessarily as a replacement of, but as an alternative to the primary history. The Chronicler's employment of mimesis or *imitation* . . ., the deliberate reuse of older works, expresses his respect for and admiration of a variety of older biblical writings . . . . By the same token, the author's skillful reuse, reinterpretation, rearrangement, and major supplementation of sections within the primary history all conspire to create a very different work. The parallels position the author's writing, defining and yet bringing recognition to his own work. The new traditions incorporated within the body of the text, coupled with the reworking of selections from older biblical texts, contribute to the creation of a new literary work that is designed to suit the writer's own times and interests in the Second Commonwealth.

Within this play between continuity and discontinuity with the past, the exegete of Chronicles can venture into the very difficult task of identifying the bias or ideology behind this book.

In previous studies on Chronicles I have indicated that I find the vantage point of identity (re)formulation quite a useful one when trying to interpret the play between continuity and discontinuity with past traditions that we witness in

---

3 For a discussion of historiography in the post-apartheid South Africa, cf. the different essays in *Toward New Histories for South Africa. On the Place of the Past in Our Present* (ed. S. Jeppie; Landsdowne: Juta, 2004). Particularly the essay by A. Grundlingh (ch. 15) titled "Some trends in South African academic history: changing contexts and challenges" is relevant to our study.

4 S. Japhet, *I & II Chronicles* (Louisville: Westminster John Knox, 1993), p. 49.

5 G. N. Knoppers, *1 Chronicles 10–29* (AB; New York: Doubleday, 2004), pp. 133–4.

Chronicles.[6] I do not suggest that other attempts at defining the ideology behind Chronicles (such as Dyck's suggestions[7] of a theocratic ideology) are wrong or superfluous. However, my own social location, being a South African living in a changed socio-political and socio-religious landscape in the post-apartheid era, sensitizes me for the fact that there is a close relationship or interaction between historiography and identity (re)formulation (particularly in times of change and reconstruction).

In previous studies I pursued two aims: (i) To experiment with different methodological approaches in order to determine whether the enrichment of our traditional scholarship on Chronicles could help us to identify those elements or trends in the texts that can be associated with a process of identity (re)formulation; (ii) To probe different sections in the books of Chronicles for this purpose.[8] My aims are nothing different in this contribution. In the next main section I will give an overview of my methodological presuppositions. Thereafter I will analyze the lists of David's officials in 1 Chronicles 23–27 in order to determine whether they reflect anything about the identity (re)formulation among (particularly) the priesthood in Second Temple Yehud. This analysis will then be allowed to interact with the reconstructed socio-historical (in particular, cultic) circumstances of this period during Ancient Israel's past. The last main section will try to answer the question of the subtitle of this contribution, namely "Do we see here a reflection of self-categorization during the Second Temple period?"

This contribution therefore does not purport to offer new analyses of the texts under discussion, or about their history of origin. The majority of the textual phenomena that will be discussed here are already described aptly in the variety

---

6 L. C. Jonker, *Reflections of King Josiah in Chronicles. Late stages of the Josiah Reception in 2 Chr 34f* (Gütersloh: Gütersloher Verlag, 2003); idem, "The Rhetorics of Finding a New Identity in a Multi-Religious and Multi-Ethnic Society: The Case of the Book of Chronicles," *Verbum et Ecclesia* 24/2 (2003), 396–416; idem, "Reforming History: The Hermeneutical Significance of the Books of Chronicles," *VT* 57/1 (2007), 21–44; idem, "Refocusing the Battle Accounts of the Kings: Identity Formation in the Books of Chronicles," in *Behutsames Lesen. Alttestamentliche Exegese im Gespräch mit Literaturwissenschaft und Kulturwissenschaften* (eds. A. Ruwe *et al.*; Leipzig, Evangelische Verlagsanstalt, 2007), pp. 245–74; idem, "Textual Identities in the Books of Chronicles: The Case of Jehoram's History," in *Community Identity in Judean Historiography: Biblical and Comparative Perspectives* (eds. G. N. Knoppers and K. Ristau; Winona Lake: Eisenbrauns, 2009), pp. 197–217; idem, "Who Constitutes Society? Yehud's Self-Understanding in the Late Persian Era as Reflected in The Books of Chronicles," *JBL* 127/4 (2008), 707–28.

7 J. E. Dyck, "The Ideology of Identity in Chronicles," in *Ethnicity and the Bible* (ed. M. G. Brett; Leiden, Brill, 1996), pp. 89–116; idem, *The Theocratic Ideology of the Chronicler* (Leiden, Brill, 1998).

8 See the works mentioned above.

of good Chronicles commentaries that appeared in the past fifteen years.[9] This contribution offers, however, an alternative methodological vantage point that could potentially enrich our understanding of Chronicles.

Methodological Reflections

In this section I would like to motivate why I find the vantage point of identity (re)formulation such a useful one when trying to interpret Chronicles. A few methodological remarks should suffice for this purpose.[10]

In earlier contributions I have argued that developments in social psychology[11] could potentially enrich our readings of the books of Chronicles.[12] I have found the

---

9 P. B. Dirksen, *1 Chronicles* (Leuven: Peeters, 2005); Japhet, *I & II Chronicles*; R. W. Klein, *1 Chronicles* (Hermeneia: Minneapolis: Fortress, 2006); G. N. Knoppers, *1 Chronicles 1–9* (AB; New York: Doubleday, 2003); Knoppers, *1 Chronicles 10–29*; S. L. McKenzie, *1–2 Chronicles* (AOTC; Nashville: John Knox Press, 2004).

10 Since I have given overviews of the social identity theories with which I am working in other studies (cf. Jonker, "Reforming History"; idem, "Textual Identities"; idem, "Who Constitutes Society?"), I will not repeat all aspects here. I will just emphasize those aspects that have become more prominent in my methodological approach since the writing of those contributions, as well as those aspects that are considered to be appropriate for the analysis of 1 Chronicles 23–27.

11 For an overview of developments in the field of social psychology see: D. Abrams, "Social Identity, Psychology of," in *International Encyclopedia of the Social and Behavioral Sciences. Vol 21* (eds. N. J. Smelser and P. B. Baltes; Amsterdam, Elsevier, 2001), 14306–9; D. Abrams and M. A. Hogg, "An Introduction to the Social Identity Approach," in *Social Identity Theory. Constructive and Critical Advances* (eds. D. Abrams and M. A. Hogg; New York, Harvester Wheatsheaf, 1990), ch. 1; C. Fraser and B. Burchell (eds.), *Introducing Social Psychology* (Oxford: Polity, 2001); M. A. Hogg, "Intragroup Processes, Group Structure and Social Identity," in *Social Groups and Identities: Developing the Legacy of Henri Tajfel* (ed. W. P. Robinson; Oxford, Butterworth-Heinemann, 1996), pp. 65–93; M. A. Hogg and D. Abrams, "Intergroup Behavior and Social Identity," in *The Sage Handbook of Social Psychology* (eds. M. A. Hogg and J. Cooper; London, Sage, 2003), ch. 19; J. Shotter, *Conversational Realities. Constructing Life Through Language* (London: Sage, 1993); J. Shotter and K. J. Gergen (eds.), *Texts of Identity* (London: Sage, 1998); R. Stainton Rogers *et al.*, *Social Psychology: A Critical Agenda* (Cambridge: Polity, 1995); idem, "Henri Tajfel: An Introduction," in Robinson, *Social Groups and Identities*, pp. 1–23; idem, *Rediscovering the Social Group: A Self-Categorization Theory* (Oxford: Basil Blackwell, 1987); M. Whitebrook, *Identity, Narrative and Politics* (London: Routledge, 2001).

12 Cf. particularly Jonker, "Reforming History"; idem, "Textual Identities." In those publications I have expressed my indebtedness toward the dissertation of Bosman that was later published as J. P. Bosman, *Social Identity in Nahum: A Theological-Ethical Enquiry* (Piscataway: Georgias, 2008). His study introduced me to this methodological perspective. In Jonker, "Textual Identities" I have interacted with Berquist's views that the majority of studies working with the notion of identity in Chronicles do not take the fluid nature of identity formation processes adequately into account. See J. L. Berquist, "Constructions of

social-psychological notion of "textual identities" quite a useful one for explaining the relationship between textual material and the (re)formulation of identity. The turn toward textual identities in social psychology lets us understand the following: (i) "Textual identities" emphasize the fluid, dynamic and discursive nature of processes of identity formation; (ii) This notion emphasizes the close interrelationship between the social environment within which a group exists, the textual resources that are available in the given culture, and the role that renewed textual construction plays in the process of identity formation; (iii) It therefore provides us with a firmer theoretical basis for relating the issue of identity formation to our literary and textual sources. De Fina *et al.*,[13] for example, emphasize: "(I)dentities are seen not as merely represented in discourse, but rather as performed, enacted and embodied through a variety of linguistic and non-linguistic means." The textual products that develop in a given situation (such as in Second Temple Persian Yehud) could therefore be studied in order to get a better understanding of the social identity (re)formulation processes that lie behind them; (iv) It cautions us not only to take into account multiple motivational factors that could have contributed to self-categorization, but also to view those motivational factors in a discursive framework.

For the purpose of this study, I would like to elaborate a bit more on the last-mentioned sub-field in social identity theory, namely self-categorization theory (SCT). The texts that will be analyzed in this contribution (1 Chronicles 23–27) very clearly reflect the categorization of officials during the final part of David's reign (as the narrative setting suggests). In order to analyze these texts, it might be helpful to involve certain distinctions made in SCT.

Self-categorization theory (developed by Turner) extends social identity theory by describing the way social identity regulates behavior. Hogg[14] summarizes this as follows:

> When we categorize others as ingroup or outgroup members we accentuate their similarity to the relevant prototype — thus perceiving them stereotypically and ethnocentrically. When we categorize ourselves, we define, perceive and evaluate ourselves in terms of our ingroup prototype and behave in accordance with that prototype. Self-categorization produces ingroup normative behavior and self-stereotyping, and is thus the process underlying group behavior.

Identity in Postcolonial Yehud," in *Judah and the Judeans in the Persian Period* (eds. O. Lipschits and M. Oeming; Winona Lake: Eisenbrauns, 2006), pp. 53–66.

13 A. De Fina *et al.* (eds.), *Discourse and Identity* (Cambridge: Cambridge University Press, 2006), p. 3.

14 M. A. Hogg, "Social Identity Theory," in *The Blackwell Encyclopedia of Social Psychology* (eds. A. S. R. Manstead and M. Hewstone; Oxford: Blackwell, 1995), p. 559.

A very important aspect of SCT is the notion of depersonalization. Hornsey[15] explains this notion as follows:

> Proponents of SCT argue that people cognitively represent their social groups in terms of prototypes. When a category becomes salient, people come to see themselves and other category members less as individuals and more as inter-changeable exemplars of the group prototype. *The prototype is not an objective reality, but rather a subjective sense of the defining attributes of a social category that fluctuates according to context.* The group identity not only describes what it is to be a group member, but also prescribes what kinds of attitudes, emotions and behaviors are appropriate in a given context [italics added].

Hornsey[16] indicates that, whereas the more general social identity theory was more preoccupied with *inter*group relations, SCT heralded a more thorough investigation of *intra*group processes. Therefore this theory could provide us with a potentially helpful vantage point when dealing with texts such as 1 Chronicles 23–27 where intragroup relations are clearly the theme.

Another elaboration on this theory could be helpful. Different factors are normally identified by theorists that serve as motivation behind these processes of self-categorization. Brewer[17] discusses, for example, the following motivational theories: (i) Common fate (where perceived interdependence among individual members of a collective is seen as the defining characteristic of a social group); (ii) Self-esteem (where individual members maintain a positive self-esteem by means of the group's successes and achievements); (iii) Self-verification or uncertainty reduction (where people are motivated to belong to a group in order to reduce uncertainty, and that clarification of group membership, adherence to group norms, and associating positive group features with the self are ways to achieve this); and (iv) Optimal distinctiveness (where two powerful social motives are held in balance, namely the need for inclusion, which is satisfied by assimilation of the self into larger collectives, and the opposing need for differentiation, which is satisfied by distinguishing the self from others).

In conclusion of this methodological section it should also be emphasized that self-categorization always takes place in interaction with a concrete context. The

15 M. J. Hornsey, "Social Identity Theory and Self-Categorization Theory: A Historical Review," *Social and Personality Psychology Compass* 2/1 (2008), 208–9.

16 Ibid., 204–22.

17 See M. B. Brewer, *Intergroup Relations* (2nd edn.; Philadelphia: Open University Press, 2003), pp. 36–9; also M. A. Hogg, "Intergroup Relations," in *Handbook of Social Psychology* (ed. J. Delamater; New York: Plenum Publishers, 2003), pp. 479–502.

implication would then also be that changes in context would result in adaptations in the self-categorization processes prevalent among a group.

In what follows below, my endeavor will be to apply these insights from social psychology (particularly from SCT) to our reading of the lists of David's officials in 1 Chronicles 23–27. This text was chosen since it is generally considered to be a very prominent reflection of the Chronicler's views held on the priesthood and cultic organization.[18] These chapters are almost in their entirety part of the non-synoptic material, i.e., own material of the Chronicler. The insights from SCT will be used to extend the results of a very basic narrative analysis of these chapters from the level of the story-world onto the level of the world-of-origin. Let me explain this in more detail: Since these lists are embedded in a broader narrative about David's reign and the transition to the reign of Solomon his son, a narrative analysis is appropriate to describe those features that make up the narrative world which is constructed by the author(s)/editor(s) for the intended reader(s).[19] Particularly the way in which characters are introduced, and the way in which they relate to other characters, will form the focus of the analysis below. Insights from social-categorization theory will then be used to extend these results from the story-world to the world-of-origin of the texts in order to theorize about the interaction between these two worlds. Whereas the basic narrative analysis helps us to answer the question "*How* was the narrative world constructed?" SCT assists us to answer the question "*Why* was this specific narrative world constructed?"

---

18   Cf. the above-mentioned commentaries, as well as the more detailed studies by G. N. Knoppers, "Hierodules, Priests, or Janitors? The Levites in Chronicles and the History of the Israelite Priesthood," *JBL* 118/1 (1999), 49–72; R. Nurmela, *The Levites. Their Emergence as a Second-Hand Priesthood* (Atlanta: Scholars Press, 1998); J. Schaper, *Priester und Leviten im achämenidischen Juda* (Tübingen: Mohr-Siebeck, 2000); T. Willi, "Leviten, Priester und Kult in vorhellenistischer Zeit. Die chronistische Optik in ihrem geschichtlichen Kontext," in *Gemeinde ohne Tempel. Zur Substituierung und Transformation des Jerusalemer Tempels und seines Kults im Alten Testament, antiken Judentum und frühen Christentum* (eds. B. Ego et al.; Tübingen: Mohr-Siebeck, 1999), pp. 75–98; idem, "Guarding the Gates: 1 Chronicles 26.1-19 and the Roles of the Gatekeepers in Chronicles," *JSOT* 48 (1990), 69–81; idem, "The Legacy of David in Chronicles: The Narrative Function of 1 Chronicles 23–27," *JBL* 110/2 (1991), 229–42; idem, "From Center to Periphery: 1 Chronicles 23–27 and the Interpretation of Chronicles in the Nineteenth Century," in *Priests, Prophets and Scribes. Essays on the Formation and Heritage of Second Temple Judaism in Honour of Joseph Blenkinsopp* (eds. E. Ulrich, J. W. Wright, R. P. Carrol, and P. R. Davies; Sheffield: Sheffield Academic Press, 1992).

19   See Wright "Gaurding the Gates"; idem, "The Legacy of David in Chronicles"; idem, "From Centre to Periphery" for illustrations of this methodological approach.

Analysis of 1 Chronicles 23–27

My analysis will proceed in two steps: First, I will provide an overview of the history of interpretation of this section of Chronicles. By doing so, I will situate my own approach in contradistinction to traditional and more recent approaches. Secondly, I will analyze the text in these chapters according to a very basic scheme of identifying who the agent(s) and affected parties are in the various texts. I have indicated above in my methodological explication that the basic characterization techniques in the narrative surrounding (or inserted into) the lists could help us to a more precise description of the relationship/interaction between individuals and/or groups reflected in these texts. But first, the history of interpretation.

HISTORY OF INTERPRETATION

Until fairly recently the majority of studies on 1 Chronicles 23–27 have focused on the history of origin of these chapters.[20] Questions such as "What sources underlie these chapters?" and "What redaction processes can be detected in this literature?" formed the main interest of many Chronicles scholars. Klein[21] summarizes the three basic positions taken in the debate on the origin of these texts: First, some scholars[22] consider all of the lists in chs 23–27 to be secondary. On account of the repetition of 23:2 in 28:1 this group of scholars argue that the five chapters in between form an interruption of the narrative about David. The inconsistency of the materials in these five chapters are furthermore seen as an indication that these interrupting lists were not added at the same time and by the same hands.[23]

---

20   For more elaborate discussions, cf. the various commentaries on Chronicles: Japhet, *I & II Chronicles*; S. S. Tuell, *First and Second Chronicles* (Louisville: Westminster John Knox, 2001); Knoppers (*1 Chronicles 1–9* and *1 Chronicles 10–29*); McKenzie, *1–2 Chronicles*; Dirksen, *1 Chronicles*; and Klein, *1 Chronicles*. Cf. also Wright, "From Centre to Periphery," a study that focuses specifically on the history of interpretation of the section 1 Chronicles 23–27 during the nineteenth century.

21   Klein, *1 Chronicles*, 445–7; Cf. also the very helpful excursus on these chapters offered in Knoppers, *1 Chronicles 10–29*, pp. 788–98.

22   Klein (*1 Chronicles*, p. 445) puts Welch, Noth, Rudolph, Mosis, and Braun in this category.

23   Knoppers (*1 Chronicles 10–29*, p. 790) summarizes the arguments normally used for attributing the material in these chapters to later hands in five points: (i) Although the accession of Solomon to the throne is only addressed in 28:5-21, 23:1 already mentions that David appointed his son to rule over Israel; (ii) The repetition of 23:2 in 28:1; (iii) The repetition among the speeches surrounding 1 Chronicles 23–27 (particularly in chs. 22 and 28–29); (iv) The internal inconsistency of the lists; and (v) The inconsistency of the content of these chapters with the Chronicler's work as a whole.

Secondly, some scholars[24] argue that certain lists are original, but others belong to a secondary level. These scholars do not understand 28:1 to be a duplicate of 23:2, but that it is rather a repetitive resumption of the narrative after some lists that were inserted by the Chronicler himself. Williamson, for example, takes his point of departure in the census list of 23:3-6a in determining which lists are original. He argues that a fourfold division of the Levites is made there and that for each of these divisions a list was appended. According to him 23:4a refers to those Levites who were in charge of the work in the house of YHWH and this reference corresponds to the lists found in 23:6b-13a, 15-24. First Chron. 23:4b refers to those Levites who were officers and Judges and this reference correlates to the list in 26:20-32. The third reference, in 23:5a, is to the Levitical gatekeepers, with a corresponding list in 26:1-3, 9-11, 19. The last reference, in 23:5b, is to Levitical singers and musicians. This reference correlates with 25:1-6. These references and lists are, according to Williamson, part of the Chronicler's own composition. The following parts are then considered to be secondary: 23:13b-14, 25-32; 24:1-19, 20-31; 25:7-31; 26:4-8, 12-18; 27:1-32 (about two-thirds of the material in these chapters).

A third position adhered to by some scholars[25] is the originality of all or almost all lists. The main argument here is again that the repetition in 23:2 and 28:1 should not necessarily be interpreted as an indication of composite sources. Knoppers, for example, confirms this when he argues: "1 Chronicles 23–27, no less than other materials in Chronicles depicting the careers of David and Solomon, contribute to a larger picture of the United Monarchy as a golden age for the people of Israel."[26]

More recently, particularly through the work of Wright[27] and Knoppers,[28] scholars have started moving away from a preoccupation with sources and redactions, and have shifted their attention to the social, political, and religious concerns reflected in the final composition. Knoppers states:

> One unfortunate consequence of this preoccupation with sources and redactions over the course of the past two centuries is that the larger picture becomes lost as scholars focus on the origins and date of individual textual fragments. I wish

---

24 Williamson is the main proponent of this category. See H. G. M. Williamson, "The Origins of the 24 Priestly Courses: A study of 1 Chronicles 23–27," in *Studies in Persian Period History and Historiography* (ed. H. G. M. Williamson; Tübingen: Mohr-Siebeck, 2004), pp. 126–40. Klein (*1 Chronicles*, p. 445) also puts Allen and De Vries in this category.

25 Klein (*1 Chronicles*, p. 447) refers mainly to Japhet in this category.

26 Knoppers, *1 Chronicles 10–29*, p. 798.

27 Cf. Wright, "Guarding the Gates"; idem, "The Legacy of David in Chronicles"; idem, "From Center to Periphery".

28 Cf. Knoppers "Hierodules, Priests, or Janitors?"; idem, *1 Chronicles 10–29*.

to return to the social, political, and religious concerns raised by these chapters, specifically, how the materials relating to administrative appointments made at the close of David's reign contribute to the larger picture of his legacy.[29]

Knoppers then comes to the conclusion: "In 1 Chronicles 23–27, the appointment of various leaders and the assignment of courses to such officials contribute to the larger picture of David's reign as a time of significant change for Israel."[30] Wright states his point of view similarly:

> 1 Chr 23–27 is not marginal to the Chronicler's Davidic narrative. The passage and its characters do not interrupt the narrative, but complete the story. David, ever the good king, arranges and orders his kingdom down to the last detail in preparation for his death and Solomon's accession. 1 Chr 23–27 emerges as a pivotal passage within the Chronicler's account of the reign of David.[31]

Although I completely agree with Knoppers and Wright on this point, I would like to take the analysis one step further by asking: *Why was it* — particularly during the time of origin of Chronicles — *necessary* to portray David's reign as a time of significant change? And *how does that relate to the interests, biases, or ideologies* behind the construction of this national epic (as Knoppers calls it) in late Persian Yehud?

The answering of these questions could start with our analysis of intergroup relations reflected in our text.

INTERGROUP RELATIONS REFLECTED IN THE TEXT

The delimitation of this section, as we have seen above, is normally done according to the repetition of David's assembling of the people in 23:2 and 28:1. After the opening notice in 23:1 which situates the following passages at the end of David's reign and in preparation of Solomon's succession, the narrator indicates that David gathered (אסף) three goups, namely the commanders[32] of Israel, the

---

29 Knoppers, *1 Chronicles 10–29*, p. 789.
30 Ibid., p. 797.
31 Wright, "The Legacy of David in Chronicles," p. 233.
32 The term שר is difficult to translate. "Commanders/officials/princes" are the translation options offered by translations. It occurs 14 times in 1 Chronicles 23–27, 11 times in the plural (23:2; 24:5[2 times], 6; 25:1; 26:26[2 times]; 27:1, 3, 22, 31) and 3 times in the singular (27:5, 8, 34). In five cases it is used in a construct relationship with הצבא in the singular (25:1; 26:26; 27:5, 34) or plural (27:3). In these cases, as well as in 26:26 (the other occurrence), 27:1, and 27:8, the term is clearly associated with a military leadership role (with "commander" an appropriate translation option). In 23:2; 24:6; 27:22, 31, however, it

priests, and the Levites before him. The counting and division of the Levites and others then start from there.

Wright differs from traditional scholarship in that he does not agree with the view that 23:2 and 28:1 are doublets.[33] He points out that the verbs differ in these two sections. Whereas 23:2 employs אסף, 28:1 uses קהל. Wright explains the difference as follows:

> In the Hebrew Bible, קהל generally means to gather persons for social purposes, either legal, military, or religious. In nondeuteronomistic passages, however, the Chronicler uses קהל to connote a formal assembly that culminates in a cultic ceremony — the procession of the ark into Jerusalem (1 Chron. 13:5; 15:3); the blessing of YHWH by David and all Israel before the anointing of Solomon and Zadok (1 Chron. 28:1); the blessing of YHWH by Jehoshaphat and his people following their annihilation of the Moabites and Ammonites in battle (2 Chron. 20:26). In contrast, the Chronicler does not use the verb אסף to convey the gathering of a formal cultic convocation. In Chronicles אסף occurs ten times in non-synoptic sections. The term has the more general connotation of the gathering of goods or persons into a specific location.[34]

Since the list genre is overwhelmingly utilized in this section, there is not much of a narrative line here. *Wayyiqtol* forms of the verb are sparsely distributed throughout these chapters. David, being the subject of some of the key verbs, is indicated to be the main figure according to the narrative line. He makes Solomon, his son, king over Israel (23:1), he assembles the commanders, priests, and Levites (23:2), and he organizes them in divisions according to the sons of Levi (23:6). David is also the one organizing them in their appointed duties (24:3), he sets apart the sons of Asaph, Heman, and Jeduthun for special service (25:1) and he appoints officials (26:32). In the conclusion to these lists (27:23) it is mentioned that he did not number those below 20 years of age, for "YHWH has promised to make Israel as many as the stars of the heavens."

David is also the subject of the only direct speech section in these chapters, namely 23:25-26 and 28-32. There he is indicated to have announced a new dispensation for the Levites. This direct speech section will be examined in more detail below.

---

is not absolutely clear what category of the leadership is mentioned. In two cases (both in 24:5) it seems clear that the term is associated with cultic service. The expression שרי־קדש ושרי האלהים suggests two groups with distinct cultic functions. It is important to keep this variation in mind when interpreting these texts.

33 Cf. Wright, "The Legacy of David in Chronicles"; Knoppers (*1 Chronicles 10–29*, pp. 788–98) follows Wright in his commentary.

34 Wright, "The Legacy of David in Chronicles," p. 230.

In order to come to a better understanding of the intergroup relations reflected in these texts, we should turn our attention now to the different kinds of power relations (or, to put it in a milder form, the different directions of influence) portrayed in these sections. We will start off by looking at David's relationship with the Levites and Aaronites.[35] Thereafter the relationship between Aaronites and Levites will be investigated before this analysis will be brought to a synthesis.

DAVID AND THE "LEVITES" IN 1 CHRONICLES 23–27

Two verbs describe David's actions with reference to the Levites: ויחלקם "and he divided them" (in 23:6) and ויבדל "and he (together with the commanders) set apart" (in 25:1).

The verb חלק which occurs in many different contexts in the Hebrew Bible normally denotes an action where somebody has the authority over something or someone to apportion/divide. It is clear from the Chronicler's text that David is explicitly emphasized as the king of Israel to whom the organization of the Levitical cultic personnel should be attributed. The organization is done according to the tripartite segmentation which is also attested in earlier sources, namely Exod. 6:16-19, Num. 3:17-39 and 1 Chron. 6:1-33. Although it is quite obvious, one should not overlook the fact that the description of these families in 23:6-27 is not an indication of the divisions that David made — those divisions were inherited by tradition — but rather an indication of the genealogical norm that David used when organizing the Levites into divisions. By presenting it in this way, the Chronicler portrayed David to be acting in accordance with tradition. Moreover, the Levites are presented as being organized in correspondence with tradition.

In 25:1 the text states that David (together with the army officers) set three Levitical families of singers, the sons of Asaph, Heman, and Jeduthun, apart for special duty (בדל).[36] It remains uncertain why the army officers were required to perform this task together with David.[37] However, what remains clear is that

---

35 Different spellings are used for this collective. In this contribution the noun will be spelled "Aaronite," but when used adjectivally it will be rendered as "Aaronide".

36 Cf. L. C. Jonker, "Another Look at the Psalm Headings: Observations on the Musical Terminology," *JNSL* 30/1 (2004), 65–85; idem, "Revisiting the Psalm Headings" for a description of Gese's theory about the development of the three branches of Levitical musicians.

37 Knoppers (*1 Chronicles 10–29*, pp. 846–7) offers the following explanation: "Many commentators have expressed astonishment that army commanders should have a say in the establishment of courses for the singers. But both the army commanders and the Levitical choristers are state employees. The projected sanctuary is to be paid for and endowed by the head of state with unbelievable amounts of wealth. The Chronicler's temple, when built, will

this setting apart is paralleled in the text by 23:13 where it is indicated that the Aaronites were to consecrate the most holy things, and to make offerings before YHWH for all times, as well as to minister to Him and to pronounce blessings in his name. Knoppers states the following about the usage of the verb בדל in this context:

> The verb denotes separation, whether of the priests from the Levites for their duties (23:13), of the priests (or the priests and/or the Levites) from the people at large (Num. 8:14; 16:9, 21; Deut. 10:8), or of Jewish husbands from their foreign wives (Ezra 10:8, 16). Using the verb in this particular context establishes a parallelism between David's choice and investiture of the singers, of the Levites, and of the priests.[38]

The most prominent section that elaborates on David's relationship with the Levites is the direct speech section in 23:25-26, 28-32.[39] The speech is introduced with כי אמר דויד. The function of כי remains conspicuous here. It seems that it picks up from v. 6 in order to motivate why the division of the Levites was done by David, and why they were assigned new functions (indicated in vv. 3-5).[40] The new dispensation for the Levites is motivated with reference to the rest that YHWH the God of Israel has given to his people, and to the fact that He now dwells (שכן) in Jerusalem forever. A correspondence is then created by using וגם at the beginning of the next sentence.[41] In correspondence to the rest that YHWH

be the most valuable edifice in the land. Who gets to serve in that institution is, therefore, not simply a sacerdotal or aesthetic issue but also a security issue. In this context, it is worth noting that some of the traditional Levitical duties, such as guard duty (23:32), are military in nature. Indeed, the book devotes significant attention to the gatekeepers, whom David appoints as the temple's police force (26:1-19)." One could ask whether Knoppers is not applying a too modern understanding of security to this text. Should the guards and gatekeepers be understood in a military, security context, or were they rather "cultic inspectors"?

38 Knoppers, *1 Chronicles 10–29*, p. 847.

39 I see 23:27 as the conclusion to the previous section in which the counting of the three branches of Levitical families is indicated. It should rather be positioned between vv. 24 and 25.

40 In this statement I argue against Dirksen and Klein who are of the opinion that the כי refers back to v. 24. According to Dirksen (*1 Chronicles*, p. 286) "כי refers back to the mention in v. 24 of the temple service of the Levites and introduces the explanation for their position." Klein (*1 Chronicles*, p. 455) agrees: "David's words here explain 'the work of the service' rather than the age of the Levites at the beginning of their service."

41 The most likely function of וגם in v. 26 is to create correspondence between YHWH giving rest to his people by dwelling in Jerusalem (v. 25) and the changed duties of the Levites. For this function of the particle, cf. C. H. J. van der Merwe, J. Naudé and J. H. Kroeze, *A Biblical Hebrew Reference Grammar (BHRG)* (Sheffield: Sheffield Academic Press, 1999), par. 41.4 (5.2 iii).

has given to his people (the Hiphil verb הניח is used), and to the fact that He now
dwells in Jerusalem, the Levites are assigned new duties. Their old dispensation
is summarized with reference to their carrying of the tabernacle (המשכן) and all
the utensils for its service. This duty will end now, and will be replaced by new
responsibilities (put in contrast by the כי at the beginning of v. 28).[42] They will
now be serving (cf. the use of the participle) next to the Aaronites (ליד־בני אהרן).
Both Knoppers[43] and Klein[44] point out that the expression used here emphasizes
"a coordinate relationship" and not subordination.[45]

Knoppers has done a thorough investigation into the terminology used in
this direct speech as descriptions of the Levites' new duties. He has shown that,
although there is a clear overlap between the terminology used in this section and
that used in the priestly work and Ezekiel, there are also significant differences.
He argues convincingly:

> The Chronicler draws on priestly terminology, but he does so to expand leviti-
> cal responsibilities and to blur some of the clear distinctions advanced by the
> priestly writers and defended by Ezekiel. In Chronicles the Levites take part in
> the preparation of certain sacrifices, the maintenance of a standard system of
> measurements, the watch of the sanctuary and the service of the temple. Given
> that some of the levitical duties are at variance with the work profiles found in
> P and Ezekiel, the claim that this roster is pro-priestly in orientation has to be
> reconsidered. If a writer wished to stress the subordination of the Levites to the
> priests, it is unlikely that he would stress their proximity to the priests (v. 28) and
> increase their involvement at the temple (vv. 28-32).[46]

Knoppers continues to show that there are four cases where the terminology in
this direct speech section is unparalleled in the Priestly writing (P) or Ezekiel.
The most significant of these is the indication in v. 30-31 that the Levites had

---

42 Dirksen (*1 Chronicles*, p. 286) emphasizes: "The direct speech gives כי a meaningful
adversative function: David's statement does not so much mean negatively that the Levites
need no longer carry the ark as positively that it is their duty to assist the priests."
43 Knoppers, "Hierodules, Priests, or Janitors?" 59.
44 Klein, *1 Chronicles*, p. 455.
45 According to Knoppers ("Hierodules, Priests, or Janitors?" 59) and Klein
(*1 Chronicles*, p. 455) subordination would have been indicated with the expression על יד־
which is used in quite a few instances in Chronicles. Dirksen does not agree with this view.
He is of the opinion that the expression indeed denotes subordination. However, he continues: "Of course this does not mean less respect. The writer holds that priests and Levites
both have their indispensable function within the order of the cult, while emphasizing only
the prerogatives of the priests" (Dirksen, *1 Chronicles*, p. 286).
46 Knoppers, "Hierodules, Priests, or Janitors?" 64.

to give thanks and to praise YHWH (להדות ולהלל ליהוה). This appointment of Levitical singers and musicians "is a case in which the Chronicler goes beyond Deuteronomic and priestly precedent."[47] This evidence, together with the other terminology considered by Knoppers, brings him to the following conclusion:

> In discussing whether the original Chronicler was pro-priestly or pro-levitical, many scholars have assumed that the Chronicler was a follower of either the Deuteronomic or the priestly traditions on the issue of cultic practice. This assumption needs to be questioned, because it sets up a false and misleading dichotomy . . . The Chronicler is heir to and interpreter of both traditions . . . Given the Chronicler's highly nuanced presentation, informed by the work of a variety of earlier biblical writers, it is too simplistic to maintain that the Chronicler's work reifies either Zadokite dominance or levitical ascendancy during the postexilic period. The Chronicler, or any writer for that matter, does not present an unmediated view of either the past or the present. To be sure, the Chronicler's work is inevitably affected by his own time and social circumstances, but his presentation is also affected by his tradition, outlook, commitments, and imagination . . . Indeed, one could argue that in writing about the past, the Chronicler attempts to shape the present.[48]

This point of Knoppers' will be taken up in the further development of my argument below. What remains in this subsection, however, is a summary of the observations made with reference to the relationship between David and the Levites reflected in 1 Chronicles 23–27: First, according to the Chronicler's understanding, the Levites' status in the cult is closely related to their great King David's appointments for the temple at the end of his reign. Secondly, the Chronicler shows David's respect for the traditions of old as the basis for the Levites' division into different family units. And thirdly, via David's speech the Chronicler closely associates the change of duties of the Levites with YHWH's role in the history of his people (giving them rest), and his dwelling in Jerusalem.

DAVID AND THE "AARONITES" IN 1 CHRONICLES 23–27

First Chron. 24:1-19 concentrate on the organization of the Aaronide families in twenty-four divisions. This was done by David, with the assistance of Zadok and Ahimelech[49] (v. 3) who are both indicated to be descendants of Aaron. The same

---

47 Ibid., 67.
48 Ibid., 68 and 71.
49 Klein (*1 Chronicles*, p. 467) remarks: "The Chronicler's connection of Ahimelech with the sons of Ithamar — and therefore a descendant of Aaron — is without precedent or

verb is used here than in 23:6, namely חלק, where it is indicated that David did
the division of the Levitical families. On account of 23:13 where it is mentioned
that the Aaronites were not counted because of their special status in the cult,
the section in 24:1-19 seems odd. Here in ch. 24, the families are listed in great
detail.[50] The motivation for the organization of the Aaronites is provided in
verse 19: So that they could perform their duties in the cult in accordance with
the regulations (כמשפטם) that were given by their father, Aaron, and that were
commanded (צוה) by YHWH, the God of Israel himself. The Chronicler therefore leaves no doubt that the Aaronide families (through the lines of Eleazar and
Ithamar) were legitimated by their great king, David, and that this was done so
in obedience to YHWH's command.[51]

THE "LEVITES" AND THE "AARONITES" IN 1 CHRONICLES 23–27

The most prominent aspect in terms of the relationship between the Levites and
the Aaronites reflected in 1 Chronicles 23–27 is the fact that the Aaronites are
portrayed as Levites. In 23:13 Aaron, together with Moses, are indicated to be
sons of Amram, the son of Kohath. As we have seen above, the line of Aaron
remains undeveloped on account of their special dedication to cultic ministry.
However, it remains clear that the Aaronites are considered to be Levites.[52]

The direct speech in ch. 23 also sheds interesting light on the relationship
between the Levites and Aaronites. We have seen above that this section in
23:25-26,[53] 28-32 portrays David announcing a new dispensation for the Levites

any other attestation in the Old Testament. Had the Ithamarite priests come to see themselves
as heirs of the house of Eli?"

50   A comparison of this list with other similar lists attested in the Old Testament is not
necessary for my argument here. Cf. ibid., p. 463 for a comparison of this list to those offered
in various sections in Nehemiah.

51   Knoppers (*1 Chronicles 10–29*, p. 834) points out that "(t)he recourse to an otherwise
unattested divine command to Aaron is unusual."

52   A distinction made by Schaper (*Priester und Leviten*, p. 294) that is not often taken
note of in scholarly discussions, should be brought in here. According to Schaper the term
"Levite" could refer, on the one hand, to somebody descending from the tribe of Levi. On
the other hand, the term could also refer to those cult officials that were subordinated to the
altar priests (according to Schaper's view). He refers to our text in 1 Chron. 23:13f. to sup-
port his point: "Wohl sind Gerschon, Kehat und Merari sowie ihre Nachkommen allesamt
Mitglieder des Stammes Levi, doch wird innerhalb der Kehatiten zwischen den Amram-
Söhne Aaron und Mose differenziert: Die Nachkommen des ersteren sind die Priester, die
Nachkommen des letzteren die 'Leviten' im technischen Sinne des Wortes" (*Priester und
Leviten.*, pp. 294–5). This helpful distinction can bring more precision into our discussions.

53   The most likely function of וגם in v. 26 is to create correspondence between YHWH
giving rest to his people by dwelling in Jerusalem (v. 25) and the changed duties of the

in which they should be assisting (ליד־בני אהרן — v. 28) and guarding (משמרת —
v. 32) the Aaronites in various duties in the sanctuary.

Another small indication in the text links the Levitical family organization to
that of the Aaronites. We have seen already that 24:1-19 lists the Aaronide family
groups in relation to certain duties in the temple. From v. 20 in the same chapter
the Levite organization is given. Verse 31 closes this section with the indication
that "also they" (גם־הם) were appointed by the lot. The particle here certainly
has the function of correspondence,[54] linking the organization of the Levites not
to the immediately preceding text, but rather to v. 1-19 where the organization
of the Aaronites is given.[55]

There are therefore not any indications in the text that would put the Levites
and Aaronites in opposition to one another. Knoppers summarizes this position
as follows:

> The Chronicler stresses cooperation and complementarity, not competition
> and hierarchy. The Chronicler maintains a basic kinship between the Levites
> and Aaronides . . . the Chronicler does not jettison all distinctions between the
> two . . . There is no firm evidence to suggest that the Chronicler holds to an
> absolute equality between priests and Levites. Nevertheless, the author does not
> emphasize hierarchy. Both the priests and the Levites are essential to the success
> of the temple cult.[56]

SYNTHESIS OF THE INTERGROUP RELATIONS REFLECTED IN
1 CHRONICLES 23–27

The present form of 1 Chronicles 23–27, whether it is a unity or a composite
text, portrays a discourse on what it means to be of Levitical descent. And let
me indicate from the start that I find Schaper's distinction between a more generic use of the term "Levite" (referring to the tribal background of a part of the
Judean society), compared with a more technical use (referring to a part of the

Levites. For this function of the particle, Cf. C. H. J. van der Merwe, J. Naudé, and J. H.
Kroeze, *BHRG*, par. 41.4 (5.2 iii).

54 Again, גם־הם expresses correspondence. However, the antecedent does not occur
immediately before the expression, but it rather refers to the information provided in vv. 1-19.

55 In support of Dirksen (*1 Chronicles*, p. 295) who states: "This verse, which refers
back to v. 6, is even less applicable to the preceding passage than v. 30b. The idea must be
that the Levites, too, like the priests, were organized into 24 divisions, and then incorporated
by lot into a roster." Cf. also Knoppers (*1 Chronicles 10–29*, p. 836) and Klein (*1 Chronicles*,
p. 471).

56 Knoppers, "Hierodules, Priests, or Janitors?" 70–1.

temple clergy), quite convincing.[57] The text indicates King David of old to be the one assembling before him certain categories from the city elite: Commanders of Israel, the priests, and the Levites (presumably used here in a technical sense). These are the groups that are also represented when the Aaronide divisions are made (cf. 24:3), as well as the division of the rest of the Levites (generic) (cf. 24:31). The part about the census in 23:3-5 introduces four categories of Levites (generic), namely those who had to conduct (לנצח) the work in the house of YHWH (24,000 in number), the officers and Judges (6,000), gatekeepers (4,000), and musicians (4,000). The division into these four groups is done by David, analogically to the Levite families (generic), going back to Levi. Three famil-ies, namely Gershon, Kohath, and Merari (23:6-24, 27) are mentioned. How the tripartite family division relates to the fourfold function division is not explained in the text. However, the aim of the census and division was that all the Levites (generic) were to do the work for the service of the house of the YHWH.

Within the Kohathite family description the focus is placed on Aaron (23:13).[58] Aaron's line is not mentioned, since they were set apart for very specific functions in the cult. The new dispensation announced by David for the Levites (technical) explicitly puts them in close association with the Aaronites by indicating that they had to assist them (ליד-בני אהרן) in various duties in the sanctuary (23:25-26, 28-32). Although the view could be accepted that this relationship does not entail subordination, a distinction of function is clear. The Levite (technical) tasks did not include service at the altar.

Although the previous chapter does not elaborate on the Aaronide line, 24:1-19 now focuses specifically on the Aaronites. David, together with Zadok and Ahimelech, organize them for their duties (24:3), and a whole entourage is present when the lot is cast to determine their twenty-four divisions (24:6). This entourage again includes — apart from David — commanders, Zadok the priest, Ahimelech the son of Abiathar, the heads of the ancestral houses of the priests, and Levites (presumably technical). A Levite (technical) acts as scribe for the occasion. And the whole procedure is completed according to how it was established for them by their ancestor Aaron, as the Lord God of Israel had commanded him (24:19).

From 24:20 the division of the rest of the Levites (generic) (ולבני לוי הנותרים) takes place. It becomes clear from 24:31 that this division is presented in corres-pondence (cf. גם-הם) with the division of the Aaronites in 24:1-19. More or less the same entourage is also present at the casting of the lot for these Levites (generic).

At this point it becomes clear that the Aaronites (together with the Levites

57 For references, see footnote 52 above.
58 Knoppers (*1 Chronicles 10–29*, pp. 807–8) indicates that this type of digression was not uncommon in ancient Near Eastern genealogies.

[technical] who are closely associated with them) are actually the 24,000 mentioned in the opening census in 23:3-5. They are clearly those Levites (generic) who had to take charge of the work in the temple. Their division and function go back to David who, together with Zadok and Ahimelech, has assigned them this function. They stand as one focal group among the Levites (generic), with the rest of the Levites (generic) who are discussed from 24:20-31 being the other focal group. What applies to the Aaronites (together with the Levites [technical]) in terms of their being appointed by David (with the cooperation of Zadok and Ahimelech), also applies to the rest of the Levites (generic).

The following chapters then describe the rest of the Levites (generic) in more detail: ch. 25 focuses on the musicians (associated with the fourth group of 4,000 mentioned in 23:3-5), 26:1-19 on the gatekeepers (associated with the third group of 4,000 mentioned in 23:3-5) and 26:20–27:34 on various officials, Judges, treasurers, commanders, and counselors (associated with the second group of 6,000 mentioned in 23:3-5).[59]

These observations should now be discussed in terms of the identity (re)formulation processes that can be detected here. However, before that can be done, it could be useful to take notice of the reconstructions of the historical context (particularly that of the Second Temple priesthood) that are undertaken by scholars in the field. In doing so, one should be well aware of the looming danger of circular argumentation where a world-of-origin is reconstructed from the textual witnesses and afterward the textual witnesses are read against the background of this reconstructed world. Below more will be said about this issue.[60]

---

59 This view relates to the indications Williamson has given for the compositeness of the texts under discussion. Cf. Williamson, "The Origins of the 24 Priestly Courses."

60 This circularity can in part be avoided when the reconstruction of the world-of-origin is done from more sources other than the biblical witnesses. For a discussion of how this view impacts on the writing of a history of biblical times, such as the Second Temple period, see L. L. Grabbe's introduction to his work, *A History of the Jews and Judaism in the Second Temple Period* (London: T&T Clark, 2004), ch. 1.

Overview of the History of the Second Temple Priesthood

A few classic studies have been done on the history of the priesthood in Ancient Israel. Gunneweg,[61] Cody,[62] Blenkinsopp,[63] and Grabbe,[64] to mention only a few, are often-quoted sources in this respect. Since the publication of Blenkinsopp's and Grabbe's books, a few other influential descriptions have appeared. Nurmela (*The Levites*) dedicated a full study to the Levites, Schaper (*Priester und Leviten*) spent a volume on "Priester und Leviten im achämenidischen Juda," and Hunt[65] dedicated a study to the Zadokites, whom she calls "the missing priests."[66] This is not the place to interact with all those studies in an in-depth discussion. The purpose of this section is more modest, namely to provide an overview of the developments in the Second Temple priesthood (up to the end of the Persian era) in order to allow our textual analysis of 1 Chronicles 23–27 to interact with this background.

Grabbe starts his discussion of the priesthood with the view that

> [a]lthough the biblical text gives an overall impression of a priestly structure that goes back to Moses, many discrepancies between texts leave the critical scholar with no doubt that the temple priesthood reached a fairly stable configuration early in the Second Temple period only after a long period of struggle between rival factions.[67]

Some of the problems summarized by Grabbe are the following: First, the common view is that the pre-exilic priesthood was Zadokite. The problem is, however, that Zadok seems to be a latecomer in history.[68] The only biblical

---

61 A. H. J. Gunneweg, *Leviten und Priester: Hauptlinien der Traditionsbildung und Geschichte des israelitisch-jüdischen Kultpersonals* (Göttingen: Vandenhoeck & Ruprecht, 1965).

62 A. Cody, *A History of the Old Testament Priesthood* (Rome: Pontifical Biblical Institute, 1965).

63 J. Blenkinsopp, *Sage, Priest, Prophet: Religious and Intellectual Leadership in Ancient Israel* (Louisville: Westminster John Knox, 1995).

64 L. L. Grabbe, *Priests, Prophets, Diviners, Sages: A Socio-Historical Study of the Religious Specialists in Ancient Israel* (Philadelphia: Trinity, 1996).

65 A. Hunt, *Missing priests: The Zadokites in Tradition and History* (LHBOTS 452; New York: T&T Clark, 2006).

66 Cf. also some of the more general studies, such as T. Willi, *Juda — Jehud — Israel. Studien zum Selbstverständnis des Judentums in persischer Zeit* (FAT 12; Tübingen: Mohr-Siebeck, 1995); idem,"Leviten, Priester und Kult in vorhellenistischer Zeit"; E. Gerstenberger, *Israel in der Perserzeit. 5. und 4. Jahrhundert v.Chron.* (Stuttgart: Kohlhammer, 2005).

67 Grabbe, *A History of the Jews and Judaism*, p. 225.

68 Hunt's book (*Missing priests*) elaborates on this problem. She suggests that there was

book where the altar priests are presented as exclusively Zadokite is Ezekiel. In this biblical book the Levites are also clearly a lower level clergy. Zadok has no ancestors indicated in the earlier traditions — it is only in the Chronicler's genealogies where Zadok is given a prominent place.

A second problematic issue is the fact that the Bible in general considers the priesthood to be Aaronide. However, Grabbe[69] points out that the statements about Aaron as a priest or as the ancestor of the altar priests are primarily from late texts — mainly from the P tradition and rarely in the Deuteronomistic History. The Chronicler takes his picture of the altar priests as being Aaronide from the P tradition, it seems. According to Grabbe:

> . . . the picture that emerges in the analysis of these texts is that Aaron was a
> priestly group, perhaps based in Bethel, but opposed by other groups who also
> had a hand in the process of transmitting the tradition. It was only in the post-
> exilic period that the Aaronites became the dominant group and impressed their
> identity on all the altar priests.[70]

A third area concerns the Levites: Who were they, and who were included under this rubric? In order to answer these questions, I will focus here on Grabbe's interaction with Schaper on this issue. Grabbe[71] summarizes Schaper's description of the developments in the priesthood. The following beacons along the way are identified:

- At the time of Josiah, the "Zadokite" priesthood[72] was in charge of the Jerusalem Temple. The priests supported Josiah's reform and were able to control it. Although the Deuteronomic law included an attempt to reform the system by giving the priests of the local YHWH shrines ("the Levites") equal rights with the "Zadokites" to preside at the Jerusalem Temple, it did not succeed, and the Levites acquired only second-class status.
- With the Jerusalem priesthood deported during the exile, the Aaronites of Bethel seem to have stepped into the breach and served as priests to those left

---

never a Zadokite dynasty before the late Second Temple Hasmonean era. Cf. also Schaper (*Priester und Leviten*, p. 270) who calls Zadok a *homo novus* in the tradition.

69 Grabbe, *A History of the Jews and Judaism*, p. 225.

70 Ibid., p. 226.

71 Ibid., pp. 228–9.

72 Whether one can call the earlier priesthood "Zadokite" has been questioned by Schaper (*Priester und Leviten*) himself by highlighting the fact that Zadok is a *homo novus* in the tradition. Cf. also Hunt's thesis (*Missing Priest*) that there was no monarchical Zadokite dynasty. Schaper's use of the term "Zadokite" here presumably gives expression to the understanding created by the biblical witnesses, particularly the Deuteronomistic tradition.

in the land; however, the status of the Levites continued to decline during the exilic and early postexilic period.

- When the exiled priests returned, they reasserted their traditional rights over the altar but were countered by a coalition of opponents. The main critics were the country Levites who had set up the cult in the ruins of the temple during the exile, but along with them were the Abiatharites of Anathoth and perhaps also the Aaronites of Bethel.

- The Persian government supported the Zadokite priests; however, the Levites and others cooperated in the rebuilding of the temple because it was also in their interests.

- It was during the time of Nehemiah (who came in 445 BCE) and Ezra (who is dated to 398) that the Levites were able to gain status. Nehemiah did not trust the high priest and the upper class of priests but used the Levites as his allies, making them guards at the city gates. The priests retaliated by not passing on the support needed by the Levites from the temple tithes and offerings, forcing many Levites to turn to farming to have enough to eat . . .; however, Nehemiah set this right on his return and established a committee equally of Levites and priests to oversee the collection and distribution of the temple dues. Ezra continued to favor them, which gave the Levites a new status and confidence. The singers, gatekeepers, and Netinim were separate from the Levites until the time of Ezra, but they became merged with them toward the end of the Achaemenid period. This was partly because of the increased importance of singing in the temple liturgy and would not have been seen as a demotion of the Levites.

Although Grabbe is in agreement with Schaper's broad argument, he questions the sharp division between altar priests and the Levites that Schaper is supporting. He states:

> Although there is evidence in the text of disputes between the two groups — disputes that eventually led to the Levites' being relegated to lower clergy — it is not so clear when these occurred; for example, they could already have been settled before the Persian period. The main arguments centre on whether Nehemiah raised the status of the Levites at the expense of the priests.[73]

Grabbe's own description of priests and Levites is the following:

> The priests were the only ones allowed to preside at the altar . . . Their main function was to carry out the sacrificial cult . . ., but they had other duties as well. They

---

73 Grabbe, *A History of the Jews and Judaism*, p. 229.

were the custodians of the written law with responsibility to teach it to the people and make cultic rulings where needed . . . They had to pronounce on all matters of ritual purity, including certain diseases . . . According to some texts, they also functioned in a wider civic context in such things as judging lawsuits and acting as appeal Judges for lower courts . . . It is also claimed that they had custody over the sacred objects of priestly divination called the Urim and Thumim . . . The duties of the 'Levites' included a variety of functions. Their most important task was to assist the priests in carrying out the sacrificial cult, though they were not to carry out the ceremonies at the altar itself . . . They also had other duties such as maintaining security and evidently a variety of administrative duties . . . (C)ertain groups of temple personnel, such as the gatekeepers, singers, Netinim and temple servants alongside the Levites were eventually assimilated into the Levites. There is also evidence that the Levites were especially drawn on for the scribal skills necessary to run the nation as well as the temple . . . The divisions of the priests evidently developed during the Persian period.[74]

It seems then that Grabbe, in reaction to Schaper's views, would rather emphasize the difference in function between priests and Levites in the Second Temple period, and not so much a difference in status.

This brings us now to the point where the methodological vantage point of identity (re)formulation, particularly the issue of self-categorization, will be probed on the chosen text and its background context.

A Case of Self-Categorization?

Before presenting a perspective on this text that involves the social-psychological notion of self-categorization, it should be clarified how this presentation will avoid the danger of circular argumentation to which I have referred above. I am well aware of the fact that the views of Schaper, Grabbe, and others that were summarized in the previous section are theoretical reconstructions from the textual witnesses at our disposal. Although these scholars utilize more textual witnesses than merely biblical material in their reconstructions, one should remember that the texts — also the texts under discussion here — underpin the reconstructions that are made there. It would therefore be irresponsible scholarship to merely turn the direction of investigation around in order to show how the biblical material reflects the realities of the past. More sophistication is needed in our argumentation. I would therefore like to propose that what follows in this section would be no different from the previously mentioned scholarship in terms of the direction of investigation. I am also working from the textual

---

74 Ibid., pp. 229–30.

witnesses toward a theoretical reconstruction of the Second-Temple-period society in Yehud. However, the methodological framework that I am offering here is informed by social identity theory (with an emphasis on self-categorization theory, as discussed above), rather than by historiographical interests. The reconstruction offered here does not aim at supplanting those historiographical descriptions of other scholars. It rather purports to be complementary in order to come to a richer understanding of the period and society under discussion. The unique contribution of this alternative methodological angle is namely that it focuses on the *process* of identity (re)formulation, rather than on the *end product* of such a process. The *pragmatic-rhetorical* aspect of the textual communication witnessed in the biblical texts is highlighted here. Historiographical reconstructions could treat textual material as if they reflect static realities. By approaching the reconstruction task from the angle of social identity theory, the textual materials are regarded as those communicational artifacts of the past that were part and parcel of the dynamic process of identity (re)formulation. The construction and editing of these texts in the past contributed to the *process* (not the end product) that we endeavor to describe here.

Do we witness any self-categorization process in the very intricate pattern of relationships that we observed in 1 Chronicles 23–27? Or to put the question somewhat differently: Is there any indication that some sort of a prototype is being constructed by means of these texts? And are there any indications that such a prototype regulated the ingroup categorization? The following points are preliminary attempts to answer these questions:

(i)   Those who constructed (and/or edited) these texts were engaged in discourse about what it means to be a Levite in the generic sense. It seems that those engaging in this discourse, as well as the presumed audience, considered Levitical descent as something significant for their own time.

(ii) The prototype of a Levite (generic) is traced back to the ancestral past. The model, according to which divisions of the Levites are made, is seen to be in continuity with the family divisions of the past. The remark in the last chapter of this section (27:23) about David not counting those below 20 years of age because YHWH has promised to make Israel as numerous as the stars of the heavens, might even be a hint that the Levites (generic) are understood to be the fulfillment of this promise to the ancestors.

(iii) The prototype of a Levite (generic) also includes respect for the royal authority of the past. David, being one of the great and successful kings of their past, is portrayed as having been instrumental in all the subdivisions and assignment of duties that they are continuing in their own day. Continuity with David's time (as a time of preparation for the building of the First Temple) would have been an important impetus for the Second Temple community during their restoration process. It would also have provided some sort of a judicial basis during a time when there was no Davidic king on the throne, but Persian imperial dominance formed the socio-political context.

Whereas, the above points emphasize the marks of *inclusion* into the proto-type being constructed here, there are also clear indications that an *intragroup self-categorization* is made here.[75] Different Levitical (generic) groupings are mentioned, and they are portrayed in very specific relationships to one another. The following points describe the self-categorization taking place through this literature:

(i)   The Levites (generic) consist of two major groups, namely first the Aaronites (with the Levites [technical] closely associated with them) and secondly the rest of the Levites. The organization of both these groupings was done with Davidic authority and in the presence of other parties.

(ii) Among those responsible for the original organization of both these groups were Zadok and Ahimelech (who are both indicated to be Aaronites and therefore Levites [generic]). The insinuation, it seems, is therefore that the adherents to the traditions of Zadok and Ahimelech (whatever that might have entailed) should realize that they were instrumental in legitimating the status and functions of the different parts of the Levites (generic). (This point confirms that the Zadokites are not portrayed as a separate or rival priestly grouping here. Reference to "priests" in this context rather refers to Aaronites. However, the mentioning of Zadok shows the need during the time of origin of this text to emphasize that the Zadokites actually confirm — or, are supposed to confirm — the present cultic order.)

(iii) The focus is very much on the Aaronites whose position is certainly being bolstered by this discourse on self-categorization. They have been set apart for special functions in the temple service and liturgy. However, the Levites (here definitely in the technical sense) serve next to them, although a differentiation of function is clearly made. Of all the groupings mentioned in these texts only the Aaronites (in 24:19) and the Levites (technical; in the direct speech in 23:25-26) are indicated as having received their function and assignment from YHWH.

(iv) The rest of the Levites (generic) consist of musicians, gatekeepers, and all kinds of officials, commanders, and counselors. Although their organization also goes back to David and their ancestral past, YHWH's direct role in their

---

75 Cf. J. Kessler, "Persia's Loyal Yahwists: Power Identity and Ethnicity in Achaemenid Yehud," in *Judah and the Judeans in the Persian Period* (eds. O. Lipschits and M. Oeming; Winona Lake, Eisenbrauns, 2006), pp. 91–121 where movements toward inclusion and exclusion are seen as simultaneous processes in identity formation.

assignment is not indicated. They are also clearly differentiated from the Levites (technical) who are associated with the Aaronites (see above).

What factors could have motivated the construction of such a prototype and such an intragroup self-categorization process? Against the background of Persian-period Yehud, one could theorize about the following possibilities:

(i)   One may assume that the common fate of all the subgroupings of the Jerusalemite society could have contributed to such a self-understanding. During the time of restoration where the community in Jerusalem and Yehud was still struggling to come to grips with their changed political, social and cultic realities, it could have been a motivation for finding continuity in the ancestral and royal past. In those circumstances, the common fate of all subgroupings would have drawn them together in anticipation of a new present and especially, new future under Persian dominion.

(ii) The way in which the Aaronites and Levites (technical) are presented in these chapters, could be an indication that there was a need to building self-esteem within the cultic sphere. By emphasizing their special position and function and by indicating that their status within the cult was legitimated by YHWH, these specific subgroupings would have bolstered their position over against other contenders.

(iii) In the very unstable conditions of the restoration period of Persian-period Yehud the need for self-verification or uncertainty reduction could have been a real need. Adherence to the group norms as spelled out by these chapters would have assisted individuals to verify themselves against the background of a bigger structure in order to find their rightful place in the changed society.

(iv) The process of self-categorization that we witness in the texts under discussion could have been motivated by the need for optimal distinctiveness. By means of this self-categorization process which builds on continuity with other groups in society, but also clarifies the discontinuities, would help the group behind this section in Chronicles to a better understanding of their distinct role and status, and would certainly assist to enforce that understanding onto society!

Conclusion

We examined one prominent section in the books of Chronicles in order to determine the self-categorization processes reflected in them. Although this section, 1 Chronicles 23–27, is very prominent in this regard, it should be kept in mind that Chronicles includes diverse descriptions that could be related to the context of the Second Temple priesthood. This study therefore does not want to offer general conclusions for the books of Chronicles as a whole. Other studies on different parts of Chronicles should append my contribution to enrich our understanding of the identity (re)formulation processes in the Late Persian Yehud.

But this should not prevent us from speculating, even a little bit. If the Chronicler had the opportunity to append a note on historiography at the beginning of his work, would that note be the same as that in Giliomee and Mbenga's *New History of South Africa*:

> We are also aware of some of the distorted historiography of the past. We have set out to redress past distortions and biases. This . . . book draws on the perspectives of different 'schools' of historians . . . We tried to synthesise the material and to make it accessible to both the academic and the general reader [my adaption – LCJ][76]

Maybe there are some things that do not ever change in history. One of those, it seems, is that there is always a relationship between historiography and identity (re)formulation!

---

76 H. Giliomee and B. Mbenga, *New History*, p. x.

Otherness and Historiography in Chronicles

Christine Mitchell

Introduction

The very first work of "history" penned in the Western tradition begins its first paragraph with setting the context of the work as the conflict between Greek and Persian. Herodotus of Halicarnassus, an Ionian Greek from the fringes of the Persian Empire, constructed his *historie* as an account of the formation of Greek identity in relation to the Other. This tendency may also be found in the annals and royal inscriptions of the ancient Egyptian, Mesopotamian, and eastern Mediterranean cultures that preceded the creation of historiography in the Persian period. We may also find this tendency in the biblical narratives of Kings and Ezra-Nehemiah. The book of Chronicles, however, has not been investigated from this perspective. Previous generations of scholarship were apt to see the Other in Chronicles as Samaritans, but this construction was based on the assumed common authorship of Chronicles and Ezra-Nehemiah. In this essay I will explore another possibility for the Other against whom Israel is constructed in Chronicles. One possibility that I raise further in the conclusion is that Chronicles is not a work of historiography at all, or, if it is, it is a radical innovation in the fundamental rules of the genre as understood in antiquity.

Historiography and the Other

In this first part of my essay, I will argue that Otherness was an integral part of the construction of the genre of historiography in the ancient world in the Persian and Hellenistic periods. I will begin with the discussion of annals and inscriptions, move to the Greek histories, and finally turn to the biblical texts. If genre is not only form but also context and significance, as I have argued previously, then this particular thematic focus deserves further discussion and reflection.[1]

There is a vast amount of inscriptional material available from the ancient cultures of Egypt and Mesopotamia. Closest temporally and developmentally to historiography as it came to be understood are the Assyrian annals and royal inscriptions and the Neo-Babylonian chronicles. The Persian Empire has little preserved except royal inscriptions and these too need to be discussed as providing context. In order to fully explore this topic, a monograph-length work would need to expand upon the comparative work I will sketch below; perhaps something along the lines of David Carr's *Writing on the Tablet of the Heart*.[2] The sketch below, therefore, should be seen as suggestive and programmatic, rather than exhaustive.

Assyrian Annals and Royal Inscriptions

It has been suggested that even from an early period (Old Akkadian) Mesopotamian identity was being constructed in relationship to an Other.[3] The chronicles preserved from this period suggest that a certain core group was seeing itself in opposition to the outside groups. This tendency may be seen in the Neo-Assyrian-period royal inscriptions and chronicles. A chronicle from this period preserved in fragmentary form lists the revolts against the Assyrian kings and their campaigns against various enemies during the period 858–699 BCE. Although there are a few mentions of other events (e.g., solar eclipse, dedication of a new temple, restoration of a palace), the vast majority of the events recorded deal with the king's military endeavors against the Other who is outside the land, or against the Other who has rebelled.[4] A similar pattern may be seen in the royal inscriptions given in annal form from the reigns of Shalmaneser III and Shamshi-Adad V (good representative examples are the so-called "Khurkh Monolith" of Shalmaneser III, and the text of Shamshi-Adad V from Calah).[5] The Others in these texts are detailed at length, making it clear that the Other is multiple, nefarious, and spread

---

1 C. Mitchell, "Power, *Eros*, and Biblical Genres," *The Bible and Critical Theory* 3/2 (2007), 18.1–11 (http://publications.epress.monash.edu/toc/bc/3/2); also in idem, *Bakhtin and Genre Theory in Biblical Studies* (SemeiaSt 63; ed. R. T. Boer; Atlanta: SBL, 2007), pp. 31–42.

2 D. M. Carr, *Writing on the Tablet of the Heart: Origins of Scripture and Literature* (New York: Oxford University Press, 2005).

3 J.-J. Glassner, *Mesopotamian Chronicles* (WAW 19; ed. B. R. Foster; Atlanta: SBL, 2004), p. 98.

4 Ibid., pp. 164–77.

5 A. K. Grayson, *Assyrian Rulers of the Early First Millennium BC, II (858–745 BC)* (RIMA 3; Toronto: University of Toronto Press, 1996), pp. 11–24, 180–8.

throughout the land. A particularly interesting text was prepared for Shamshi-ilu, the field marshal of Adad-narari III; it was carved on two stone lions and described his campaign against an Urartian king, who "had not *had relations with* (lit. 'stretched out his hand to') any previous king." The two lions' names were given as "who [. . .] angry demon, unrivalled attack, who overwhelms the insubmissive, who brings success" and "who charges through battle, who flattens the enemy land, who expels criminals and brings in good people."[6] The specific descriptions of enemy kings and territories are here generalized as criminals and insubmissive, contrasted with good people and successful conquerors.

From the many royal inscriptions of the Assyrian kings, I now turn to focus on the well-known Sennacherib inscriptions. The introduction to the Sennacherib Prism is a general panegyric to the king and the conclusion focuses on his build-ing projects, followed by a general benediction. However, the majority of the text is made up of accounts against various enemies, both those who had rebelled ("did not submit to my yoke") and those whom he defeated ("made submit to the yoke"). The Babylonians come in for special mention as "wicked devils" and are the people against whom he especially defined Assyrian rule.[7] The strategy of demonizing the Babylonians, turning them into the Other that must be defeated, is consistent with the Assyrian historiographic tactics.[8] The historically most-dangerous Others were not only subjected to attack and devastation, but also to the destruction of their central temples to the national god.[9] Laato suggests that the use of pejorative language in Sennacherib's inscriptions is most acute when the enemy was not completely defeated;[10] this makes sense, as the Other that has been defeated cannot be set up against the self as an identity-forming object. In fact, for the Western kingdoms absorbed by Assyria, there was no sense that they had a history prior to being conquered:[11] they are Othered and absorbed all at once.

The fate of Judah, Jerusalem, and Hezekiah has come in for much analysis, especially in the area of historical reconstruction.[12] This is not my concern in this

---

6 Ibid., pp. 231–3.

7 D. D. Luckenbill, *The Annals of Sennacherib* (Chicago: University of Chicago Press, 1924), pp. 24–7.

8 S. W. Holloway, *Aššur is King! Aššur is King! Religion in the Exercise of Power in the Neo-Assyrian Empire.* (SHANE 10; Leiden: Brill, 2002), p. 93.

9 Ibid., pp. 116–17.

10 A. Laato, "Assyrian Propaganda and the Falsification of History in the Royal Inscriptions of Sennacherib," *VT* 45 (1995), 198–226 (213).

11 M. W. Hamilton, "The Past as Destiny: Historical Visions in Sam'al and Judah Under Assyrian Hegemony," *HTR* 91 (1993), 215–50 (219).

12 See recently Laato, "Assyrian Propaganda"; W. R. Gallagher, *Sennacherib's Campaign to Judah: New Studies (*SHANE 18; Leiden: Brill, 1999); L. L. Grabbe (ed.),

essay, but rather how Hezekiah is constructed in the inscriptions. Sennacherib describes shutting up Hezekiah in his city "like a bird in a cage," and while what this means historically has been extensively discussed, I would like to focus on the simile itself. Gallagher points out that this simile is also used in an inscription of Tiglath-Pileser, but more importantly for my purpose, that it comes from hunting descriptions of the Assyrian king killing lions.[13] The enemy, in our case Hezekiah, is likened to an animal, made not-human and thus Other.

Cynthia Chapman has shown how gender also works as an Othering device in the Neo-Assyrian inscriptions and iconography. The foreign king and subjects (especially the military) are likened to women in their defeat. Women are constructed as the opposite of the hyper-masculine Assyrian king and the identification of the foreigner as Other is heightened by this gendered Othering.[14] It seems, from these brief examples, that Otherness in terms of nationality or ethnicity is constructed from other binaries: the binaries of human–animal and man–woman. Ethnicity in and of itself was perhaps not enough to construct the Other.

Neo-Babylonian Chronicles

The Neo-Babylonian chronicles do not use the more vivid imagery that is found in the Neo-Assyrian inscriptions, but follow the same pattern found in the earlier Assyrian chronicles. In this case the core group, the Babylonians (defined as the Akkadians), is positioned against the Assyrians first and then the Medes/Persians. Glassner suggests that it is curious that at a certain point in the chronicles, the Medes are no longer called Medes, but "Ummān-manda," a pejorative term.[15] Perhaps it is at this point, when the Assyrian defeat is assured, that the Medes now become the Other. Unlike the royal inscriptions of the Neo-Assyrians, the Neo-Babylonian inscriptions are more concerned with building activities and expressions of devotion to the gods than with detailing the military campaigns, although this may be an argument from silence.

Persian Royal Inscriptions

Persian-period Zoroastrianism was well known as highly dualistic. While this might be the "cause" of a certain dualism or Othering found in the Persian

---

'Like a Bird in a Cage': The Invasion of Sennacherib in 701 BCE (JSOTSup 363; ESHM 4; London: T&T Clark, 2003).

    13 Gallagher, *Sennacherib's*, p. 133.

    14 C. R. Chapman, *The Gendered Language of Warfare in the Israelite-Assyrian Encounter* (HSM 62; Winona Lake: Eisenbrauns, 2004), pp. 20–59.

    15 Glassner, *Mesopotamian*, p. 218.

royal inscriptions, the fact that the earliest Persian inscription, the Bisitun inscription, was written also in the language of Babylon, should keep us from leaping immediately to this conclusion; as we have seen, there is Othering in the Akkadian-language inscriptions without the influence of a necessarily dual-istic religious ethic. However, as Bruce Lincoln has recently shown, there was a strong link forged between the Lie (as a religious concept) and the enemies of Darius in the Bisitun inscription. As in the Neo-Assyrian materials, the Other is constructed by analogy. In this material, the analogy is not with animals or with women, but with a religious concept of the Lie. The Lie in its very nature is constructed as that which is opposed to justice, righteousness, and the divine. Darius is called by Ahura Mazda to oppose the Lie, and in a syllogism those that oppose Darius are part of the Lie.[16] Darius' rise to power is thus recounted in a series of Othering moves.

Greek Histories

As I noted in the introduction, the very first work of history, Herodotus' *historie*, constructs Greek identity in relation to the Other, most notably the Persian Other, but also the Egyptian Other (Book 2), the Lydian Other (Book 1), and so on. There is a vast amount of scholarship on the relationship of Greek and Barbarian in a variety of texts in a variety of genres, growing yearly. My purpose in this essay is not to look at the subject from the broader context of identity forma-tion (see the excellent collection edited by Harrison),[17] but rather at the Other in historiography.

Francois Hartog's book, *The Mirror of Herodotus,* was the first to examine this concept of the Other in Greek historiography, although the earlier work of Arnaldo Momigliano had certainly provided some groundwork.[18] In his more recent work, *Memories of Odysseus*, Hartog notes that the Barbarians form an antonymic pair with the Greeks in Herodotus, "as they stand in opposition they define each other."[19] However, there were no "Barbarians" in the earlier

16 B. Lincoln, *Religion, Empire and Torture: The Case of Achaemenian Persia, with a Postscript on Abu Ghraib* (Chicago: University of Chicago Press, 2007).

17 T. Harrison (ed.), *Greeks and Barbarians* (New York: Routledge, 2002).

18 F. Hartog, *The Mirror of Herodotus: The Representation of the Other in the Writing of History* (trans. J. Lloyd; Berkeley: University of California Press, 1988; French orig. 1980); idem, *Alien Wisdom: The Limits of Hellenization* (Cambridge: Cambridge University Press, 1975); idem, *Essays in Ancient and Modern Historiography* (Middletown: Wesleyan University Press, 1977); idem, *The Classical Foundations of Modern Historiography* (Berkeley: University of California Press, 1990).

19 F. Hartog, *Memories of Odysseus: Frontier Tales from Ancient Greece* (trans. J. Lloyd; Chicago: University of Chicago Press, 2001; French orig. 1996), p. 79.

Homeric epics. Hartog also notes that Thucydides construes an earlier time when the Greeks themselves were "Barbarians" (Thucyolides 1.3.3), but that without Barbarians there could be no Greeks.[20] The Persian Wars of the fifth century BCE were the catalyst for making the opposition between Greek and Barbarian. Although this opposition was also found in Aeschylus;[21] we might compare Momigliano's suggestion that it was the Persian imperial presence that fostered the development of historiography in both Greece and Judah.[22] Herodotus' work places the Barbarian in Asia with a Persian face, but the primary opposition in Herodotus is a political one, not a moral/ethical one: the Greek is part of the *polis*, i.e., free, while the Barbarian is subject to a king. The Barbarians were all Others, but the Barbarian *par excellence* was the Great King of Persia.[23]

Herodotus used a system to depict the various cultures in his work: using Greek ways of seeing the world as the defining categories, a series of opposi- tions were set up. This macro-system of oppositions can be used as a base for various micro-systems of local oppositions. Thus, within the structure of Greek– Barbarian, there were a series of inner-Greek oppositions set up: the Athenians/ Ionians were contrasted to all other Greeks, and the Athenians were contrasted to all other Ionians; his historical framework was, above all, patterned.[24] The Greek *nomos* or worldview (language, religion, and customs) was the master key.[25] It is possible that this series of oppositions are embedded into the style of classical Greek prose, which uses the μέν . . ., δέ construction (on the one hand . . ., on the other hand) to balance opposites. This was characteristic of the Sophists' teaching of rhetoric, and marks the style of Thucydides just as much as Herodotus — it was an Athenian style.[26] Thucydides' ability to undercut

20 Ibid., p. 80. Cf. D. Shanske, *Thucydides and the Philosophical Origins of History* (New York: Cambridge University Press, 2007), pp. 25–6.

21 Hartog, *Memories*, pp. 81–2.

22 Momigliano, *Essays*, pp. 27–33; idem, *Classical*, p. 12.

23 Hartog, *Memories*, pp. 81, 84. Cf. "When the Greeks refer to non-Greek people under the Hellenic sphere of influence, these people are not called barbarians, but ἀλλόφυλοι. Barbarians are people who lived in the Persian Empire" (J. M. Alonso-Núñez, "Herodotus' Conception of Historical Space and the Beginnings of Universal History," in *Herodotus and His World: Essays from a Conference in Memory of George Forrest* [eds. P. Derow and R. Parker; Oxford: Oxford University Press, 2003], pp. 145–52 [148]).

24 C. Sourvionou-Inwood, "Herodotos (and Others) on Pelasgians: Some Perceptions of Ethnicity," in *Herodotus and His World: Essays from a Conference in Memory of George Forrest* (eds. P. Derow and R. Parker; Oxford: Oxford University Press, 2003), pp. 103–44 (122–4); R. Fowler, "Herodotos and his Contemporaries," *JHS* 116 (1996), 62–87, (82).

25 Hartog, *Memories*, pp. 91–2, 95; Alonso-Núñez, "Herodotus," 148; T. Harrison, *Divinity and History: The Religion of Herodotus* (Oxford: Oxford University Press, 2000), pp. 214–16.

26 T. J. Luce, *The Greek Historians* (London: Routledge, 1997), pp. 72–3; Shanske,

his oppositional pairs — seen also in Herodotus — should not blind us to this important structuring device.[27]

In the third and fourth centuries, the Persians of the past continued to be depicted in historiographic works, but contemporary Persians and their institutions were not.[28] The Greek–Barbarian opposition also continued to be operational, but now it was modified so as to be less political and more moral/ethical/cultural. It was at this point that the Persians truly became "Orientalized," i.e., portrayed as effeminate, "soft," and so forth.[29] However, Hartog's presentation may be an oversimplification. Returning to Thucydides, a fifth-century author, we may note that the major structuring opposition in his work was not Greek–Barbarian, but an inner-Greek Athens–Sparta. Persians appear, to be sure, but in much more of the cultural sense; their role in the politics of the Athens–Sparta conflict is played down.[30] So already, the Greek–Barbarian opposition became less political, perhaps at a time contemporary with Herodotus. Nevertheless, the oppositional form of identity formation in historiography is apparent in Thucydides' work. Even Xenophon's work, which is often credited with at least part of the Orientalizing of the Persians in Greek discourse, has been reassessed. While his *Cyropaedia* is certainly set in the past, his depiction of Persian customs is drawn much more from his own experiences and imagination.[31] Yet Robin Lane Fox has shown the link between Barbarian and woman in the *Anabasis*, in a way similar to Chapman's work about the Assyrians' portrayal of their enemies. Fox argues that Xenophon's encounter with the Other while on the march through the Persian Empire shaped his entire depiction of Cyrus the Great in the *Cyropaedia*, especially the different construction of the masculine subject.[32] The evidence,

Thucydides, p. 27.

27 Ibid.; Sourvinou-Inwood, "Herodotos," 125–6.

28 Momigliano, *Alien*, p. 138.

29 Hartog, *Memories*, pp. 96–8. Ctesias bears much of the blame for this: cf. D. G. Levine, *Xenophon's Cyropaedia: Style, Genre, and Literary Technique* (Oxford: Oxford University Press, 1993), p. 106; H. Sancisi-Weerdenburg, "Exit Atossa: Images of Women in Greek Historiography on Persia," in *Images of Women in Antiquity* (eds. A. Cameron and A. Kuhrt; London: Routledge, 1993), pp. 20–33 (32).

30 J. Wiesehöfer, "'. . . Keeping the Two Sides Equal': Thucydides, the Persians and the Peloponnesian War," in *Brill's Companion to Thucydides* (eds. A. Rengakos and A. Tsakmakis; Leiden: Brill, 2006), pp. 657–67 (657–58).

31 Cf. S. W. Hirsch, *The Friendship of the Barbarians: Xenophon and the Persian Empire* (Hanover: University Press of New England, 1985), p. 13; he argues that Xenophon is a reliable source on Persian customs and was an admirer of things Persian.

32 R. L. Fox, "Sex, Gender and the Other in Xenophon's *Anabasis*," in *The Long March: Xenophon and the Ten Thousand* (ed. R. L. Fox; New Haven: Yale University Press, 2004), pp. 184–214.

therefore, leads to differing interpretations of the role of the Persian/Barbarian as the Other, while leaving the basic Self–Other dichotomy intact.

Beginning in the fourth century, we find many expressions of historiography written in Greek that were less "universal" (as Herodotus' work basically was, even though it dealt with one particular encounter), and more specific. Thus, contemporary with Xenophon was the physician Ctesias, who wrote his *Persika* after having spent time as the personal physician of the Persian king Artaxerxes I. His complete history of the Persian Empire, including its predecessor Assyrian empire, has not survived, but its basic contents and some indication of its style has. In this case, the Other, as defined by Herodotus, was more fully (and luridly) described to Greeks. Ctesias' claims to personal knowledge of Persian customs and history through his sojourn in Persia gave his work an authority that was not matched by the native informants who wrote their own histories in Greek. For example, the history of Babylon written by Berossus, a native Babylonian who wrote in Greek, was not the authority for Babylonian customs; Ctesias was.[33] Even when Berossus specifically contradicted Ctesias' claims, and presumably had an authority as a native informant, Ctesias' version became the accepted one.[34] Even though Ctesias' *Persika* has not been preserved, the accounts of Persians and Babylonians that have been preserved from the Greek world were all written by Greeks (notably Herodotus). Greeks (even Hellenistic Greeks), it seems, preferred their accounts of the Other to be written by themselves.

Judahite Historiography

Beginning with John Van Seters' *In Search of History*,[35] there has been considerable interest in the problem of what I will call Judahite historiography, by which I mean Judahite historiographic texts prior to the fourth century BCE. I have tried to coin a term that does not presuppose the canon of the Bible, because I do not want to include Chronicles in this investigation. I want the ability to use a term that describes texts such as Kings that the Chronicler used, without presupposing that Chronicles belongs to the same genre. This starting point is in direct contrast to, for example, Marc Zvi Brettler, who begins his book on historiography with the supposition that Chronicles is a work of historiography, and in fact is the example from which to begin discussing Judahite historiography more generally.

---

33   G. P. Verbrugghe and J. M. Wickersham, *Berossos and Manetho, Introduced and Translated: Native Traditions in Ancient Mesopotamia and Egypt* (Ann Arbor: University of Michigan Press, 1996), p. 27.

34   Ibid., pp. 21–2.

35   J. Van Seters, *In Search of History: Historiography in the Ancient World and the Origins of Biblical History* (New Haven: Yale University Press, 1983).

Brettler takes issue with Van Seters and others who begin with a discussion of the Deuteronomic History, suggesting that because we can see how Chronicles operates as a text and with respect to its sources, it is a more appropriate beginning point for exploring earlier Judahite historiography.³⁶ Brettler has been hampered by his definition of historiography, "a narrative that presents a past" as opposed to ideology.³⁷ He suggests, in his conclusion, that "[b]iblical historical texts reflect a combination of genuine interest in the past, strong ideological beliefs and refined rhetorical devices,"³⁸ yet his operational definition separates out these three features and emphasizes only the first.

One of the criticisms leveled at Van Seters' work is his uncritical use of genres.³⁹ Indeed, all of the scholars surveyed so far have an uncritical use of genre. Definitions of biblical historiography as a genre that is some variation of "a narrative that recounts a past" are uncritical in their use of content to determine genre. I have argued elsewhere that genre is both form and content.⁴⁰ In that article, I suggested that the source citations in Chronicles and Kings are an index of the form of a genre to which both works belong, although Chronicles should be seen as an innovation within that genre. I would suggest that another index of the genre (anachronistically named historiography) would be the use of the Other against which the main group is constructed. Thus, I agree with John Frow that a definition of any genre must include both its formal features and its thematic content.⁴¹ A formal feature of Judahite historiography would be the use of source citations; a thematic feature of Judahite (and other ancient historiography) would be the use of the Other. Whether and how Judahite historiography uses this Other requires further investigation, but I will suggest — based on some preliminary evidence — that it does.

Scholars have examined the role of identity formation in the so-called biblical historiographic texts. Van Seters and Thomas L. Thompson, for example, see identity formation as the primary role of biblical historiography.⁴² E. T. Mullen

36 M. Z. Brettler, *The Creation of History in Ancient Israel* (London: Routledge: 1995), pp. 20–1.
37 Ibid., p. 12.
38 Ibid., p. 138.
39 L. Younger, review of John Van Seters, *In Search of History: Historiography in the Ancient World and the Origins of Biblical History*, JSOT 40 (1988), 110–17 (113–14).
40 Mitchell, "Power."
41 J. Frow, *Genre* (New Critical Idiom; London: Routledge, 2006), pp. 74–7. Frow defines genre as combining formal organization, rhetorical structure, and thematic content. Rhetorical structure is taken to mean the relations between speaker and hearer; in texts, that would mean "formal expression in the syntactic and intonational nuances of discourse" (p. 75). For biblical texts I think it is hard to disentangle rhetorical structure from formal organization.
42 Van Seters, *Search*, pp. 1–6; T. L. Thompson, *Early History of the Israelite People*

has read the entire Deuteronomic History as promulgating ethnic identity, with
Deuteronomy as the charter for the identity. He makes the distinction between
Israelite and non-Israelite (which is a form of Othering), but does not really
define the Other.[43] Following Mullen's work is that of James Linville, who sees
Kings as a project of identity formation, but, again, defines Israel in the positive
(community of Yahwists) rather than over against an Other.[44]

It seems to me that more attention should be paid to the oppositional form
of identity formation in these texts: there is a great deal of negative language in
Judges and Kings, especially. For example, the formulaic language of "his heart
was not true to Yhwh" (e.g., 1 Kgs 15:3), "he did not turn aside from the sins"
(e.g., 2 Kgs 10:29), "the high places were not taken away" (e.g., 2 Kgs 12:3), and
the negative rhetorical question form of the source citation, "are they not written?" (e.g., 2 Kgs 12:19). In fact, a quick tally suggests that the books of Judges
and Kings use the negative markers לא, אין and אל almost twice as much as does
Chronicles or Ezra-Nehemiah (uses per verse). Notably, Deuteronomy uses those
negative markers at a higher rate than does Leviticus. Perhaps, rather than looking
at Israel in the Deuteronomic materials as being positively constructed, we could
consider Israel as being negatively constructed: what it is *not* rather than what it
is. The work begun by Hartog on the classical historiographic material could be
extended to examine the material of Kings.

Oppositional identity formation is well-recognized as present in Ezra-
Nehemiah.[45] The identity of the Judean community in that text is created by
separation of that group from other groups, and by the definite Othering of the
excluded groups. Unlike Deuteronomy or Kings, being true to YHWH and wishing
to participate in worship at Jerusalem are not sufficient for inclusion in the community. The "peoples of the land" do include those who are YHWH-worshippers
(cf. Ezra 4:1-5, Neh. 13:4-9). Saul Olyan has drawn attention to the manner
in which purity regulations were applied to YHWH-worshippers who were
"aliens" in such a way as to exclude them from the community.[46] Nehemiah's

From the Written and Archaeological Sources (SHANE 4; Leiden: Brill, 1992), pp. 353–4.

   43 E. T. Mullen, Jr., *Narrative History and Ethnic Boundaries: The Deuteronomistic
Historian and the Creation of Israelite National Identity* (SemeiaSt 24; Atlanta: Scholars
Press, 1993).

   44 J. R. Linville, *Israel in the Book of Kings: The Past as a Project of Social Identity*
(JSOTSup 272; Sheffield: Sheffield Academic Press, 1998).

   45 Cf. S. Japhet, "Postexilic Historiography: How and Why?" in *From the Rivers of
Babylon to the Highlands of Judah: Collected Studies on the Restoration Period* (Winona
Lake: Eisenbrauns, 2006; repr. from *Israel Constructs Its History: Deuteronomistic
Historiography in Recent Research* [eds. A. de Pury, T. Römer, and J.-D. Macchi; JSOTSup
306; Sheffield: Sheffield Academic Press, 2000], pp. 144–73), pp. 307–30 (312–13).

   46 S. M. Olyan, "Purity Ideology in Ezra-Nehemiah as a Tool to Reconstitute the

wall-building activity is typological for the wall-building between Judean and "peoples of the land," the Other. Presumably only those whose names could be found in the genealogical lists of the book might be inside the wall, the rest would be part of the "peoples of the land."[47] The "nations round about" are also cast as the Other in the Nehemiah Memoir.[48] Just as in the Neo-Assyrian materials, in Ezra-Nehemiah there is also a pronounced gendering of the Other: except where the Neo-Assyrian texts say the defeated enemy has become *like* a woman,[49] Ezra-Nehemiah says the defeated enemy *is* a woman. Because the Other is found within, it must be expelled.[50] It is interesting to note with Harold Washington that priestly texts (he seems to mean legal material) do not treat Other foreigners the way that Ezra-Nehemiah does.[51] Is this perhaps, a pronounced marker of the genre of historiography found in Ezra-Nehemiah? If this is the case — that the Other is a generic feature of ancient historiography — then Ezra-Nehemiah would need to be interpreted in this light.

Chronicles and the Other

Sara Japhet and Hugh Williamson suggest that identity in Chronicles is not constructed by boundary-setting and exclusion, but by inclusion, in contrast to Ezra-Nehemiah.[52] This view of Israel in Chronicles is in contrast to an earlier view that Chronicles was constructed as an anti-Samaritan polemic. Williamson in particular has shown how the Chronicler's view of the inhabitants of the former Northern Kingdom was welcoming and inclusive, although this has been qualified to see non-Jerusalem Israel as peripheral.[53] However, if it is the case that the northern inhabitants are Israel, and if the genre of historiography requires the construction of the Other, then what might that Other be? Perhaps, the narrowing of the focus from all of humanity down to Israel in 1 Chronicles 1 might show Israel as being constructed against the Other of all the nations. This should be

Community," *JSJ* 35 (2004), 1–16 (11–13).

47 P. F. Esler, "Ezra-Nehemiah as a Narrative of (Re-Invented) Israelite Identity," *BibInt* 11 (2003), 413–26 (422–3), 420.

48 Knoppers, "Nehemiah and Sanballat," 305–31 (312–13).

49 Cf. Chapman, *Gendered*.

50 H. C. Washington, "Israel's Holy Seed and the Foreign Women of Ezra-Nehemiah: A Kristevan Reading," *BibInt* 11 (2003), 427–37 (431).

51 Ibid., 434 n. 21.

52 Japhet, "Postexilic," 321; H. G. M. Williamson, *Israel in the Books of Chronicles* (Cambridge: Cambridge University Press, 1977).

53 E. Ben Zvi, *History, Literature and Theology in the Book of Chronicles* (London: Equinox, 2006), pp. 198–9.

understood as not the same entity as the "peoples of the lands" of Ezra-Nehemiah, as there is no "inside-outside" distinction made[54] — all Yahwists may be Israel.

It has been argued that in Chronicles there is a tendency to "Israelitize" the foreigner. Examining the portrayal of foreign monarchs who speak to Judah, these monarchs are found to act in ways consistent with following YHWH.[55] If this argument is accepted, then the Other is not all the nations, or is not not-Israel. Yet this argument does not deal with the genealogies, which, whatever else they may be, are such an arresting feature of the book. As well, alliances with foreign rulers are consistently presented as contrary to following YHWH.[56] Contrary to Williamson's assertion that the Northern Kingdom was in some way also Israel, alliances with kings of the Northern Kingdom by Judahite kings are always condemned.[57]

Recently, Julie Kelso has examined what appears to be a lack of the feminine in Chronicles. By using the work of Luce Irigaray, she is able to read the Other in Chronicles as the repressed feminine. The maternal body as a producer of the sons, so important to the patrilineal genealogies is repressed by the use of the birthing verb ילד by masculine subjects. Bodies themselves, particularly diseased bodies, become feminine as well.[58] Kelso argues that "women have been silenced to enable the phantasy of mono-sexual, masculine production required to sustain this particular (masculine) literary (re)production of Israel's social, political, and cultic past."[59] In this reading, the feminine is made so Other that it cannot even be spoken. The absence of women characters in the narrative and genealogies is in stark contrast to the preoccupation with women in Ezra-Nehemiah or the feminizing metaphors of the Neo-Assyrian texts. Yet somehow, gender difference, femininity, is found here as well. If the feminine is the Other against which the subject is constructed, then the identity that is being constructed for that subject in this historiography is — what? Men? This is an intriguing possibility. If "Israel" is read as a largely inclusive label, what is it inclusive of? When Other

---

54 A. Siedlecki, "Foreigners, Warfare and Judahite Identity in Chronicles," in *The Chronicler as Author: Studies in Text and Texture* (eds. M. P. Graham and S. L. McKenzie; JSOTSup 263; Sheffield: Sheffield Academic Press, 1999), pp. 229–66 (237); J. E. Dyck, *The Theocratic Ideology of the Chronicler* (BibIntS 33; Leiden: Brill, 1998), pp. 117–18, 121.

55 E. Ben Zvi, "When the Foreign Monarch Speaks," in *The Chronicler as Author: Studies in Text and Texture* (eds. M. P. Graham and S. L. McKenzie; JSOTSup 263; Sheffield: Sheffield Academic Press, 1999), pp. 209–28.

56 G. N. Knoppers, "'Yhwh Is Not with Israel': Alliances as a *Topos* in Chronicles," *CBQ* 58 (1996), 601–26 (611).

57 Knoppers, "Yhwh," 621.

58 J. Kelso, *O Mother, Where Art Thou? An Irigarayan Reading of the Book of Chronicles* (London: Equinox, 2007).

59 Ibid., p. 213.

= women, and Other = not Israel, then Israel = men. In fact, when we look at the place where women figure significantly and consistently in Chronicles, it is in the regnal notices at the beginning of each reign, when the name of the king's mother is given. Rehoboam's mother is an Ammonite (2 Chron. 12:13) and Ahaziah's mother is a Northerner (2 Chron. 22:2); while both kings are not judged positively, it is nowhere suggested that they are not of Israel. Therefore, Israel = men.

Nevertheless, if we look at ancient historiography, usually the Other is marked fairly clearly near the beginning of the text. In that case, we might turn to the beginning of Chronicles, where there is an Esau/Seir/Edom genealogy before the Israelite genealogy in 1 Chron. 1:35-54. The purpose of this genealogy has long puzzled commentators.[60] Gary Knoppers asks, "If Israel is the focal point of the Chronicler's interests, why mention the descendants of Esau at all?"[61] The Chronicler does consistently deal with the segments of the genealogy that do not lead to Israel prior to those that do, but the descendants of Japhet, Ham, Qeturah and Ishmael are all recounted much more briefly than the descendants of Esau (Ham is given more space than Ishmael, so it is not necessarily a matter of genealogical proximity to Israel). Edom/Seir — the link being made by para-taxis in 1 Chronicles 1 — is also mentioned a few more times in Chronicles, as well as "Edom's servant" — Obed-edom — in two different parts of the book. Examining Edom as a potential Other might seem to select only one of "the nations" that seem to most scholars to be constructed as the Other,[62] yet Edom is a most interesting possibility.

First, the lengthy genealogical excursus on Esau/Seir/Edom in 1 Chronicles 1 has been read typically as a positive construction by the Chronicler. Since genealogies are typically seen as a way of creating a community and weaving in various new groups, the inclusion of a long Edomite genealogy is seen as a way of cementing the relationship between Israel and Edom.[63] However, given the largely negative way that Edom is seen in other biblical texts and that Edom is not, in fact, Israel, it might be a possibility to read the genealogy as an Othering move. The note introducing the list of kings indicates that these kings ruled "before a king ruled over the Israelites" (1 Chron. 1:43). In some ways, this brings to mind the antiquity of Egypt as compared with Greece for Herodotus. Yet the period of the kings devolved into a period of chieftains who are not even named indi-

60 See the bibliographies in G. N. Knoppers, *I Chronicles 1–9: A New Translation with Introduction and Commentary* (AB; New York: Doubleday, 2004); and E. Assis, "From Adam to Esau and Israel: An Anti-Edomite Ideology in I Chronicles i," *VT* 56 (2006), 287–302.

61 Knoppers, *I Chronicles 1-9*, p. 287.

62 Cf. Siedlecki, "Foreigners."

63 J. M. Tebes, "'You Shall Not Abhor an Edomite, for He is Your Brother': The Tradition of Esau and the Edomite Genealogies From an Anthropological Perspective," *JHS* 6 (2006), article 6.27 (http://www.arts.ualberta.ca/JHS/Articles/article_56.pdf).

vidually. Edom is therefore constructed as the opposite of Israel, the Other. Elie Assis argues that the chieftains are not meant to be read as following the kings, but as a separate list (reading the words "and Hadad died" in 1 Chron. 1:51 as the conclusion of the list of kings rather than the heading of the list of chieftains),[64] but I find this unconvincing, seeing rather a devolution. What Assis does note, correctly in my opinion, is that this genealogy is constructed as an anti-Edomite genealogy rather than one merely showing Edom's relationship to Israel.

The next mention of Edom is actually within the name Obed-Edom (עבד-אדם), which may be construed as "Edom's Servant" or as "Servant Edom," and which name is the only one in Chronicles to include the name of a non-Israelite people.[65] When reading this name in conjunction with the Edomite genealogy in 1 Chronicles 1, we must discount the suggestion that it means "Servant of Edom's God."[66] This figure appears in 1 Chronicles 13, 15 and 16 as a Gittite (a Philistine from Gath?) on whose property the Ark of the Covenant rests, and may or may not be the same figure as one of the two Levites by the same name who appear in 1 Chronicles 15 and 16, one as a lyre-player and the other as a gatekeeper.[67] In the family of Obed-Edom the gatekeeper also appears in 1 Chronicles 26 in the list of gatekeepers and their rotations. Such a multiplication of Obed-Edoms! Rather than seeing their inclusion as a measure of Chronicles' inclusiveness,[68] perhaps there is an anxiety at work here: David's testing of the Ark in 1 Chronicles 13 is done on the servant-Other within, and when the Ark brings blessing even on the Other, then there is textual anxiety about the servant-Other having been blessed. The multiplication of Obed-Edoms then serves to mask their Otherness and to draw them into Israel.[69]

Edom appears next in 1 Chron. 18:11-13 in the more typical role as one of David's enemies that he has vanquished. The Other here is relegated to its appropriate place on the outside of Israel, after having been found within 1 Chronicles 13–16. Similar is the mention of Edom in 2 Chron. 8:17 as the launching place for Solomon's ships — on the outside of Israel, showing Solomon's reach.

In 2 Chronicles 20, Jehoshaphat faces the inhabitants of Mount Seir. The metonymy of the genealogy might allow us to construe them as Edomites. However, more interesting is the "rebellion" of the Edomites against Judah in the time of Jehoram in 2 Chron. 21:8-10. There it is noted that Edom has been in revolt "until

---

64 Assis, "From Adam," 301.

65 Siedlecki, "Foreigners," 248.

66 *Contra* N. Tan, "The Chronicler's 'Obed-edom': A Foreigner and/or a Levite?" *JSOT* 32/2 (2007), 217–30 (218), and the references given there.

67 G. N. Knoppers, *I Chronicles 10-29: A New Translation with Introduction and Commentary* (AB; New York: Doubleday, 2004), p. 624.

68 As does Tan, "Chronicler's 'Obed-edom'," 227.

69 Cf. Ibid., 228.

this day." The Edomites are outside the land (where they belong), but they no longer are in an appropriate subordinate relationship with Judah. The Other must always be subordinated in some way, as we saw in the Neo-Assyrian texts. Even if the Other is not subordinated, their subjectivity must be constructed in such as way as to subordinate them (e.g., foreigners constructed as women).

Not long afterward in the text, the Edomites are violently subjected. As Knoppers points out, Chronicles picks up this battle from the text of 2 Kings 14, but makes it much greater in terms of textual space and importance.[70] While the importance of the attempted alliance between Amaziah and Israel should not be dismissed, the violence of the domination of Judah over the Edomites should be noted. The Edomites who had asserted their own subjectivity in 2 Chronicles 21 are now firmly subordinated and subjected to Judah again. The Other has now been put in its proper place. The only other mention of the Edomites, in 2 Chron. 28:17 has them again rising up against Judah — and not put back down again.

Yet the episode found in 2 Chronicles 25 has a rather interesting epilogue. After Amaziah's defeat of the Edomites, he brings back their gods and begins to worship them. He imports the Other again into the midst of Judah,[71] where they might again be asked to be "servants of Edom." This irruption of the Other within is then further signaled by the very odd occurrence of the name Obed-Edom in 2 Chron. 25:24. It is as if the Other brought within by Amaziah is so disturbing that it raises the specter of that other Other, "Servant Edom" that is now no longer servant.

Suggestions

In Japhet's fine summary of the various scholarly positions on Chronicles as historiography, she takes the *a priori* assumption that Chronicles is a work of historiography and then seeks to demonstrate by nature of its structure and content that it is.[72] She is most concerned to counter the claim that Chronicles is some kind of "free" history or midrash. She suggests that because Chronicles begins with a genealogy, continues to tell a story about the past in periodized form, uses sources and selects from them, sees causation as important (the "doctrine of immediate retribution"), and evaluates sources based on "historical probability," that it is "history."[73] Most telling about her discussion is the statement in her

---

70 Knoppers, "Yhwh," 619.
71 Siedlecki, "Foreigners," 264.
72 S. Japhet, "Chronicles: A History," in *From the Rivers of Babylon to the Highlands of Judah: Collected Studies on the Restoration Period* (Winona Lake: Eisenbrauns, 2006), pp. 399–415.
73 Ibid., pp. 404–8.

conclusion that "the Chronicler was a historian in the *modern* sense of the term, and the book of Chronicles is a 'work of history,' no more and no less."[74] Although she considers that she has drawn her conclusions from "reverting to the book itself and trying to uncover its nature and characteristics,"[75] she has not raised the larger question of what historiography in the *ancient* sense of the term might be. We might contrast her definition of history with that of John Frow:

> . . . the writing of history is generically structured by the narrative problems of binding the singularities of events and their multiplicity of times into the coherence of a structural explanation. Everything else follows from this . . .[76]

This definition effectively denies the difference between "historiography" and "ideology" that Brettler construes.

In this essay, I have sought to demonstrate that if we consider genre to be both form and content, that the Other was an important feature of ancient historiography. Having discussed a variety of ancient texts with respect to their Others, I turned to Chronicles. The problem with Chronicles is that it seems to be so positive in its construction generally, so inclusive, so single-minded in its focus on Israel, that there seems to be not much room for an Other. Even my discussion of the Edomites, as much as they may run through the entire book, falters on the fact that the Edomites simply do not appear all that often. Although Ammonites, Moabites, Philistines, etc. do not appear with the extensive genealogy that Edom is given, it would be possible to examine a variety of foreign nations as the Other,[77] and to then extrapolate a broader Other in Chronicles of not-Israel. However, most of the Chronicles is just not that concerned with foreigners. They are present, but do not form an antagonistic pair in the way the Persians/Barbarians do in Herodotus. In this case, perhaps we should look elsewhere for an explanation.

One possibility is to suggest that perhaps Chronicles is not historiography at all. This possibility has not been thoroughly explored by scholars (midrash/ rewritten Bible is the only other possibility that is generally discussed). I have argued in the past that Chronicles is political philosophy, based on formal and thematic features and on a comparison with Xenophon's *Cyropaedia*.[78] I have also argued in the past that Chronicles is an innovation in the genre to which

---

74   Ibid., p. 415, italics added.
75   Ibid., p. 403.
76   Frow, *Genre*, p. 99.
77   As does Siedlecki, "Foreigners."
78   C. Mitchell, "Bakhtin and the Ideal Ruler in 1-2 Chronicles and the Cyropaedia," in *The Bakhtin Circle and Ancient Narrative* (ed. R. B. Branham; Groningen: University of Groningen Library/Barkhuis, 2005), pp. 297–319.

Samuel-Kings also belongs, without naming that genre.[79] In a way, I think that Chronicles is both. If genre is descriptive rather than prescriptive, then there must be room for both understandings of Chronicles. As comparatist Wai-Chee Dimock has recently written, genre is "more . . . a self-obsoleting system, a provisional set that will always be bent and pulled and stretched by its many subsets."[80]

Another possibility is to suggest that Chronicles is historiography, but in a sense different from that which Japhet uses the term "history," and more like that which Frow uses: a narrative that presents a coherent structural explanation of events. I noted above that Hartog suggests that while the Greek–Barbarian pairing was operational in the third–fourth centuries, it became modified. If in Herodotus the Barbarian had a Persian face, perhaps we could consider that in Chronicles the non-Israelite had an Edomite face — the non-Israelite certainly did not have a Persian face, even though the text was probably written during the era of Persian sovereignty. Yet perhaps (as Chronicles is generally dated to the third–fourth centuries) a distinctive feature of earlier historiography, the Other, was also modified in Chronicles, and instead of being an overriding thematic fascination the Other was included as a nod to generic conventions. Or, perhaps the later works of historiography no longer constructed the self in relation to the Other, but were inward looking rather than outward, as was possibly the case with Berossus, and as often seems with Chronicles.

All of this rumination is really about meaning: how do we construe meaning from a text? Genre is the framework for the contract between author/text and reader, but when the socially–grounded basis for the framework is not shared, in essence the contract is broken. As the reader tries to reconstruct the contract, the meaning, there are only reconstructions of the social context to guide the reconstruction. Yet those reconstructions are constructs grounded in the social context of the reader. As we stare in the window through to the text, ultimately we see our own reflection first. The Other is us.[81]

79 Mitchell, "Power."

80 W.-C. Dimock, *Through Other Continents: American Literature Across Deep Time* (Princeton: Princeton University Press, 2006), pp. 73–4.

81 My thanks go to the other panelists in Auckland for a stimulating discussion on the topic of historiography, and for their pertinent questions.

PART II

RESPONSES

"IDENTITY (RE)FORMATION AS THE HISTORICAL CIRCUMSTANCES REQUIRED"

Raymond F. Person, Jr.

Introduction

In *The Deuteronomic School: History, Social Setting, and Literature*,[1] I argued — on the basis of text-critical evidence and a re-appraisal of themes found in the Deuteronomic History — that the Deuteronomic school's redactional activity continued into the Persian period. I reconstructed the redactional history of the Deuteronomic History as follows. The Deuteronomic school emerged from the exiled community of scribes in Babylon. Using preexilic sources, the Deuteronomic school produced the first redaction of the Deuteronomic History, providing theological justification for the destruction of Jerusalem and the Babylonian exile as well as their place within the exiled Judean bureaucracy. This theology of God using foreign nations for God's own purpose (including submitting to Babylon) provided the theological basis for cooperation with the Persian Empire, when Cyrus's defeat of Babylon and the first return to Jerusalem were understood as a part of God's plan for the punishment of Babylon and the restoration of Israel (similar to Second Isaiah). The Deuteronomic school returned to Jerusalem to provide scribal support for the rebuilding of the temple and temple cult under Zerubbabel (similar to the contemporary mission of Udjahorresnet to rebuild the temple-related scribal institutions in Sais, Egypt). I then demonstrated how passages in the Deuteronomic History could be interpreted in the Persian period during the time of Zerubbabel and later. The Deuteronomic school became disillusioned with its cooperation with the Persian-controlled bureaucracy and the delay of the full restoration of Israel and, as such, became increasingly

---

1 R. F. Person, Jr., *The Deuteronomic School: History, Social Setting, and Literature* (Atlanta: Society of Biblical Literature, 2002).

problematic from the perspective of the empire. The Persian Empire reasserted its control over Jerusalem in the form of the mission of Ezra. Ezra's "introduction" of the law and the related control of the scribal and religious institutions in Jerusalem was clearly the Persian Empire's attempt to replace one legal system (within the Deuteronomic canon) with another (Ezra's law). Thus, Ezra's mission led to the demise of the Deuteronomic school as the official scribal guild of the Jerusalem bureaucracy.

In *The Deuteronomic History and the Books of Chronicles: Scribal Works in an Oral World*[2] I argue that the relationship between the Deuteronomic History and the books of Chronicles requires a reassessment, because of the following recent developments: (1) arguments for a Persian setting for the Deuteronomic History,[3] (2) the contribution of the study of oral tradition to understand the composition and transmission of biblical texts in ancient Israel,[4] and (3) the reassessment of the relationship between Standard Biblical Hebrew and Late Biblical Hebrew.[5] I conclude that the Deuteronomic History and the book of Chronicles are competing contemporary historiographies that descended from a common source. The common source was the exilic form of the Deuteronomic History and the divergence occurred when the exilic Deuteronomic school divided into two groups, (1) the scribal group that returned to Jerusalem under Zerubbabel (the Deuteronomic school) and produced the later version of the Deuteronomic History and (2) the scribal group that remained in Babylon (the Chronistic school) and later produced the books of Chronicles (and even later Ezra-Nehemiah). That is, both scribal groups continued to redact the common source in isolation from each other. When Ezra returned to Jerusalem, the two scribal groups and their

---

2 R. F. Person, Jr., *The Deuteronomic History and the Book of Chronicles: Scribal Works in an Oral World* (Atlanta: Society of Biblical Literature, forthcoming). Portions of this monograph first appeared in idem, "The Deuteronomic History and the Books of Chronicles: Contemporary Competing Historiographies," in *Reflection and Refraction: Studies in Biblical Historiography in Honour of A. Graeme Auld* (VTSup 133; eds. R. Rezetko, T. H. Lim, and W. B. Aucker; Leiden: Brill, 2006), pp. 315–36.

3 See idem, *The Deuteronomic School*, especially ch. 2; T. C. Römer, *The So-Called Deuteronomistic History: A Sociological, Historical and Literary Introduction* (London: T&T Clark, 2007) especially ch. 6; J. L. Berquist, "Identities and Empire: Historiographic Questions for the Deuteronomistic History in the Persian Period" in this volume.

4 See S. Niditch, *Oral World and Written Word: Ancient Israelite Literature* (Louisville: Westminster John Knox, 1996); R. F. Person, Jr., "The Israelite Scribe as Performer," *JBL* 117 (1998), 601–9; D. M. Carr, *Writing on the Tablet of the Heart: Origins of Scripture and Literature* (Oxford: Oxford University Press, 2005); K. van der Toorn, *Scribal Culture and the Making of the Hebrew Bible* (Cambridge: Harvard University Press, 2007).

5 See I. Young (ed.), *Biblical Hebrew: Studies in Chronology and Typology* (London: T&T Clark, 2003), and I. Young, R. Rezetko, and M. Ehrensvaard, *Linguistic Dating of Biblical Texts: An Introduction to Approaches and Problems* (London: Equinox, 2009).

literatures once again came into contact. Because of the Deuteronomic school's prolonged history in Persian Jerusalem, the Deuteronomic History kept the place of honor in the tradition as the more authoritative story from Moses to the destruction of Jerusalem and the Babylonian exile. However, due to the demise of the Deuteronomic school, the Chronistic school had the opportunity to write the first complete history from Adam to Nehemiah (1–2 Chronicles and Ezra-Nehemiah) to rightfully take its place alongside Genesis–2 Kings.

Below, I will discuss how the essays published in this volume provide additional support for and/or challenges to my own understanding of the Deuteronomic History, the books of Chronicles, and Ezra-Nehemiah.

The Deuteronom(ist)ic History[6]

In his essay "Identities and Empire: Historiographic Questions for the Deuteronomistic History in the Persian Period," Jon Berquist dates the final redaction of the Deuteronomistic History to the early Persian period. He concludes as follows:

> The Deuteronomistic History, as a narrative, is an evolutionary story of state formation, moving from simple forms such as chiefdoms to true states such as the monarchy, and eventually to the post-state realities of imperial domination. (p. 11)

As such, the Deuteronomistic History narrates the failure of the judges and later the kings to provide political stability, in order to present "a story in which the Yehudites are not capable of self-governance" (p. 7) and, therefore, are in need of Persian imperial rule. Thus, "the Deuteronomistic History serves an imperial function" (p. 7), by advocating a colonial identity of submission to the Persian Empire. The Deuteronomists' identity was imperial and their literary work promoted the same for their audiences.

Berquist notes that there is a certain ambiguity in the text, that "the text offers conflicting opportunities for identity, imperial or postcolonial" (p. 11); however, the postcolonial reading he reconstructs for the later Persian period is a re-reading not by the Deuteronomists, but by others.

Although there is much I agree with in his reconstruction (for example, a Persian setting), I think that Berquist unnecessarily levels out the understanding of

---

6 Since I do not share Noth's clear distinction between "Deuteronomic" and "Deuteronomistic," I prefer to use "Deuteronomic" as the simpler of the two terms to refer to all of the literature and its various redactional layers. However, when discussing others' work, I will use whatever term they choose to use.

the Deuteronomic school in relationship to issues of human leadership. Certainly, there are anti-monarchic sections in the work, but there are also pro-monarchic sections. In other words, the multivalence that Berquist allows in the text was not simply something created by readers after the Deuteronomists, but exemplified a tension that existed within the ideology of the Deuteronomic school itself, most likely due to differing historical circumstances (exilic versus postexilic) but possibly due at times to conflicting ideologies within the school itself in the same temporal period. In fact, it is quite possible that such conflicting tendencies could exist within a single Deuteronomist.

Based on his reading of 2 Kgs 24:9, Berquist concludes that the Deuteronomists understood Jehoiachin as an "evil" king. This is certainly true; however, the Deuteronomic understanding of Jehoiachin can certainly be more complex than simply that. If the Lord used Babylon as his tool to punish Judah, we must note that Jehoiachin was not killed by the Babylonians like the other "evil" last kings of Judah, but in fact was elevated above other exiled kings (2 Kgs 25:27-30). Therefore, another understanding of Jehoiachin in the early Persian period most certainly could have provided hope that one of Jehoiachin's descendants (including especially his grandson Zerubbabel) would restore the monarchy (see similarly Haggai).[7] In other words, it is certainly possible that the Deuteronomic school was, on the one hand, critical of the monarchy as practiced during the preexilic period and advocated submission to the imperial power of first the Babylonians and then the Persians, but, on the other hand, hoped for the Lord's intervention to overthrow the imperial administrations in order to restore Israel fully, including overcoming the obvious limitations of depending on human leadership. In my own reconstruction of the Deuteronomic school's theology I understand that this tension of caution and hope existed during the time of Zerubbabel, but later, due to its disillusionment with the failure of Zerubbabel and others to restore Israel fully, the Deuteronomic school placed less and less trust in human institutions and became more eschatological in its views.[8] In short, both of Berquist's readings, imperial and postcolonial, can be understood within the ideology of the Deuteronomic school itself.

In his essay "The Book of Judges as a Late Contruct" Klaas Spronk builds upon some recent arguments against the hypothesis of a Deuteronomistic History (especially those of Guillaume and Auld[9]), concluding that the book of Judges

7 On 2 Kgs 25:27-30, see further Person, *The Deuteronomic School*, pp. 119–20.

8 See further ch. 5: "Deuteronomic Literature during the Time of Zerubbabel" and ch. 6: "Deuteronomic Literature after the Time of Zerubbabel" in ibid.

9 P. Guillaume, *Waiting for Josiah: The Judges* (JSOTSup. 385; London: T&T Clark, 2004) and A. G. Auld, *Samuel at the Threshold: Selected Works of Graeme Auld* (SOTS Monographs. Aldershot: Ashgate, 2004).

was created in the Hellenistic period to provide a literary bridge between the Hexateuch and Auld's "Book of Two Houses," the common source for material in both Samuel-Kings and the books of Chronicles.

Since I have responded to some of the recent critics who have rejected the Deuteronomistic History hypothesis to some depth elsewhere,[10] I will respond here only to Spronk's comments concerning Judges. Spronk describes well the many connections between the book of Judges and the book of Joshua, on the one hand, and the book of Judges and the books of Samuel and Kings, on the other. However, Noth's original thesis of a Deuteronomistic History takes note of such connections, so these connections do not necessarily support Spronk's thesis of a late book of Judges. Determining the direction of literary influence of roughly contemporaneous ancient texts is difficult, if not impossible, and Spronk acknowledges this when he discusses the "compositional knot" of the relationship of the end of Joshua and the beginning of Judges.[11] In fact, I suspect that, because of the long span of redactional activity within the Deuteronomic school, the direction of literary influence among the books in the Deuteronomic History ran in multiple directions. Certainly some books must have been written first in some early form; however, the complex intertextuality between the various books suggests to me that at times, for example, Judges influenced Joshua and at other times Joshua influenced Judges, so much so that we probably never will be able to conclude which book was written first. Because of this complexity, I find Spronk's arguments unconvincing.

Spronk's argument is not based strictly on his discernment of the direction of literary influence. He also draws some parallels between Hellenistic literature and the book of Judges as evidence of a late dating for the composition of the book. Although some of his parallels are interesting, I do not find that they require a Hellenistic date for the composition of the book of Judges. In fact, even if I were convinced of the validity of many of his parallels, such observations would not necessarily require a Hellenistic dating of Judges. As has been argued by others, the influence of Hellenistic culture in Israel began before Alexander the Great defeated the Persians.[12] Furthermore, Spronk's argument that the book of Judges was written to provide a bridge from the Tetrateuch to Auld's "Book of Two

---

10 Person, "The Deuteronomic History and the Books of Chronicles: Contemporary Competing Historiographies," 316–24.

11 Spronk (p. 19 fn. 12) borrows the term from E. Blum, "Der kompositionelle Knoten am Übergang von Josua zu Richter: Ein Entflechtungsvorschlag," in *Deuteronomy and Deuteronomic Literature: Festschrift C. H. W. Brekelmans* (BETL 133; eds. M. Vervenne and J. Lust; Leiden: Brill, 1997), pp. 181–212.

12 e.g., L. G. Perdue, *Wisdom Literature: A Theological History* (Louisville: Westminster/John Knox, 2007), p. 176: "While the rapid expansion of hellenization was due to the military conquests of Alexander, this does not mean there was negligible Greek

Houses" requires that even the early forms of both the Deuteronomic History and the books of Chronicles be dated even later in the Hellenistic period.

The Books of Chronicles

In her essay "Otherness and Historiography in Chronicles" Christine Mitchell surveys the genre of historiography in the ancient Near East and then concludes that "Otherness was an integral part of the construction of the genre of historiography in the ancient world in the Persian and Hellenistic periods" (p. 93). She then concludes that "[a] formal feature of Judahite historiography would be the use of source citations; a thematic feature of Judahite (and other ancient historiography) would be the use of the Other" (p. 101). She discusses the importance of oppositional language in the Deuteronomistic History (especially Judges and Kings) and in Ezra-Nehemiah and contrasts these works with the books of Chronicles. Agreeing with Japhet and Williamson she concludes that "Chronicles is not constructed by boundary-setting and exclusion, but by inclusion, in contrast to Ezra-Nehemiah" (p. 109).[13] This could lead one to conclude that the books of Chronicles are not historiographic, but Mitchell offers another suggestion: "perhaps the later works of historiography no longer constructed the self in relation to the Other, but were inward looking rather than outward" (p. 109).

Although Mitchell does not elaborate on what the "inward looking" issues specifically were, Louis Jonker in his essay "David's Officials according to the Chronicler (1 Chronicles 23–27): A Reflection of Second Temple Self-Categorization?" provides an insightful suggestion. Drawing from the work of Knoppers,[14] Jonker concludes that the Chronicler's description of David's relationship with the Levites and the Aaronides emphasizes cooperation between the two groups of temple servants with neither having a subordinate role. That is, the Chronicler replaced the emphasis of the Other as opponent in historiography with the

---

influence in the ancient Near East, including Israel, prior to this time." Perdue then provides examples of Hellenistic influence during the late Persian period.

13 S. Japhet, "Postexilic Historiography: How and Why?" in *From the Rivers of Babylon to the Highlands of Judah: Collected Studies on the Restoration Period* (Winona Lake: Eisenbrauns, 2006; repr. from *Israel Constructs Its History: Deuteronomistic Historiography in Recent Research* [JSOTSup 306; eds. A. de Pury, T. C. Römer, and J.-D. Macchi; Sheffield Academic Press, 2000], pp. 144–73), pp. 307–30; H. G. M. Williamson, *Israel in the Books of Chronicles* (Cambridge: Cambridge University Press, 1977).

14 G. N. Knoppers, "Hierodules, Priests, or Janitors? The Levites in Chronicles and the History of the Israelite Priesthood," *JBL* 118/1 (1999) 49–72; idem, *1 Chronicles 1–9* (AB; New York: Doubleday, 2003); and idem, *1 Chronicles 10–29* (AB; New York: Doubleday, 2004).

de-emphasizing of the Other, so much so as to emphasize cooperation with those who at other times may have been constructed as the Other.

Mitchell's and Jonker's emphasis on cooperation in the books of Chronicles have helped me formulate my own understanding of Ezra's mission better. I reconstruct the redaction of the books of Chronicles in the late Persian period probably closely associated with Ezra's mission.[15] Although Ezra was certainly functioning as an appointed official of the Persian Empire and would have been seen by some (if not all) of those who had been functionaries of the temple cult from many years as an outsider imposing his own ideology on them, the self-understanding of Ezra and his supporters who returned with him would not necessarily be understood in such antagonistic ways.[16] If this is so, then one could easily understand why the group of Ezra's supporters would produce a historiographic work that minimized conflict with the Other and emphasized cooperation between opposing groups. Although Ezra's mission certainly was one of taking control of the Jerusalem temple cult, Ezra could only succeed with the cooperation of some of those who had served in the temple cult for years. Therefore, although Ezra's mission may have led to the demise of the Deuteronomic school by the displacement of its leadership, Ezra needed to gain the support of at least some lower level scribes in the Deuteronomic school in order to succeed. The identity (re)formation that Jonker describes as the motivation behind the historiographic description of David's officials in 1 Chronicles 23–27 would certainly be an important aid in Ezra's and his supporters' attempt to overcome the inevitable conflict that his mission created between those who had been in Jerusalem for generations and the recent returnees.

Ezra-Nehemiah

As noted above, Mitchell contrasts the books of Chronicles with Ezra-Nehemiah in relationship to oppositional language. Unlike other Persian and Hellenistic historiographies, the books of Chronicles are focused on internal group dynamics rather than the external Other. Ezra-Nehemiah, on the other hand, includes the oppositional language typical of historiographies of this period, targeting the "aliens" as Other (pp. 103–7). Drawing from Mitchell's work, I argued that the minimization of the oppositional language in Chronicles may reflect an effort

15 See similarly R. Klein, "Chronicles, Books of 1-2," *ABD* I (1992), 995–6 and K. Peltonen, "A Jigsaw with a Model? The Date of Chronicles," in *Did Moses Speak Attic? Jewish Historiography and Scripture in the Hellenistic Period* (JSOTSup 317; ed. L. L. Grabbe; Sheffield: Sheffield Academic Press, 2001), pp. 225–71.

16 As we will see below in my discussion of Leuchter's essay on Ezra-Nehemiah, this reconstruction is consistent with the portrayal of Ezra's mission in Ezra-Nehemiah.

by Ezra and his supporters to manage the conflict that Ezra's mission necessarily would provoke when he and his supporters took control of the Jerusalem
bureaucracy.

Despite the oppositional language aimed at the foreigner in Ezra-Nehemiah,
the portrayal identified by Jonker of the Chronicler emphasizing cooperation between the Aaronides and Levites has, as identified by both Brett and Leuchter, its
counterpart in Ezra-Nehemiah. In his essay "National Identity as Commentary
and as Metacommentary" Mark Brett describes well the tension in "Ezra's 'egalitarian' impulse." On the one hand,

> Ezra's "egalitarian" impulse in the discourse of the "holy seed" would appear to be
> shared, at first blush, with both the Holiness Code and with Deuteronomy. (p. 34)

That is, in Ezra-Nehemiah, Ezra's construction of the people of Israel appears
to be portrayed in a way that might suggest to those of what may have been in
competing groups that their understandings have been taken seriously. This certainly suggests an attempt at cooperation between potential rivals. On the other
hand, Brett notes that,

> the ethnic or "nativist" purity imagined by Ezra seems to promote one model of
> horizontal solidarity at the expense of other models that could have been derived
> from Deuteronomy or from the Holiness Code. The Persian period seems there-
> fore to provide evidence of competing models of horizontal solidarity. (p. 35)

Here Brett recognizes that the rhetoric of cooperation between competing groups
was strategically an effort to create one authoritative ethnic identity by subsuming
the competing ones within it.

In his essay "Coming to Terms with Ezra's Many Identities in Ezra-Nehemiah"
Mark Leuchter reaches a similar conclusion:

> Ezra-Nehemiah confirms that Ezra was a royal administrative emissary that both
> Zadokite priests and Deuteronomistic Levite scribes saw as a suitable vehicle to
> advance their respective traditions. Though the specifics of this administrative
> characteristic remain elusive, neither group is presented as independent of his
> official imperial status. (p. 60)

Of course, it is a completely different matter whether or not the statement that
"both Zadokite priests and Deuteronomistic Levite scribes saw [Ezra's mission]
as a suitable vehicle to advance their respective traditions" accurately reflects
the ideology of these two rival groups. Nevertheless, Ezra-Nehemiah asserts that
these groups cooperated with Ezra and his mission.

Since, in my opinion, the books of Chronicles date to the late Persian period and Ezra-Nehemiah to the early Hellenistic period, I can easily explain the different emphases on the Other as described by Mitchell. During the time of Ezra when the books of Chronicles were likely written, the Chronistic school produced literature that emphasized the need to overcome the rivalries between competing groups of Jewish bureaucrats, thereby resulting in a reduction of oppositional language concerning the Other. However, when the history of Ezra and his mission was written later by this same scribal guild, the rivalry between these Jewish groups had for the most part ceased to be a significant issue, so much so that the characteristic oppositional language of the Other returned once again to the historiographic work of Ezra-Nehemiah. With the demise of the Deuteronomic school the Chronistic school could change its focus from the inward to the outward as it strove to (re)formulate the ethnic identities of the people of Israel, especially since this (re)formation was now taking place in the context of a different empire.

Conclusion

I attended the lively session at the International Meeting of the Society of Biblical Literature in Auckland, New Zealand, in July 2008 and enjoyed the papers as presented. Therefore, I was especially pleased when Louis Jonker invited me to prepare this response to the revised papers. Each of the papers has helped me to (re)formulate my understanding of the relationship of historiography and identity (re)formation, especially as it relates to the Deuteronomic History, the books of Chronicles, and Ezra-Nehemiah.

In sum, the identity (re)formation of these historiographies differed as the historical circumstances required. The Deuteronomic History in the early Persian period promoted a self-identification that is both imperial and postcolonial, thereby allowing cooperation with the Persian administration while at the same time longing for the Lord's intervention to fully restore Israel. The books of Chronicles in the late Persian period promoted a self-identification that attempted to overcome the conflict between rival groups of Jewish bureaucrats by claiming a common history for the competing groups going back to the time of David. Ezra-Nehemiah in the early Hellenistic period promoted a self-identification that, like that in the books of Chronicles, overcame the division between different Jewish groups, but once again emphasized the Otherness characteristic of historiography in the Persian and Hellenistic period by drawing boundaries to exclude the foreigner.

"Persian Period Studies Have Come of Age"

Armin Siedlecki

Persian period studies have come of age. Until a few decades ago, postexilic texts were generally viewed as less significant, theologically inferior, and in some cases — most notably Chronicles — historically unreliable degenerations of earlier narratives. Gunkel, writing in 1906, expresses a view characteristic of much of the century that followed: "The literature of ancient Israel experienced its classical period before the great catastrophes [the destruction of Jerusalem and the subsequent exile]. The spiritual life (*geistiges Leben*) of Israel was in full bloom in almost all of its aspects, but was now followed by a long winter."[1] However, a reassessment of historical assumptions as well as the development and application of new methodologies, especially in the areas of social scientific and literary studies have prompted new ideas and shifts in interpretative paradigms.[2] Among the results of these changes were a re-evaluation of the Persian period as a formative time for the composition of many biblical texts or even for the formation of the Hebrew biblical canon in general, as well as an increased ideological awareness both with regard to the production of texts (and the social structures of the communities that produced them) and their reception and interpretation by readers and exegetes. As a result, there has been a wealth of studies about the

---

1 H. Gunkel, "The Literature of Ancient Israel," in *Relating to the Text: Interdisciplinary and Form-Critical Insights on the Bible* (eds. T. Sandoval and C. Mandolfo; London and New York: T&T Clark, 2003), pp. 26–83 (74).

2 Cf. M. Z. Brettler, *The Creation of History in Ancient Israel* (London and New York: Routledge, 1995), p. 2: "Biblical books that were previously viewed as history in the sense of a generally accurate depiction of the Israelite past are now seen as historiography, literally 'history writing,' a term typically used to emphasize the creative nature of historical texts. This change is not entirely new; in many ways, it is a return to the position espoused by Julius Wellhausen over a century ago. Wellhausen's position, however, was relatively short-lived due to the tremendous influence of scholars such as Albrecht Alt and William Foxwell Albright."

community of the returning exiles, the Persian province of Yehud, and the political interaction between its capital Jerusalem and the Achaemenid empire. These studies have revealed a higher degree of politicization and of social complexity with regard to the community of Yehud than had previously been assumed.

As different methodologies began to proliferate, questions about identity became a dominant discourse in biblical studies and other academic disciplines. This development was in part prompted by the aforementioned reassessment of historical assumptions but also by self-reflexive considerations about the study of biblical texts itself. As scholars were in search of ancient Israel[3] they were at the same time in search of modern biblical studies. Furthermore, the very notion of a stable, monolithic self (social or psychological) was increasingly deconstructed during the last few decades of the twentieth century. Thus, as the identity of the biblical authors and their original audience is as much in question as the identity of the modern reader, interpretation has become the negotiation of meaning through a complex interplay of various considerations and approaches.

A good example of such negotiation is Jonker's paper on David's officials according to 1 Chronicles 23–27. Jonker begins and ends his study with reflections about his own point of departure. Writing in the context of post-apartheid South Africa and citing the example of a recent revisionist history of his country, he suggests that "no historiography can ever be objective" (p. 66). His own context of a society trying to reformulate its identity after drastic political and social change offers a good point of comparison for the Chronicler's context. To be sure, the comparability is limited, as the fall of apartheid ended a period of legislated discrimination and oppression, leading to a more pluralistic type of society, while Chronicles was written in the wake of a period of restoration following geographic displacement and the subsequent integration into a larger imperial administration. However, Jonker does not seek to establish parallels between specific details, but rather to examine ideological or structural dynamics involved in revisionist history writing. In other words, he is less concerned with "how" a particular narrative was assembled than with "why" it was assembled in a particular way. This emphasis is also hermeneutically significant, since the focus on structural dynamics not only allows for the comparison of historically and geographically different contexts, it also provides for a way to make the text applicable to contemporary readers.

Jonker's use of self-categorization theory (SCT) takes the discussion about identity beyond the traditional focus of *inter*group relations, generally associated with Fredrik Barth,[4] toward "a more thorough investigation of *intra*group

---

3 Cf. P. R. Davies, *In Search of Ancient Israel* (Sheffield: Sheffield Academic Press, 1992).

4 F. Barth, *Ethnic Groups and Boundaries: The Social Organization of Culture*

processes" (p. 70). Barth himself had argued vehemently against older, mono-lithic views "that a race = a culture = a language and that a society = a unit which rejects or discriminates against others,"[5] which have since largely been abandoned by social scientists. This expansion of the discourse of identity is most welcome, since it adds depth and complexity to the discussion.

The possibility of drawing comparisons between the dynamics of ancient contexts and later periods in history is also a central theme in Brett's discussion of "National Identity as Commentary and as Metacommentary." While Jonker's approach addressed the specifically diachronic problem of negotiating continuity and change, Brett is initially more concerned with the synchronic issue of how a community can view itself (imagine itself) as continuous, despite the fact that its constituent members do not (and cannot) in fact all know each other, a condition that describes virtually any community larger than an extended family, modern as well as pre-modern. Benedict Anderson had advanced the now commonly accepted idea that nationalism is a modern phenomenon that finds its origin in the early development of print capitalism. Bringing Anderson into conversation with David Goodblatt and other critics of his view, who have argued that it is indeed possible to speak of national identity with regard to ancient Israel, Brett offers a useful critique of both positions. Most notably he identifies the common ground constituted by Anderson's concept of "imagined communities" that is shared by ancient and later communities. The idea that communities are imagined con-structs, defined and guarded by ideological concepts and practices that function to ensure the loyalty of its members, is by no means limited to the socio-economic conditions that define the modern nation state. Thus, Goodblatt's "linking of national consciousness to a mass audience is lent plausibility . . . in part because Benedict Anderson laid the foundations of this conceptual link. . ." (p. 31).

Following this discussion, Brett pursues several different directions. He discusses the idea, raised in part by Daniel Smith-Christopher and John Kessler and more fully discussed in his *Decolonizing God*,[6] that Ezra-Nehemiah's understanding of ethnic identity could be seen as a nativist response to Persian hegemony. While there may be good arguments for the presence of subversive elements in Ezra-Nehemiah, he may be overstressing this idea. Considering the infrastructure of writing, it is more likely that the authors of the text had Persian imperial interests in mind, as is well argued in the contributions by Leuchter and Berquist.[7] Furthermore, Ezra-Nehemiah generally takes an antagonistic position

---

Difference (Bergen-Oslo: Universitets Forlaget, 1969).

   5 Ibid., p. 11.

   6 M. G. Brett, *Decolonizing God: The Bible in the Tides of Empire* (Sheffield: Sheffield Phoenix Press, 2008).

   7 See my discussion of their contributions later in this chapter.

not toward the Achaeminid administration but rather toward close neighbors, a stance which itself can be seen to reflect Persian interests.

The second idea discussed by Brett is Charles Taylor's concept of the "secular self," which he contrasts with the "enchanted self" that characterized pre-modern identity. It is not entirely well integrated into the larger discussion and connects only loosely to his discussion of Goodblatt and Anderson or of Ezra-Nehemiah as a nativist response. Nevertheless, the theory merits further exploration with regard to biblical concepts of identity and posits an important cautionary idea against the dangers of anachronistic comparisons.

Klaas Spronk and Jon Berquist both call for a reassessment of the Deuteronomistic History. Both express dissatisfaction with the consensus view that has existed since Noth, that the Deuteronomistic History is a sixth-century composition written to provide a theological explanation for the fall of Jerusalem. However, the two papers take very different approaches to this re-evaluation. Spronk focuses in particular on the book of Judges and argues that it should be seen as a relatively late addition to the canon. This suggestion goes against the common assumption that Judges contains some of the oldest stories in the Hebrew Bible, folkloric hero tales going back to Israel's pre-monarchic past, that were incorporated into a Deuteronomistic framework, but which nevertheless preserved a window to Israel's earliest, reconstructable history. Spronk resists resorting to an exclusively literary reading, citing Scherer's warning that synchronic approaches tend to lead to "eisegesis" rather than exegesis, but he is rightly wary of placing too much emphasis on redaction-critical theories, noting that "almost every redaction critic nowadays seems to have his or her own Deuteronomist" (p. 16). This point is important, especially since the Deuteronomistic History — more than any other text — has attracted critics who are quick to "discover" a new redactional layer whenever a particular idea does not seem to fit their idea of what the text should have said. There is arguably a greater danger to read one's own ideas into the text in uninhibited redaction criticism, than in synchronic readings, which tend to be more concerned with aesthetic or ideological structures than historical reconstructions.

For Spronk the point is neither to seek (or invent) new redactional layers nor to ignore the history of the text altogether, but to situate the text in an altogether different redactional context. His analysis seeking to show that the author of Judges was aware of Joshua as well as 1–2 Samuel is plausible, even compelling, but not necessarily requisite. There are several alternative solutions to explain the parallels between the birth stories of Samson and Samuel, to name but one example. His reading may fall into the same trap as the one he posits for synchronic readings of Judges which "usually leads to beautiful results: clear structures around interesting themes. But other synchronic studies lead to other structures and other central themes . . ." (p. 16). Nevertheless, it provides an important new impulse for approaching both Judges and the Deuteronomistic History, especially when viewed in conjunction with Spronk's second major point, the presence of linguistic and thematic connections to Greek literature in the book of Judges. While comparisons between Hebrew biblical literature and Greek literature are hardly a new idea, they have not received as much consideration as they should have, being generally restricted to late wisdom literature. Spronk has shown that this connection can be fruitfully explored and one can hope that future research will devote more attention to this link. In particular in studies concerned with genre in the way in which it is used by Berquist and Mitchell, Greek literature may become an important point of reference.

Like Spronk, Berquist also challenges conventional assumptions about the Deuteronomistic History, but is less concerned with the history of the text than with the use of the text in the Persian period. The conventional (exilic) understanding of the Deuteronomistic History places priority on the institution of the monarchy and the monarchic period as Judah's golden age. Berquist proposes that rather than being a nostalgic account of a lost monarchy, the Deuteronomistic History is an account of failed self-governance, justifying Persian imperial government and Yehud's status within the Persian Empire. He rightly wonders why Judah's monarchy is posited as a glorious institution, when almost every king is said to have done what was evil in the eyes of YHWH. Furthermore, he suggests that the infrastructure of writing required for the composition of a work like the Deuteronomistic History is more plausibly found in the Persian imperial context than during the exile. Both points seem surprisingly obvious, and reading Berquist's analysis one does indeed get the impression that the consensus view that has dominated the Deuteronomistic History for much of the twentieth century is an unnecessarily complex construction that obscures some very basic problems, like the two cited here, in order to satisfy theological expectations. These expectations were largely based on an exaggerated emphasis on the Babylonian exile as the watershed experience in the history of Judah, which had prompted a view that still persists to some extent that the destruction of Jerusalem and the end of Judah's political independence led to theological introspection and the reformation of the people into a largely apolitical community that was content to have its religious autonomy within the Persian Empire.

At first glance Berquist may seem to share common ground with some minimalist historians, especially with regard to his later dating of texts, in this case the Deuteronomistic History, and the de-emphasis of the exile experience, but he is much more nuanced than that. His reading calls for much more than a reevaluation of historical and literary details and proposes a completely different way of looking at the Deuteronomistic History. He is not primarily interested in the history of the text, but rather the use of the text within a particular historical context. Likewise, he does not speculate about the degree of continuity between the preexilic and postexilic communities, but is rather concerned with the political realities that existed in the province of Yehud. His reading is also methodologically highly complex, including political theory, cultural theory, literary theory, and postcolonial theory. This complexity is also reflected in his awareness of the ambivalence contained in the relationship between the Deuteronomistic History and the Persian context in which it was read. While the Deuteronomistic History reflects Persian imperial interests in providing a historical justification for Yehud's lack of political autonomy, it also gives expression to a desire for such autonomy, or as Berquist puts it, "[t]hey long for independence, even though the text shows self-reliance to be miserable" (p. 10). In other works, Berquist had described this ambivalence as a subversive element within texts that are otherwise supportive of Persian imperial interests.[8]

His suggestion that the Deuteronomistic History was read as a kind of fantasy literature by the scribes of the Persian period emerges directly from this ambivalence. Even if his hypothetical reconstruction of the composition and transmission of the Deuteronomistic History is not entirely convincing, it is no less plausible than the consensus view, once the approach to the text is reframed. It is certainly much more congruent with the political realities of the time. Perhaps even more important is the metacommentary implicit in his analysis, since he applies his suggestion, that the Deuteronomistic History was read as fantasy in the Persian period, also to recent scholarship. The impossible dream of an autonomous, monarchic government in Yehud is paralleled by the equally impossible dream of a theologically motivated reconstruction of Judah's history with the exile as the watershed experience that led to an apolitical reconstitution of the community.

By focusing on uses of the text within an interpretive community, Berquist appeals to "genre recognition as a basis for producing certain readings of texts" (p. 13). In doing so, he is relying to a large extent on Mikhail Bakhtin, whose work is also central to Christine Mitchell's paper "Otherness and Historiography in Chronicles." Bakhtin's theory of genre as a dialogic connection between author, reader, and text provides a prime opportunity to conduct both commentary and metacommentary, since the identity of the ancient as well as the modern reader is influenced by the text, while also shaping the reading of the text itself. An exegete must therefore apply the same critical questions to the modern, scholarly audience of the text as to the presumed ancient audience (and by extension author). Mitchell can find the same dynamic of "Othering" in Mullen's

---

8 Cf., e.g., idem, "Postcolonialism and Imperial Motives for Canonization," *Semeia* 75 (1996), 15–35, or his "Psalms, Postcolonialism, and the Construction of the Self," in J. L. Berquist (ed.), *Approaching Yehud: New Approaches to the Study of the Persian Period* (Atlanta: Society of Biblical Literature, 2007), pp. 195–202.

interpretation of the Deuteronomistic History (p. 102), as she does in Herodotus or the Neo-Babylonian chronicles.

Like Berquist, Mitchell's analysis displays a high degree of methodological complexity. Her understanding of "Othering" is influenced by feminist theory and cultural studies and her analysis of historiography displays much sensitivity to both historical and literary questions, a combination that also reflects her understanding of genre as both form and content (p. 108). Her conclusions are surprisingly (or perhaps not surprisingly) open-ended. Rather than offering a clear answer to such questions as to whether Chronicles should be understood as historiography, or what Chronicles says about Israelite identity, she offers various considerations that are neither contradictory nor complementary. Chronicles may be seen as political philosophy, comparable to Xenophon's *Cyropaedia*, or it may be seen as an innovative genre shared by Samuel-Kings. Her statement "[i]f genre is descriptive rather than prescriptive, then there must be room for both understandings of Chronicles" (p. 109) is congruent with Berquist's observation: "A single text reflects multiple possible genres, depending upon the reading strategy. In a postmodern sense, no text contains unambiguous clues as to how it should be read" (p. 12).

A different approach is offered by Mark Leuchter's paper "Coming to Terms with Ezra's Many Identities in Ezra-Nehemiah." At first glance, the paper appears to be the most traditional among the contributions in this volume. The trend in biblical scholarship has been to focus on institutions at the expense of individual biblical figures who have proven too elusive over the years. However, even though Leuchter's paper is framed as an analysis of personal identity, he is in fact much more concerned with religious, political, and social questions pertaining to the office of Ezra than with the man himself. Furthermore, Leuchter's analysis is deeply infused with an awareness of the Persian imperial context governing the text. Ezra's identity as a Zadokite and as a Deuteronomistic Levite must be understood within the context of his identity as an imperial emissary. Leuchter's confidence in the authenticity of diplomatic correspondence in Ezra 4–6 and Ezra 7 (p. 58) may not be shared by everyone, but his argument is not dependent on this detail, since the imperial context may be presumed even if the letters are literary constructs.[9] Similarly, Ezra's ambivalent identity is a literary construct by the redactors, who sought to undercut what Morton Smith had called the beginnings of Jewish sectarianism.[10] Ezra's policies, representing imperial interests,

---

9 A good approach to this issue that is actually more in line with Leuchter's argument is offered by D. Janzen, "The 'Mission' of Ezra and the Persian-Period Temple Community," *JBL* 119 (2000), 619–43. Janzen suggests that the letters are plausible, regardless of their historical authenticity.

10 Cf. M. Smith, *Palestinian Parties and Politics that Shaped the Old Testament* (New

needed to be seen as in line with both Zadokite and Deuteronomistic Levitical concerns, which were instituted as a model prior to Nehemiah's mission, at least on a literary level. Leuchter's conclusion reflects the same pluralism and complexity found in other papers in this book. He is not in search of the "real" Ezra, but rather tries to explain why the multiple personalities of Ezra had to exist simultaneously for rhetorical reasons.

Trying to formulate a concluding response to all six studies presented here, the following questions arise: What do the papers in this volume have in common, and what do they say about Persian period studies today? In response to the first question, one must observe that aside from the larger thematic foci of history and identity, the contributions in this book are both very diverse and methodologically complex. The combination of methodologies found in the contributions at hand would likely have seemed to previous generations of scholars as improper unions, perhaps comparable to the mixed marriages of Ezra 9–10 and Nehemiah 13. Ironically, it is precisely this methodological complexity that provides cohesion for this book, if not unity. Even though virtually each paper deals with a different subject matter and offers a different approach, each reading draws on a variety of methods which themselves offer connecting points, so as to form a web of interpretation. For example, Spronk and Berquist both call for a reassessment of the Deuteronomistic History, although each has a very different take on this re-evaluation. Berquist and Mitchell both rely heavily on genre, although Berquist is more socio-political, while Mitchell is more historical and literary in her analysis. In addition, one factor common to all contributions in this volume is the combination of commentary and metacommentary, specifically named in Brett's paper, but implicit in all.

The answer to the second question emerges directly from these observations. Several of the papers have noted the interaction between the understanding of history in the Persian period and the identity formation of the Persian-period writers and readers, and this analysis can be extended to include modern interpreters. The interaction of our own understanding of Persian-period history and the identity formation of twenty-first-century scholarly readers and writers points to the changing face of biblical studies. Previous generations of scholars may have had an easier time defining the Other in biblical studies. A biblical scholar is *not* a literalist reader of scripture, a biblical historian is *not* a literary critic, etc. Such dichotomies are increasingly difficult to maintain, and even though some distinctions remain in place (literalist readings being an obvious case), the identity formation of scholars working with Persian-period texts is governed by historical, political, sociological, and literary factors as well as contributions from cultural or gender studies, all of which are reflected in the papers at hand.

York and London: Columbia University Press, 1971).

This complexity is perhaps analogous to the Persian-period context itself, as the following observation by Leuchter could be easily adapted to fit the academic context in which the contributors to this book are writing: "This is the result of a new worldview that no longer understood Israel as a nation among other nations, but as a people within a pluralistic environment that could only achieve social definition in relation to the whole" (p. 61). Clearly, Persian period studies have come of age.

IDENTITY, POWER, AND THE WORLD OF ANCIENT (BIBLICAL) TEXT PRODUCTION

Gerrie Snyman

Introduction

The emphasis on an ethics of reading, in terms of doing justice *to* the text in its historical context as well as accounting *for* the researcher's methodology and the marks his or her reading will leave on others, have brought issues of identity and power into the limelight.[1] Christine Mitchell alludes to the ethics of interpretation when she concludes her essay by saying "As the reader tries to reconstruct the contract, the meaning, there are only reconstructions of the social context to guide the reconstruction. Yet those reconstructions are constructs grounded in the social context of the reader. As we stare through to the text, ultimately we see our own reflection first" (p. 109). The plotting of the socio-political location of the researcher has become of extreme importance, since social location, influenced by one's position in relationships of power, determines how one sees the world, how one constructs reality, and, eventually, how one interprets the biblical text. Biblical interpretation is never done in a political vacuum. Factors that determine identity — like race, gender, economy, age, and political power — influence interpretation. If this is true for the reader of the text, it is equally valid for the one who produced the text.

The common denominator between the essays in this volume is the focus on the world of text production: Berquist raises questions about the writing of historiography during the Persian period while postulating a world of text production for the Deuteronomistic History which he regards as a fantasy of an alternate

---

1 My understanding of an ethics of reading the Bible is based on Elizabeth Schüssler Fiorenza's seminal article "The Ethics of Biblical Interpretation: Decentering Biblical Scholarship," *JBL* 107 (1988), 3–17.

world detached from the reality of empire. Brett doubts that the Deuteronomic theologians or Second Temple historiographers engaged in forging "national identity," although he does not deny that each new historical challenge evokes a revision of identity — identity was not the overriding issue. In fact, Brett finds the use of modern theories on the construction of identity anachronistic, since he regards modern identity as being constructed in a different way. Jonker's contribution stands in contrast to Brett's point of departure. Jonker deliberately employs social identity theory and accepts that the biblical text is part and parcel of the dynamic process of identity (re)formulation. Leuchter's essay inquires into the identity of Ezra in Ezra-Nehemiah from the point of view of the socio-political context of Yehud. He acknowledges that the Persian paradigm brought a huge challenge to the descendants of ancient Israel in seeing themselves as part of and not excluded from empire while holding on to some elements of their heritage. Mitchell inquires into historiography and the process of Othering that is a prominent feature of historiography. She asks whether Chronicles presents the reader with such a process. Spronk's essay puts the book of Judges as a late construct (thus more or less contemporaneous with Qohelet) on the table. He shows how the book could have functioned if it was linked to a world of text production much later than traditionally anticipated.

The overarching theme of these essays is the relationship between identity formation and the production of texts. I will first put the hermeneutical problem on the table, namely that of relativity. Since identity plays an important role in most of these essays, I will then proceed with a discussion on identity formation, followed by a discussion of text and power, the public transcript, and memory.

Theoretical Considerations

Taking seriously Brett's warning of anachronism in rendering the socio-political location too absolute in searching for identity issues in the biblical text as if in a modern sense, the question one is stuck with is the following: How does one construct knowledge about ancient society?

Berquist refers to the distinction of *emic* and *etic*, which he does not think is sustainable, "because both ancients and moderns are involved in identity construction as they reflect on the same texts and imagine historical contexts for them" (p. 12). Mitchell's reference of seeing one's own reflection in the text becomes a problem when it happens at the cost of looking behind the text.

These remarks allude to the age-old hermeneutical problem of the biblical text belonging to one culture and the reader belonging to another. Cultural relativism holds that texts from one culture are basically inaccessible and totally irrelevant to another culture. Cultural relativity holds that texts from one culture, while tinged by that particular culture and therefore only understandable relatively to the particular culture, are nevertheless accessible to someone from another culture.

Brett seems to be wary of ignoring the historicity of the text in the Bible as well as that of the current reader. He problematizes the socio-political location of the reader by inquiring into the frameworks readers employ in the reading of the biblical text. He asks if readers bear in mind the difference between their own reading framework and the text in terms of time as well as culture. His hypothesis is that it is anachronistic to read identity issues into the biblical text if identity is understood in a modern sense. He refers to the egalitarian impulse — a characteristic of modern nationalism — that is being read into the biblical text, for example Eskenazi's understanding of Ezra-Nehemiah as a challenge to elite groups in order to promote a more egalitarian solidarity of Judeans based on ethnic affinities rather than on hierarchy.[2] His remark that it is "important to bear in mind that modern nationalisms have habitually veiled their histories of suppression" (p. 33) is of considerable value when one takes the recent history of colonialism into account. In this history, the biblical text was employed as a matrix of action for the conquest of the Americas, Africa, Australia, and Asia.

Ignorance of the historicity of the text and the readers' own historicity caused the issues of identity and power — raised in the biblical texts (such as in the story of the conquest and entrance into the Promised Land) — to find a strong structural resonance within colonial circles. For example, the Hexateuch's concern for the covenant between YHWH and Abraham, Isaac, Jacob/Israel and his progeny comes at the cost for the indigenous inhabitants of the Promised Land. In Gen. 15:13-14 it is stated clearly that the Promised Land does not belong to Israel but to various other groups (Gen. 15:18-21), yet Abram and Lot acted as if these groups do not exist in distributing the land between them! A reader might ask how would Abra(ha)m's descendants eventually take occupation of the land. From a perspective ignoring the Canaanites, the answer inevitably is the conquest, as suggested in Deut. 7:12: God will give the inhabitants over to the Israelites who will defeat and utterly destroy them; they will receive no mercy! Worse, the absence of concern for the plight of the indigenous people like the Canaanites became the matrix for an interpretation of the Bible that sanctioned colonialism.[3] Brett argues that English nationalism in the sixteenth-century was modeled on Deuteronomy.

---

2 T. C. Eskenazi, "The Missions of Ezra and Nehemiah," in *Judah and the Judeans in the Persian Period* (eds. O. Lipschits and M. Oeming; Winona Lake: Eisenbrauns, 2006).

3 M. Prior asserts in his book *The Bible and Colonialism. A Moral Critique* (Sheffield: Sheffield Academic Press, 1997), p. 39, that the notion that God instigated the Israelites to exterminate the Canaanites in fact "sanctioned the British conquest of North America, Ireland and Australia, the Dutch conquest of South Africa, the Prussian conquest of Poland and the Zionist conquest of Palestine."

The lack of concern for the indigenous inhabitants of the colonized countries reflected what Michael Prior called "a deeply ingrained Eurocentric, colonialist prejudice which characterizes virtually all historiography, as well as the discipline of biblical studies."[4] To quote Berquist: "Scholars read the Deuteronomistic History, and become imperial themselves" (p. 10). Not only do readers ignore the otherness of the text that is honored by cultural relativity, but the story's non-recognition of the legitimacy of the Canaanites inhabiting land enables them to be totalized and denied an own identity.[5]

Identities

In general, identity asserts what people have in common with one another and what differentiates them from each other. It is for this reason that an identity can be enabling as well as troubling. On the one hand they provide bedrock for a person's existence and social belonging, but on the other hand identity needs to be continuously reinvented. Subsequently, an identity that excludes, provides fuel for many violent disputes around the world whereas identity that provokes hierarchies of power within a group may turn identity itself into a battleground.[6] While the books of Joshua and Judges illustrate the violent nature of an excluding identity, Brett illustrates how identity itself became a battleground in the opposition to the foreign women in Ezra-Nehemiah. He is unable to find anything defiling about strangers in priestly theology. To him, the ethnic purity propagated by Ezra-Nehemiah is but one model with the Persian period providing evidence of *competing* models.

But identity is not always harmless or enabling. The experience of apartheid forms the socio-historical background of Jonker's essay. During apartheid and in its current aftermath blackness and whiteness still operate like a chessboard where things are strictly white and black, with no in-between. Yet both are relative conditions where identity is constructed in relation to the racial other.[7]

---

4 Ibid., p. 39.

5 I understand totalisation in a Levinas sense, namely "a denial of the otherness of the 'Other', a non-recognition that the other person is a real person existing apart from one's interpretation of him or her. With totalisation the 'Other' is reduced to something the 'Other' refuses to be reduced to." See G. Snyman, "Rhetoric and Ethics: Looking at the Marks of Our Reading/Speaking in Society," *Communicatio* 28/1 (2002), 39–48 and idem, *Om die Bybel Anders te Lees: 'n Etiek van Bybellees* (Pretoria: Griffelmedia, 2007), pp. 139–50.

6 J. Weeks, "Necessary Fictions: Sexual Identities and the Politics of Diversity," in *Sexualities and Society. A Reader* (eds. J. Weeks, J. Holland, and M. Waites; Cambridge: Polity, 2003), pp. 122–31 (123).

7 T. Morrison, *Playing in the Dark. Whiteness and the Literary Imagination* (Cambridge: Harvard University Press, 1992), pp. 44 and 59 argue that blackness in the USA, backgrounded by rawness and savagery, provides a stage for a quintessential American

Christine Mitchell employs the process of Othering as a principle of historiography. She asks whether Chronicles conforms to the principles of historiography. She argues that there is a clear link between historiography and identity formation as can be seen in the books of Kings and Ezra-Nehemiah. She is not so sure about Chronicles, since Otherness functions here in a way quite different from the way it functions in Kings or Ezra-Nehemiah. In Assyrian and Neo-Babylonian historiography Otherness in terms of nationality or ethnicity is defined along the binaries of human–animal or man–woman. In Persian historiography Otherness is depicted along a dualism of the Lie and the Divine. In Greek historiography Otherness is depicted in terms of antonymic pairs: Greeks versus Barbarians. This means that without Barbarians there would be no Greeks. It is an oppositional form of identity formation which Mitchell then sees in Judges and Kings with their negative language or negative marking. She argues "[p]erhaps, rather than looking at Israel in the Deuteronomic materials as being positively constructed, we could consider Israel as being negatively constructed: what it is *not* rather than what it *is*" (p. 102).

Opposition identity formation is at its strongest in Ezra-Nehemiah where identity is constructed by a definite Othering of excluded groups by building a wall and expelling the other from within, i.e., the strange women. Regarding Chronicles Mitchell sees that in terms of the practice of ancient historiography the Other is marked at the beginning of the text, i.e., in 1 Chron. 1:35-54 where one finds the genealogy of Edom. Edom is constructed as the opposite of Israel and eventually subjected and subordinated to Judah, thus firmly put in its proper place. However, Mitchell thinks that most of Chronicles is not that concerned with foreigners. They are present, but not in an antagonistic way. The Edomites do not appear everywhere. One possibility is to declare Chronicles as being not historiography after all. Another possibility is to see the inclusion of the Other (the Edomites) as a nod to generic conventions instead of manifesting an overriding thematic fascination with the Other like in Hellenistic historiography with its oppositional form of identity formation.

Identity assumes fixity, yet confirms diversity and difference. Once an identity is constructed, it becomes fixed and establishes a stable category for society that will then not allow a person any autonomy in choosing an identity. When an identity becomes fixed, an impersonal power structure via the public transcript starts to regulate the performance of that identity.[8] For example, the demise of apartheid did not mean that race has suddenly become a non-issue. In redressing

white male identity. Blackness forms a dark and abiding presence, without which whiteness is "mute, meaningless, unfathomable, pointless, frozen, veiled, curtained, dreaded, senseless, implacable."

8 Weeks, "Necessary Fictions," 124.

the past, racial identity remains an issue. Companies need to publish the racial composition of their employees annually. To this end, a particular form needs to be filled out in which the employee has to indicate whether he or she is African, Asian, Colored, White, or Other. These are identities fixed by a power structure and a white person who regards him- or herself as an African cannot choose to be an African.

Leuchter argues that the character in Ezra-Nehemiah should be understood as a reaction against an earlier fixity of identity that occurred in the Neo-Babylonian period. The latter caused the exiles to retreat into the older traditions where lines were drawn between disparate socio-religious groups with polemical stances taken between them. Says Leuchter, "This created a crucible for reifying older cultural and kinship-based standards of identity, regardless of whether or not they were capable of carrying on in any practical sense under the conditions of exile or forced migration" (p. 60). In the Persian period, the fixed patterns of lineage hierarchy were reinterpreted under the abiding presence of imperial power.

However, since one has multiple social belongings, identities remain provisional and cannot be treated as if they embody unique truths about people. For this reason identity acts as "relay points for a dense network of interconnected differences that involve gender, nationality and age as well as sexuality."[9] This means that, in order to hold on to his or her vulnerabilities, a person is continuously constructing and reinventing his or her identity in tandem with the demands and opportunities of a world that is in constant flux.[10] Berquist's remark about the Deuteronomistic History as a transfer of allegiance to the Persian Empire can be understood in the sense of reinventing oneself in the light of a new political reality, especially when he argues that people would have read the text as part of becoming Persian vassals, as beginning to see themselves as parts of empire rather than as members of a separate state.

The sources employed to construct an identity depend on a variety of social bonds, which present one with fragments of experience, which are glued together to construct a mosaic of images refracting the group's history. Identity is deeply historical, yet they operate on a contingent level in that the dominant form of any social position becomes the norm at any given time.[11] Its arbitrariness creates oppositional identities in a distinctive process of categorization, which, in turn, expose what has been obscured from recorded history. However, its arbitrariness and contingent nature implies that identity has a fictional nature, albeit necessary fiction! Its fictional nature enables one to challenge history's rigidity in

9 Weeks, "Remembering Foucault," *Journal of the History of Sexuality* 96 (2005), 186–201 (192).
10 Weeks, "Necessary Fictions," 125.
11 Ibid., 126.

constructing narratives of the past in order to imagine the present and the future.[12] Berquist does not employ the term fiction, but rather refers to fantasy, which he deemed important for the construction of identity.

Because of the categorization that goes with identity construction, identities are sites of contestation. As is succinctly illustrated by Ruth Frankenberg's study on whiteness,[13] the dominating identity speaks from a position of assumed naturalness that belies its historical and contingent nature. The opposing identity serves as a fiction that offers an imagined alternative. Its openness, fluidity, and conditional nature offers an opportunity of reinvention. However, once the fictional identity becomes closed, that is, the exclusive home of those who identified with it, identity becomes at that moment fixed, inexorable, and an expression of essential qualities.

Identity provides coherency to life and expresses certain values that people share with one another and which differentiate them from others with whom one cannot identify.[14] The existence of a strong identity is a precondition for social advance and for the development of an agenda.[15] Did the need for a strong identity become acute in the early years of the Persian period? When one looks at the oppositional identity formation in Ezra-Nehemiah, it is apparent that there was a group of people who assumed power in Jerusalem on behalf of the Persian imperial power. This group was in desperate need to legitimize the subordination of those around them. Subordination would only have succeeded if they could claim an authentic identity. Chronicles probably brought such authentication with a peculiar genealogical structure. Would the formation of an authentic identity have been possible without the construction of texts?

Text and the Power to Produce Texts

Christianity and Judaism are called book religions. Their sacred scriptures function as prime sources for their respective religious and theological underpinnings. Apart from being attributed divine power of some sort (different kinds of inspiration), some of the books these two traditions share (OT/HB) came into being because of political power. I think it is fair to assume that in the socio-political circumstances in which these texts originated, the author would wield

---

12 Ibid., 129.

13 R. Frankenberg, *White Women, Race Matters: The Social Construction of Whiteness* (Minneapolis: University of Minnesota Press, 1993).

14 Weeks, "Necessary Fictions," 123. The fact of multiple social belongings means that identities are hybrid and heterogeneous. A single person may establish a few possible identifications across boundaries of a lot of potential differences that refuse precise categorisations, and in the process challenging the identity enforced by the public transcript.

15 Ibid., 194.

some power based on the economic conditions required to make the activity of writing possible. Text production, being an expensive, difficult, labor-intensive, and time-consuming process, had to be an economically supported and a politically driven venture by people with ways and means. Text production required money and specialized knowledge.[16]

Texts were not written to be read at leisure. They had economic and political functions, so any scribal activities would be sought for at a scribal school linked to some kind of political administration. In keeping commercial records, they exerted control over the economy. In keeping the archives, they controlled knowledge of the past, the formation of new traditions, as well as the legitimacy of the ruling elite.

Who would have been responsible for the texts in the postexilic period? To write a text such as Chronicles would have required time, money, resources, motivation, and, above all, particular writing and text production skills. The archival nature of Chronicles suggests that the author(s) could be linked to the temple given the hierocratic governing system of the time. One would expect them to write what their paymasters told them to write, or, at least, to write in such a way that they would not endanger the power of their paymasters. These scribes were not working for government, so to speak. They were part of the governing structures, so that they were to a degree insulated from popular culture.

Given the limits of literacy levels in ancient Yehud it is fair to assume that any scribal activity lay within the hands of those who exerted political and economic power. Writing involved professional administration and the latter, in turn, related directly to the seat of power in ancient Near Eastern culture. So, the writing of books such as Chronicles or Ezra-Nehemiah would have taken place at or near the center of power. In controlling the contents, the ruling elite was able to create and establish a public transcript whereby they could explain why they were in power and why society needed to be structured in a particular way. With this public transcript, they created a portrait of themselves as they wished to see themselves and how others needed to see them.

According to Spronk, the first few chapters of Judges is a recapitulation of the book of Joshua, but not with Joshua as the main character taking over from

---

16 Reading D. W. Jamieson Drake, *Scribes and Schools in Monarchic Israel: A Socio-Archaeological Approach* (Sheffield: Sheffield Academic Press, 1991), there appears to be a definite link between literacy and the upper classes of ancient Israelite society. I. Young, "Israelite Literacy: Interpreting the Evidence, Part II," in *VT* 48/3 (1998), 408–22 attributes writing to army officers and the priests. An army tended to be bureaucratic and would guard the monopoly of the ruling elite. Priests apparently took over the administration in the postexilic period, but Young does not want to push that point too far. The use for literacy Young places at the cult as well as the administration. But he is at pains to emphasize that there was not a general literacy. Literacy was limited to the upper class of society.

Moses, but Judah taking over from Joshua. Judges attempts to put Judah in a more favorable light than the book of Joshua did. Judah is not to be blamed for failing to drive out the Jebusites from Jerusalem, but the Benjaminites. Judah conquered Jerusalem, subdued Gazah, Ashkelon, and Ekron. Judah is appointed by YHWH.[17] In Judges then, Spronk detects what Mitchell calls "oppositional identity formation" (p. 102) whereby a core group regards itself as in opposition to other groups.

What good reasons would the socio-political context in the third–second centuries have provided that warranted a public transcript that is more favorable to Judah than its portrayal in the book of Joshua? Does this focus reflect that particular consciousness that led to the formation of Judaism in the early Second Temple period?

Identity and the Public Transcript

A public transcript suggests a discourse in public by which the ruling elite maintain its power and the subordinates their position of subordination. A text as part of this public transcript presents readers thus with a *self-portrait* of those in power as well as the ideologies they want the subordinates to accept. But the text alone cannot tell the whole story about power relations, especially in a context of totalitarian or authoritarian power. The mask with which subordinates receive the text would be stereotypical and ritualistic, offering a public performance of deference and consent, but privately attempting to discern the real intentions and mood of the potentially threatening power holder.

Jonker focuses on the link between historiography and identity, or between the production of texts and identity. He uses the term *textual identity* from social psychology whereby identity is, *inter alia*, performed, enacted, and embodied through a variety of linguistic (and non-linguistic) means. Jonker alludes to the idea of a self-portrait in his use of self-categorization theory whereby similarity to a relevant prototype is being accentuated. According to self-categorization theory the in-group defines itself according to the terms of their in-group prototype, resulting in in-group normative behavior and self-stereotyping. The process is depersonalizing as the group regards themselves and others as interchangeable exemplars of the group prototype. Thus a group identity describes what it means to be a group member as well as prescribes the attitudes, emotions, and behaviors appropriate in each context.

17 Spronk also argues that the stories in Judges are modeled after similar stories in Samuel; for example, the narrative of the Levite cutting his dead wife in twelve pieces corresponds to Saul sending pieces of his oxen throughout Israel. Samson's birth story is modeled after Samuel's birth story.

James Scott[18] says the following in this regard:

> The theatrical imperatives that normally prevail in situations of domination pro-
> duce a public transcript in close conformity with how the dominant group would
> wish to have things appear. The dominant never control the stage absolutely,
> but their wishes normally prevail. In the short run, it is in the interest of the
> subordinate to produce a more or less credible performance, speaking the lines
> and making the gestures he knows are expected from him. The result is that the
> public transcript is — barring a crisis — systematically skewed in the direction of
> the libretto, the discourse, represented by the dominant. In ideological terms the
> public transcript will typically, by its accommodation tone, provide convincing
> evidence for the hegemony of dominant values, for the hegemony of domin-
> ant discourse. It is in precisely this public domain where the effects of power
> relations are most manifest, and any analysis based exclusively on the public
> transcript is likely to conclude that subordinate groups endorse the terms of their
> subordination and are willing, even enthusiastic, partners in that subordination.

However, domination does not continue on its own momentum. It has to be continuously maintained by the dominant parties by symbolizing their power and
enacting it efficiently. In violent societies, symbolization and enactment would
happen by gun-toting soldiers around a bleeding corpse. In peaceful surround-
ings, every visible act counts, such as the production of a text manifesting and
reinforcing the social order prescribed by the ruling elite.

In reading 1 Chronicles 23–27 Jonker tentatively postulates the prototype of a
Levite in a generic sense. Levitical descent still carried weight, not only as fulfil-
ment of promises to the ancestors, but being active in the time of David would
have given them some clout in the socio-political context of Persian imperial dominance without a Davidic descendant on the throne. The self-categorization that
takes place favors a particular group, the Aaronites, who claim having received
special functions and duties in the temple with the Levites. The rest of the Levites
received no such directly acclaimed duties from YHWH. In this regard Jonker
says: "By emphasizing their special position and function and by indicating that
their status within the cult was legitimated by YHWH, these specific subgroupings would have bolstered their position over against other contenders" (p. 90).
The purpose of the public transcript is not to gain agreement, but to intimidate
and to overawe the recipients into a durable and expedient compliance. Its effect
on the dominant group itself is to self-hypnotize them to buck up their courage,
display their power and convince themselves of their high moral purpose.

---

18 J. Scott, *Domination and the Arts of Resistance. Hidden Transcripts* (Yale: New
Haven, 1991), p. 4.

A successful communication of a message of power and authority will have been manifested when the subordinates start to believe that the ruling elite are indeed superior and thus powerful. This impression enables the powerful to impose themselves on the subordinates. This they do by

- creating an appearance that approximates what the dominant parties would want the subordinates to observe;
- magnifying certain aspects to create awe and keeping certain facts out of the public eye, obscuring delicate facts that may be embarrassing;
- creating the appearance of unanimity among the ruling group and the appearance of consent among the subordinates.

The ruling elite will subscribe to the values that underwrite their privileges. But the dominated, the subordinates, the unprivileged, will not necessarily participate in rituals that mark their own inferiority. However, the dominated calculates in the daily course of life the degree of power, self-confidence, unity, and determination of the dominant. On the basis of their calculation they would adjust their behavior to the reality of power. As long as they are unable to penetrate the transcript of the powerful, they are obliged to make inferences from the text of power. For this reason the powerful would watch the reception of the public transcript very closely.

Jonker also suggests that the text indicates the community (which found itself in the changed political, social, and cultic reality of Persian dominance) tried to find continuity in the royal past in order to build up self-esteem, especially that of the subgroupings. In this way they could verify themselves against a bigger structure in order to find their rightful place in society. Jonker argues that this group would have achieved a better understanding of their role and status and their construction would have assisted it most certainly to enforce that understanding on society.

Chronicles is based on the royal history found in the books of Samuel and Kings, albeit with the addition of extra material called *Sondergut*. Chronicles changes what the other two books wanted their readers to remember. It provides a new official and public memory via a written text that forms part of the public transcript.

Memory and the Public Transcript

Berquist argues that the compilation of literature in the Persian period did not intend to provide a historical reminiscence but wanted an answer to the question "Who are the Yehudites?" (p. 6). However, memory cannot be excluded here, since what is being remembered and how it is remembered eventually fill the public transcript.

The memory being referred to here can be called the official public memory that functions within a group or a collective remembering the past.[19] The construction of official public memory takes place within a particular ideological framework that ultimately determines what is being remembered. One can speak of a calculated selectivity which affirms certain aspects at the cost of forgetfulness of others. What is being remembered and how it is remembered is determined by selection. The latter is directed by ideology which makes the official public memory reductive, evacuative, biased, and intentional.[20]

Memory is a struggle over power and who gets to decide over the future. If one can inscribe a particular memory in a pervasive way in a public transcript, those who succeeded in its inscription would exert social control over a group of people in enabling them to live a structured or ordered life. What is being remembered in the public transcript serves a political objective. Thus, the public transcript does not deal with objective facts, but with a narrative that is open to reconstruction in the service of other ideological impulses. This seems to be attested to by Spronk's reading of Judges and the role Jonker attributes to Chronicles. Official public memory does not recover a literal past, but functions as an impostor whose claims cannot be forensically verified.[21] But it does not mean it cannot construct a canonical past and provide dogmatic stability. Memory is not reliable, but it is the only recourse one has to the past:

> If we can reproach memory with being unreliable, it is precisely because it is our one and only resource for signifying the past character of what we declare to remember. No one would dream of addressing the same reproach to imagination, in as much as it has as its paradigm the unreal, the fictional, the possible and other non-positional features . . . To put it bluntly, we have nothing better than memory to signify that something has taken place, has occurred, has happened *before* we declare that we remember it. False testimonies . . . can be unmasked only by a critical agency that can do nothing better than to oppose those accounts reputed to be more reliable to the testimony under suspicion.[22]

Memory in the public transcript acts as a vehicle for social action to produce social identities. Berquist brings into the equation the means of authorship and archival preservation during the Persian period, the means an exilic Jewish

---

19 B. Havel, "In Search of a Theory of Public Memory: The State, the Individual, and Marcel Proust," *Indiana Law Journal* 80 (2005), 608–9.

20 Ibid., 633.

21 Ibid., 680.

22 P. Ricoeur, *Memory, History, Forgetting* (Chicago: University of Chicago Press, 2004), p. 21.

community in Babylonia did not possess. In focusing on the literary construction of identity in the Deuteronomistic History, he brings into play the role of power in the construction: particular imperial strategies that portrayed a picture of the Yehudites incapable of self-governance. After the Persian period, the Deuteronomistic History received a postcolonial life where the text imagines a world without empire, a recounting of how all conquests fail, how genocides destroy the aggressors as well as the victims and how monarchies dwindle and consume themselves.

His remarks reminded me of the so-called "new empire" which is portrayed as a postmodern empire without colonies, yet unable to function without the logic of race and coloniality.[23] In this new empire sociological and cultural signifiers replaced biological differences as the key representation of racial hatred and fear. Although all cultural identities are equal in principle, these differences in plurality are accepted as long as people act out their race. Racial differences remain necessary markers of social separation. Subsequently, race still permeates everything and enters the stage through the backdoor! An egalitarian society remains elusive!

Similarly, is a world without empire a world where the geopolitics of expansion, power, and control are absent? Or rather present but hidden? Existing but not recognized?[24] There is a naturalness regarding one's being in the world from a position of power. The latter provides a location of structured advantages of privilege; a standpoint or a place from which the ruling elite can look at themselves, at others and at society and a set of cultural practices that remain unmarked and unnamed.[25] Any system of differentiation will shape those on whom it bestows privilege by oppression. The question is whether its shaping force is recognized. Being part of the ruling elite generates a public and a psychological wage.[26]

---

23 M. Hardt and A. Negri, *Empire* (Cambridge: Harvard University Press, 2000), pp. 190–1.

24 N. Maldonado-Torres, "The Topology of Being and the Geopolitics of Knowledge. Modernity, Empire, Coloniality," *City* 8/1 (2001), 29–56. He argues that the appearance of multiculturalism hides a multiracism that only recognizes the right for differences within a domesticated regulative ideal of capitalism, market economy, and the liberal ideas of freedom and equality.

25 R. Frankenberg, *White Women, Race Matters: The Social Construction of Whiteness* (Minneapolis: University of Minnesota Press, 1993), p. 1. Her remarks regarding power relate to whiteness as it relates to the normative racial position in the USA against which everyone is measured.

26 D. Roediger, in his book *The Wages of Whiteness. Race and the Making of the American Working Class* (London: Verso, 1991), p. 13, has shown the psychological advantage whiteness once offered capitalist and industrial society. It is the sort of advantage apartheid too once promised to its adherents. This advantage refers to the public and psychological wage the white working class, as part of the racial grouping of the ruling elite,

It is a wage Leuchter thinks the community that produced Ezra-Nehemiah would tap into. Leuchter argues that the Persian conquest brought an end to oppositional identity formation. The descendants of Israel in Persia were no longer forced to identify themselves in contradistinction to Persian imperial power, but rather as part of that power, albeit with some grip on their own heritage. The Ezra that emerges from the books Ezra-Nehemiah reflects this tendency. Ezra's Levitical and Zadokite status reflects a position where Israel is no longer a nation among other nations, but a group of people within a pluralistic environment. A new identity emerges that transcends the older divisions and renders Zadokite and Levitical leadership compatible with each other. However, in terms of Diaspora and those who remained behind, oppositional identity formation still continues: "This combination was perhaps a necessary measure to reify the Yehudite community and its parent group in the eastern Diaspora against other social collectives in Yehud who could lay claim to authentic Israelite heritage and who fostered religious traditions that left little room for the former's system of thought" (p. 62). The presence of Yehud in the Persian period necessitated a redefinition of social hierarchies. The movement that embraced this regarded Ezra as a visionary who deemed it necessary to dissolve barriers in order to address the needs of a new reality. The historical Ezra remains hidden, and one would not know what he did in real life, but his memory lives on in a literary text where he became "a character of immense hermeneutical potency that channeled their own vision of Persian-period Judaism into an accessible form and an enduring context" (p. 63).

Conclusion

In terms of cultural relativity, the reading of the biblical text by necessity entails a cross-cultural exercise. Bible reading in this sense can even be described as ethnocentric, since the reader has to compare the text's background with that of his or her own.[27] Declaring a reader's socio-political location also helps with keeping the offensiveness of the text alive, so that the text's Otherness is affirmed and not negated.

Looking at the socio-political location of the world of text production brings certain forces into play that influenced the construction of the text. From an

received from being white in spite of low economic wages. Ultimately, in a racialized world the pleasure of whiteness functioned as a wage for white workers, i.e. a status and privilege conferred by a particular race's powerful position that was used to make up for alienating and exploitative economic relationships.

27 S.-K. Wan, "Does Diaspora Identity Imply Some Sort of Universality? An Asian-American Reading of Galatians," in *Interpreting Beyond Borders* (ed. F. Segovia; Sheffield: Sheffield Academic Press, 2000), pp. 107–31 (108).

ethnocentric hermeneutical perspective it is possible to read identity issues into the text of Chronicles and Ezra-Nehemiah. While Brett's cautioning remarks about anachronism should be taken to heart, the boundary maintenance that occurs in Ezra-Nehemiah with the banning of the strange women and Chronicles' focus on genealogies for the first nine chapters may cause readers to inquire into identity issues in these texts.

But what exactly necessitated these texts? The book of Judges revealed textual affinities with other texts that were written much later than the book of Judges was thought to originate. But textual affinities are insufficient. The social location of the author would bring the context of the writing of a text under the magnifying glass.

The notion of a public transcript may be helpful in this regard. The notion assumes the written text plays its part in establishing or maintaining a particular view on those in whose midst the text functioned as an exercise in subordination. If the text is related to power, then one can assume there will be a level of self-categorization in the text that provides a self-portrait of those who think they are in command in a particular context of social belonging.

Power meant the authors or their paymasters had access to the official public memory which they then changed to suit them better in a changed socio-political context. A text like Chronicles appears to be an excellent illustration of how an official public memory can be changed when the ideological framework in which it used to function changed. However, such a memory alludes to a process of *mythopoesis*, the manufacturing of myths, i.e., the establishment of a new Torah narrative that functions as a master narrative of a new identity. Concerns with historical fidelity are less important than the construction of a narrative that simplifies a complex past.[28] History wants to discover the literal past. A text as part of the public transcript imposing itself as memory, acts as an impostor, yet constructs a canonical past.

---

28 See Havel, "Public Memory," 632.

"Continuing These Conversations"

Jacob L. Wright

I would like to begin by expressing my appreciation for the opportunity to respond to these papers. The model here of essays followed by responses has long been adopted in other disciplines, and I hope that biblical studies will increasingly take this route. If my remarks in what follows tend to be on the critical side, they should not be confused with a disparagement of the papers or what these respected scholars have otherwise contributed to the field. If I have misunderstood or misrepresented their views, I beg of them forgiveness.

Christine Mitchell's essay makes a case for "otherness" as constituting a central feature of historiography. Her aim is to raise the possibility that "Chronicles is not a work of historiography at all, or, if it is, it is a radical innovation in *the fundamental rules of the genre as understood in antiquity*" [italics added] (p. 93).

In order to establish empirically what these rules were Mitchell surveys a range of ancient chronicles and inscriptions. She begins by noting that from an early period "Mesopotamian identity was being constructed in relationship to an Other" (p. 94). This statement is, however, a truism for all identity construction. I am not sure how else the self could be affirmed, if not by affiliation or identification with someone/something and simultaneously separation from someone/something else.

It is true that the Mesopotamian chronicles and inscriptions have some sort of "Other" in view. By their very nature they focus extensively on royal activities; hence they devote a great deal of space to military feats and (subsequent) construction projects, in keeping with the long-established expectations for successful rulers.[1] Because the entries (especially the Assyrian annals and

---

1 See J. L. Wright, "Military Valor and Kingship: A Book-Oriented Approach to the Study of a Major War Theme," in *Writing and Reading War: Rhetoric, Gender and Ethics in Biblical and Modern Contexts* (eds. B. E. Kelle and F. R. Ames; Atlanta: SBL, 2008), pp. 33–56.

chronicles) deal so often with wars and campaigns, the enemy is necessarily present. Whether "the Other" plays a large role in these chronicles and inscriptions, and constitutes a constitutive element of the historiography, is, however, a different question.

Mitchell correctly observes that in many of the texts she examines "the Other is multiple, nefarious, and spread throughout the land" (pp. 94–5). In a study of *kitru* (and *puḫru*) Mario Liverani has discussed at length this aspect of enemy construction in various contexts.[2] With respect to the enemies in chronicles and inscriptions, one should, however, distinguish between "normal" foes and those who are identified as far beyond the bounds of usual deviance. In the latter case, the "Other" is regarded as not male or not human (having the physiognomy of animals, behaving like apes or dogs, not bleeding when hurt, etc.).

The inscription of Šamšī-ilu, the "field marshal" (*turtānu*) of Adad-nīrārī III, is a bit curious as an illustration of the way one constructed "the Other" in Assyria. The quoted phrase from the lion inscription (the Urartian king "had not established relations with any previous king") is a stock expression signifying something that never happened or had been achieved previously. Likewise, the names of the two stone lions are typical for apotropaic figurines.[3] Yet the most interesting feature about the Šamšī-ilu inscription is that it is not the reigning king, who was an exceptionally weak ruler, but rather his presumptuous official who "established his name" through the commissioning of these inscriptions. The text says less about the construction of a non-Assyrian "the Other" than about dividing the Assyrian "self" into two, which would potentially lead to a *coup d'état* or even civil war.[4]

Although Mitchell's discussion of the Greek material is generally helpful, one thing that needs to be noted — or at least stated more clearly — is the strikingly open, non-chauvinistic, inquisitive, and almost cosmopolitan character of Herodotus' writings on other peoples and customs. This is also the point of Hartog's *Memories of Odysseus*: It is not simply the fact that "the Other" is present in and indeed formative for Herodotus' work. What Hartog investigates is rather *how* "the father of history" represented this difference (i.e., the linguistic, rhetorical and philosophical means). In so doing, Hartog shows that Herodotus is much more fascinated with otherness and difference than in documenting Greece's great victory.

With respect to the criteria used to identify historiography, the presence of

---

2 M. Liverani, "Kitru, Katāru," in *Mesopotamia* XVII (1982), 43–66.

3 See F. A. Wiggermann, *Mesopotamian Protective Spirits. The Ritual Texts* (Cuneiform monographs 1; Groningen: Styx & PP Publications, 1992), pp. 14–15, lines 195–205.

4 On Šamšī-ilu, see now A. Fuchs, "Der Turtān Šamšī-ilu und die große Zeit der assyrischen Großen (830-746)," *Welt des Orients* 38 (2008), 61–145.

cross-references to other sources, which one finds throughout Samuel, Kings, Chronicles, and Ezra-Nehemiah, is an interesting suggestion. On the basis of this criterion, one would have to include also the Pentateuch and Joshua, yet exclude Judges, even though many would agree that the latter qualifies superbly as history writing (not least because its authors have collected local narratives and aligned them according to a collective "national" narrative, much like the early historians of Germany and Italy did). Furthermore, one would have to account for the presence of these references in biblical literature that no one would think of calling "historiography."[5]

I would argue that little is accomplished by expanding the definition of the genre "historiography" to include "the use of the Other." I am not sure what a history or a narrative of any sort would look like without the presence of some sort of "Other" in it. Conversely, I am not sure why one should confine the definition of history to narratives that focus on "the Other." To demonstrate the importance of this criterion, Mitchell appeals to Greek writings. On the basis of this material, she argues that Chronicles cannot so easily be defined as historiography since "the Other" figures here less prominently than elsewhere.[6] Even if one could agree that a focus on "the Other" is indispensable in Greek historiography, the question deserves to be asked: Why should one allow Greek history writing to be the standard according to which material from other cultures is judged?

In criticizing Sara Japhet for not defining her use of the term of "history," Mitchell remarks that one must first raise "the larger question of what historiography in the *ancient* sense of the term might be" [original italics] (p. 108). In addition to reminding the reader that Japhet's essay emphasizes method, structure, and overarching guiding principles as indispensable to history writing (and which are clearly identifiable in Chronicles), I would suggest that Mitchell's statement problematically presupposes not only that a work of literature adheres predominantly to one basic genre but also that the ancient authors thought in terms of "the fundamental rules of the genre" (p. 93). The problem with this presupposition is that after more than two millennia, one has still failed to come up with a definition of — or approach to — historiography that all can accept. That "the writing of history is generically structured by the narrative of the problems of binding the singularities of events and their multiplicity of times into the

---

5 See the discussion in K. M. Stott, *Why Did They Write This Way?: Reflections on References to Written Documents in the Hebrew Bible and Ancient Literature* (New York: T&T Clark, 2008).

6 I am not sure why Mitchell claims that "Ezra-Nehemiah says the defeated enemy *is* a woman. Because the Other is found within, it must be expelled" [original italics] (p. 103). There are several problems with this statement, but one of the most important is that *men*, not women, are identified as culpable in Ezra-Nehemiah and that women are never expelled in the book.

coherence of a structural explanation," as John Frow defines the enterprise, might apply to broader accounts of places and peoples, but it is ultimately inadequate as a definition for what many classify as history.[7] For example, T. P. Newcomb and R. T. Spurr's *A Technical History of the Motor Car* (1989) is a fine example of history writing, but it — and many other shorter works (*histoire événementielle*) on technologies, institutions, and social groups — would be disqualified on the basis of Frow's definition.

While it is a useful and important task to investigate the influences and frame-work informing the composition of a given literary work, I am not sure why one should use a body of literature from one culture as the basis for defining a genre and then conclude that a body of literature from another culture does not fit this genre. The motivation is explained in the concluding paragraph: "All of this rumination is really about meaning. . . Genre is the framework for the contract between the author/text and reader, but when the socially grounded basis for the framework is not shared, in essence the contract is broken" (p. 109).[8] This anxiety that the covenant between author and audience may be broken impels Mitchell to search assiduously for the genre that the Chronicler adopted; she finds it in "political philosophy" (p. 108) based on the model of Xenophon.[9]

Mitchell's anxiety is perplexing. Chronicles is such a fun book to teach in Intro courses because, in contrast to many other texts in the Bible, genre does not pose a major problem: the primary *Vorlage* (or at least a version of it) is there for students to see precisely where the author innovates.

Furthermore, I am not sure I can accept Mitchell's view of texts and the activity of reading. Even when sharing the same culture ("the socially grounded basis" [p. 109]), the reader must necessarily allow for freedom of the author to adopt and mix literary forms/genres/styles. Indeed, this freedom is critical to the effectiveness and longevity of a work. If there is a contract between author/text and reader, it is that the former, rather than abiding by "the fundamental rules" (p. 93), will offer the latter *rich material to play with*. Instead of having to decide between historiography or political philosophy as *the* genre for Chronicles, one can attempt to approach the work on its own terms, appreciating all its complex (material, stylistic, generic) interrelations with other texts as well as its ultimate creative distinctiveness.[10] And this approach is indeed what Mitchell models in her other studies of various issues related to Chronicles.

---

7 J. Frow, *Genre* (London: Routledge, 2006), p. 99.

8 The conception of genre as a contract is found elsewhere; see, e.g., R. Altman's *Film/Genre* (London: BFI, 1999), p. 14.

9 Mitchell does not discuss the relevant essays on this subject in M. P. Graham *et al.* (eds.), *The Chronicler as Historian* (JSOTSup 238; Sheffield: Sheffield Academic Press, 1997).

10 Here I am more sympathetic to Jon Berquist's suggestion, contained at the end of his

Like Mitchell, Louis Jonker sees identity as an important aspect of the historiography in general and Chronicles in particular. But I would once again ask: What is the alternative to "identity formulation"? (Perhaps a better term would be the more conventional "identity formation," since Jonker does not refer simply to the expression of identity but also its construction.) It is not a matter of *whether* historiography is related to identity formation but rather *how* and the *particular nature* of the identities being formed. Understood as such, all scholarship on the book of Chronicles has been concerned with various identities reflected in and constructed by the book of Chronicles; perhaps they have just not spent as much time theorizing it as such — for better or for worse.

On the assumption that Chronicles represents a Persian-period production, Jonker confines his discussion to historical dynamics shaping the Persian period. But given the fact that so many scholars agree that the chapters at issue (1 Chronicles 23–27) constitute a secondary interpolation into the book, it would have been advisable to take into consideration at least the early Hellenistic period. This wider purview would not only have extended the usefulness of the article but would also have potentially revealed that the text under discussion has much in common with Hellenistic-period sacerdotal texts and concerns.[11]

Much of this article consists of synopsis and overview of past scholarship, some of it is even explicitly second- or third-hand (see, e.g., Jonker's extended recapitulation of Lester Grabbe's view of Joachim Schaper's German monograph). The discussion here is nevertheless useful. It highlights many important research insights and introduces several new ones. Yet despite the new insights or the review of research, Jonker claims at the outset, and then again later, that his paper does not intend to offer new analyses of the text, and that most of the textual phenomena he treats have already been long described by others. Instead, he states that his aim is to offer "an alternative methodological vantage point that could potentially enrich our understanding of Chronicles" (p. 68). Herein again lies the problem: I am not sure that this "alternative methodological vantage point" (i.e., "identity formulation") (p. 68) is really all that new or an alternative to what has been done previously. No one would disagree that these chapters are related to identity construction, and the processual and pragmatic-rhetorical understandings of the way texts construct identity have long been common features of biblical interpretation. Hence what is ultimately decisive — where the rubber of this long-accepted theory meets the road of texts — is the specific

---

essay, to think of genre more as "uses of texts."

11   In addition to Jewish texts, see also the striking similarities to Seleucid Babylonian temple rosters studied by my respected teacher Laurence T. Doty ("Cuneiform Archives from Hellenistic Uruk." Ph.D. diss, Yale, 1977) as well as G. J. P. McEwan (*Priest and Temple in Hellenistic Babylonia*. Freiburger altorientalische Studien 4. Wiesbaden: Franz Steiner, 1981).

nature of the identities being constructed. It is all about the fine nuances, and these require us to focus our attention back on the literary subtleties in search of new arguments and evidence that would assist us in assessing competing interpretations. And in this respect, Jonker has a lot to offer.

Mark G. Brett's paper recognizes the problems posed by the term "identity" and its use in "metacommentaries" on ancient societies. Brett begins by discussing an important book, David Goodblatt's recent *Elements of Ancient Jewish Nationalism*. In particular, I welcome Goodblatt's departure from the modernist position in the study of nationhood and nationalism,[12] and his use of the term "nation," rather than "ethnicity," to describe the vision of political community set forth in many biblical texts. It would be interesting to learn how Brett distinguishes between "ethnicity" and "nation." In my own work, I use the term "nation" as consisting — often though not necessarily — of multiple "ethnicities" as well as socio-economic groups. According to my definition, "nation" is the ultimate category for a collective with shared patria (historic or actual), calendar, language, memory, ideals, etc.

I agree wholeheartedly with Brett's emphasis on the horizontality of the nation — the overarching *unity* of the constituent social components and the *participation* of these components in the process through which the fate of the whole is determined (i.e., enfranchisement).[13] Of course, this horizontality may often be more about self-understanding than actual practice.[14] But Brett rightly notes that one can trace a direct line from the "brother" rhetoric in Deuteronomy to the rise of conceptions of nationhood in sixteenth-century England.[15]

With Adrian Hastings, one might be able to find a connection between the

---

12 For a discussion of the modernist versus perennialist positions in research on nationhood, see A. D. Smith, *The Nation in History* (The Menachem Stern Jerusalem Lectures; Hannover: University Press of New England, 2000), pp. 27–51.

13 In the biblical vision of the nation of Israel, these components include territories, cities, towns, clans, households, tribes, classes, guilds, and even kingdoms (viz., the states of Israel and Judah).

14 National memories are inherently — or at least pretend to be — multivocal. They do not necessarily silence the voice of the king, rulers, or elites. Yet in order to be called "national," they must subsume this voice to a broader corporate perspective or amplify it with other voices. The *state* inscriptions and iconographic images found in the Iron Age Levant and throughout the ancient Near East tend to focus on the feats of the king for the people. Their subject is the "I" of the ruler. In contrast, the subject in *national* memories is the "we" of the people or the name of this collective group, very similar to what we find in the Hebrew Bible.

15 For an important study of this Deuteronomic use of "brother" and its biblical reception history, see L. Perlitt's "'Ein einzig Volk von Brüdern'. Zur dtn. Herkunft der bibl. Bezeichnung 'Bruder'," in idem, *Deuteronomium–Studien* (FAT 8; Tübingen: Mohr-Siebeck, 1994), pp. 50–73.

translation of the Bible into vernacular languages, on the one hand, and the emergence of national consciousnesses in early modern Europe, on the other.[16] Yet as I show in my current book project, *War and the Formation of Society in Ancient Israel*, the strongest expressions of nationhood are found in the face of defeat. As Ernest Renan observed in his famous essay "Qu'est-ce qu'une nation?" (1882): "Where national memories are concerned, griefs are of more value than triumphs, for they impose duties and require a common effort." Similarly Schiller wrote after the defeat of the Germans in 1801, "the German Empire and the German nation are two separate things. The majesty of the German people has never depended on its sovereigns. The strength of this dignity is a moral nature. It resides in the culture and character of the nation that are independent of its political fortunes."[17] Under such conditions of defeat, not only self-consciousness (the "imagined" aspect of community, according to Benedict Anderson) but also some attempt to foster the participation of various factions is critical if the nation is to be a successful political model. Asserting the necessity of creating a national identity in the aftermath of defeat, Rousseau wrote after the partition of Poland by Russia in 1768: "The virtue of its citizens, their patriotic zeal, the particular form that national institutions can give to their spirit, that is the only rampart always ready to defend it [Poland], and which no army could breach. If you arrange things such that a Pole can never become a Russian, then I assure you that Russia will never subjugate Poland."[18]

Rousseau's method for arranging things "such that a Pole can never become a Russian" involved not only giving him/her a voice in the political process and share in future prosperity but first and foremost shaping the individual into a citizen through *enseignement* and *éducation*, which he describes in his favorite work, *Émile, ou De l'éducation*. The collective could responsibly determine its fate only

16   A. Hastings, *The Construction of Nationhood: Ethnicity, Religion and Nationalism* (Cambridge: Cambridge University Press, 1997). Although the Shalem Center in Jerusalem and its publications (e.g., Hebraic Political Studies) have worked to awaken greater interest in the impact of the Old Testament on early modern political theory, much remains to be done in this area of biblical reception history.

17   Quoted from: E. Renan "What is a Nation?" in *Becoming National: A Reader* (eds. G. Eley and R. G. Suny; New York and Oxford: Oxford University Press, 1996), pp. 41–55, here p. 53; F. Schiller, *Sämtliche Werke. Vol. 2* (Stuttgart: I. G. Cotta'sche Buchhandlung, 1844), pp. 396–7.

18   J. J. Rousseau, *The Political Writings* (ed. by C. E. Vaughan; Cambridge: Cambridge University Press. 1915), p. 43. One could mention many more examples of defeat (sometimes more mythical than historical) inciting national consciousness; e.g., the Battle of the White Mountain (*bílá hora*) (1620) in Czech national consciousness, the Battle of Kosovo (1389) for Serbs, the Battle of Mohacs (1526) for Hungarians, or the "Genocide of 1915" for Armenians. For France in the wake of the Franco-Prussian War and Germany following World War I, see W. Schivelbusch, *Die Kultur der Niederlage* (Berlin: Fest, 2001).

if its constituent members were properly instructed in the nation's history and laws.[19] As I show in my book, similar principles may be discerned within biblical texts. The land ideal according to which each tribe, clan, and family should possess its own inalienable territorial portion is closely related to its pedagogical ideal that parents educate their children — especially the fathers teaching the male children, who are assumed to be the primary bearers of memory (cf. זכר with זכרון). This grand pedagogical project not only creates "the people of Israel" but also represents the primary force propelling the composition of the Bible itself.[20]

These ideals, along with laws that establish or maintain a balance of political and religious powers, are not features of some form of egalitarianism that many see as inherent in ancient Israelite tradition or Yahwistic religion. Nor does this vision of nationhood necessarily represent advancements toward a morally superior social order. Rather it should be seen, I argue, as a direct pragmatic response to anticipated and actual loss of territorial sovereignty,[21] similar to the way Schiller and Rousseau recognized that the German and Polish *nations*, in contrast to states and sovereigns, can withstand military defeat. Accordingly, the biblical discourse on the nature of peoplehood and Israel's collective (or national) identity — and by extension, all the various themes in this discourse, whether it be land, law, theology, ethics, calendar, national festivals, etc. — owe themselves to the encroachment of imperial powers and their ultimate subjugation of the states of Israel and Judah.[22]

---

19 A number of studies treat the place of education in the formation of nationhood; see, e.g., N. Davidson, *The Origins of Scottish Nationhood* (London: Pluto Press, 2000).

20 Although I am suggesting that this pedagogical function is already operative at the *inception* of biblical literature, see David Carr's suggestion that the final shaping of scripture should be seen in terms of a Hellenistic-style anti-Hellenistic curriculum (*Writing on the Tablet of the Heart*, New York: Oxford University Press, 2005).

21 I would offer this comment as a historical contextualization of the important observations with respect to pentateuchal polities made by J. Berman in *Created Equal: How the Bible Broke with Ancient Political Thought* (New York: Oxford University Press, 2008).

22 This statement is made in conscious departure from positions that identify the composition and compilation of much of biblical history and laws as "writing by the state." (The position has its origins ultimately in the Hegelian principle that "states make [and write] history.") See, e.g., M. A. Sweeney, *King Josiah of Judah. The Lost Messiah of Israel* (Oxford: Oxford University Press, 2001), W. M. Schniedewind, *How the Bible Became a Book: The Textualization of Ancient Israel* (Cambridge: Cambridge University Press, 2004), and I. Finkelstein and N. A. Silberman, *David and Solomon: In Search of the Bible's Sacred Kings and the Roots of the Western Tradition* (New York: Simon & Schuster, 2006). The most explicit proponent of this position is Schniedewind, who extends the position of Frank Moore Cross to encompass all of biblical literature: "Fundamentally, the writing of the exilic period was an extension of writing by the state. It was writing by and for the Judean royal family. The royal family is the only social setting suitable for writing substantive literature during the exile" (p. 164). In fairness to Schniedewind, his conclusion rests on an inability

Indeed, the Bible represents, I suggest in my book, the earliest expression of division between what political scientists would call "state" and "nation." The transmitted shape of the Primary History (Genesis-Kings) places the land and those institutions that cannot withstand the threat of imperial subjugation, such as the monarchy and a standing professional army, in relation to a prehistory when the land was not yet in possession and those institutions had not yet been established. In this way, the land and these institutions are shown to be historically important yet not essential to the identity of the nation. The Pentateuch, as well as Joshua and Judges, never refers to an Israelite standing army and has very little to say about an Israelite monarchy. While the Primary History does not forget the important role played by monarchy and the professional army, it remembers them as *secondary* socio-political developments. Even the conquest of the land and the construction of the temple, while pivotal, are presented as occurring relatively late in the nation's history. This literary arrangement underscores the point that Israel constitutes a people not limited to its historical territory and longstanding monarchies, and it can survive without its temple and armies. A simple equation between people or nation, on the one hand, and the state and land, on the other, is therewith radical.[23] This division between nation and state, which anticipates later political theory and is arguably one of the sources informing this theory,[24]

to explain who otherwise could have financially supported the scribes responsible for the formation of biblical literature. Yet in claiming that the Persian period was one not of "creativity" but of merely "retrenchment" and "preservation," Schniedewind revives the old Wellhausian stereotypes against the postexilic Judean communities.

That the biblical authors wrote history in the face of defeat makes sense from a comparative perspective; see, e.g., R. Lentin, *Israel and the Daughters of the Shoah: Reoccupying the Territories of Silence* (New York: Berghahn Books, 2000); P. Gray and K. Oliver, *The Memory of Catastrophe* (Manchester: Manchester University Press, 2004); S. M. Weine, *Testimony After Catastrophe: Narrating the Traumas of Political Violence* (Chicago: Northwestern University Press, 2006). Significantly, the first resurgence of Jewish history writing in the Common Era was in the sixteenth century, after the expulsion of the Jews from Spain. This epochal change that shifted the center of Jewish life from the West to the East provoked the composition of numerous major historical works that treated the entire course of Jewish history from the time after the demise of the Second Commonwealth up to the expulsion. The question these works attempted to answer was, as Solomon Ibn Verga wrote in his *Shebet Yehudah*, "Why this enormous wrath?"

23 As for the distinction between nation and land, the name "Israel" most often refers to a *people*, not a territory, within biblical literature. This differs strongly from the trend elsewhere to identify the name of a people in relation to its land (and/or chief city). This conception is also found within the Bible, but it is much rarer than its use as the name of a people or its ancestor (Jacob).

24 For example, just as the biblical authors tell the history of the unified Israelite people in relation to the disunity of Israel's separate monarchic houses, tribes and territories, eighteenth- and nineteenth-century German thinkers often placed the history of multiple German

takes its point of departure from the imminent or actual loss of territorial sovereignty in Israel's and Judah's history. The discovery and construction of עם ישראל in biblical literature is made in direct response to the defeat of the state; the former presupposes the latter.

This critical role played by imperial pressure in Israel's and Judah's history is appreciated by Brett, who remarks that in response to Assyrian expansionism the authors of Deuteronomy (he identifies them problematically as "theologians") "reinterpreted earlier legal traditions in a manner that established the priority of national 'brotherhood' above the obligations of clans and tribes, at the same time establishing a division of powers that decentered the role of Judah's king" (p. 39). Brett correctly notes, on the evidence of more recent history, that "national identities were produced within territorial borders defined by the colonial powers, rather than by pre-colonial cultures . . ." (p. 37).

Brett detects a "nativist" political agenda in the book of Ezra-Nehemiah, which he identifies above all in the authors' opposition to intermarriage. He compares this political agenda to "an *overt* program [in anti-colonial movements] of reinstating 'indigenous cultural tradition' which is presented as unsullied and uniquely 'authentic'" (p. 37). Although I think that this comparison is worth pursuing, I cannot follow the direction Brett himself takes. As he points out, the modern anti-colonial oppositional discourses have the massive influence of the West in their sights. But nothing in Ezra-Nehemiah polemicizes against Persia or some sort of imperial culture. For example, it is not a world language like Aramaic (comparable to English) but rather equally small languages like Ashdodite that threaten the survival of "Judean/Jewish" (יהודית) (Neh. 13:24).[25]

Issues such as language and intermarriage are often very vexing in colonized lands and diasporic communities. Throughout Jewish history these issues have persistently occupied the attention of local communities. And indeed languages can fade into oblivion; intermarriage can quickly dissolve communities. I find it difficult therefore to accept that the references to these issues in Ezra-Nehemiah

---

states and principalities in relation to the history of the German nation. Indeed, many (not least Herder) pointed to direct analogies in this respect between Israel's and Germany's histories; see F. M. Barnard, *Herder on Nationality, Humanity and History* (Montreal: McGuill-Queen's Press, 2003), pp. 38–65. The perceived parallels between the relation of nation and state in the biblical memories of Israel and the contemporary context of German unification is arguably one of the reasons why German-language scholars produced many of the most influential paradigms for studying the composition of the Bible and the history of ancient Israel.

25 We cannot be sure what exactly is meant by the term יהודית ("Judean/Jewish"). The children "did not know how to speak Judean/Jewish" (אינם מכירים לדבר יהודית) is, I suggest, a way of saying they had lost their basic sense of what it means to be Judean/Jewish that expresses itself linguistically in the act of "knowing how to speak" in a certain way.

represent mere rhetorical constructions as part of some "'nativist' politics" of "ethnic nationalism," promoted "at the expense of other models" (p. 35) of horizontal solidarity. I also find problematic the statement that Ezra-Nehemiah has *"hardened* the opposition to *foreign women* beyond anything that we find in previous laws" [italics added] (p. 33). The text consistently points the finger at *men* who intermarry or permit intermarriage; women as a specific group are rarely culpable in the book (Noadiah in Neh. 6:14 is perhaps one such rare exception).

From these and other passages in Brett's paper, one could get the impression that Ezra and Nehemiah were chauvinistic hard-liners rather than the figures who established enduring strategies for Jewish survival under foreign rule, as they are commonly viewed in later Jewish tradition.[26] The strategies for survival consist once again of features that are indispensable in projects of creating national identities. For example, we can identify in the book an emphasis on enculturation in Israel's history and legal traditions through textual learning. Indeed the community is presented as acquiring the ability to read for itself without a prominent figure or guild that could monopolize interpretation.[27] Equally pronounced in the book, although more ideal than ever really practiced in Jewish history, is the move toward what we may call "mass enfranchisement." The community as a whole constitutes a leading protagonist, and decisions are regularly made collectively in the "congregation" (קהל or קהלה), where all men, women, and "those who could understand" are present.[28]

To return to the topic of identity, Brett's main point is that even when historical challenges evoked revisions of ethnic and national identity, "the overriding issues for the historical actors themselves would not have been the making of identity as such" (p. 40). This is not simply a claim about emic versus etic distinctions, but rather about the anachronism inherent in uses of the term identity in biblical scholarship. Brett draws directly on the work of Charles Taylor to affirm that

---

26 Brett's remarkable and important work, *Decolonizing God: The Bible and the Tides of Empire* (Sheffield: Phoenix, 2008), which I read subsequently, adds many nuances to the position set for this paper.

27 See T. C. Eskenazi, *In an Age of Prose: A Literary Approach to Ezra-Nehemiah* (Atlanta: SBL, 1988) and J. L. Wright, "Seeking — Finding — Writing," in *Unity and Disunity in Ezra-Nehemiah: Redaction, Rhetoric and Reader* (Hebrew Bible Monographs 17; eds. M. J. Boda and P. L. Redditt; Sheffield: Phoenix, 2008), pp. 277–305.

28 This attention to women as participants in the decision-making process (Ezra 10, Nehemiah 10) and during the reading of the Torah (Nehemiah 8; see Deut. 31:12!) is probably not motivated by a sense of fairness but rather pragmatically by an awareness that the people as a whole are stronger when all — especially women — are also educated and given a voice in determining communal policies. (This voice becomes audible in Nehemiah 10 after the earlier passive reading in Nehemiah 8–9.)

Protestantism created conditions of "social disembeddedness" that constitutes the precondition for our modern (i.e., constructivist) formulation of identity.

I agree that social upheavals brought by modernity have introduced unprecedented changes in European history, yet rather than applying Taylor's analysis of Western history in the direction of a universal Hegelian *weltgeschichtliche Kritik*, one could alternatively seek to demonstrate the manifold ways in which many peoples and communities have undergone radical and life-changing upheavals that produced similar social changes to those in post-Reformation Europe. In particular, biblical scholars and historians of ancient Israel can show the ways in which resistance to imperial pressure elicited developments that are very similar to the demystification, secularization, breaking of older social bonds, and "abolition of the enchanted cosmos" that Taylor, Weber, Hegel, and many others note for Protestant lands after Luther's resistance to and ultimate break with Rome.

I am therefore not sure that "the characteristic inability of earlier societies to imagine themselves outside of a particular embeddedness (in clans and tribes or sacred structures)" (p. 38) or of "choosing an identity" (p. 38) applies to all times and places. At least it seems to be at variance with the evidence of many biblical authors, especially of those responsible for the very book that Brett discusses at length. Throughout its pages, Ezra-Nehemiah reflects an anxiety over competing identities and the nature of being a Judean/Jew that presupposes the intentional and pedagogical, in addition to ethnic, character of national identity in an age of great political and social flux.[29]

This emphasis on intentionality and pedagogy in Judean/Jewish ethnic identity can be witnessed above all in the portrayal of Ezra and his impact. He is privileged with a prestigious pedigree (7:1-5), but the narrative shifts attention to his performance: He "*set his heart to study* the Torah of Yhwh, and to *practice* it and to *teach* statutes and ordinances in Israel" (7:10). Nehemiah 10 tells how a community, after being taught by Ezra, follows suit and ratifies a pact that helps demarcate their collective identity. That others in Judah did not "separate themselves" (10:29) and embrace this new identity is presupposed by the language of the pact itself and the surrounding narratives.

While also treating the subject of identity, Jon L. Berquist offers a critique focusing on the interpretation of the Deuteronomistic History. According to Berquist, the Deuteronomistic History has too often been read in an exilic context,

---

29   In the later stage of the book, this Judean identity is amplified to עם ישראל. The competing identities included not only ethnicities but also social classes: the aristocrats are Nehemiah's chief nemeses and are significantly also the ones most prone to intermarry with the same class in neighboring lands (see Ezra 9–10, but especially Neh. 5:1-13; 6:17-19 and 13:4-31). See the discussion of these passages throughout J. L. Wright, *Rebuilding Identity: The Nehemiah Memoir and Its Earliest Readers* (BZAW 348; Berlin: De Gruyter, 2004).

whereas one has largely failed to ask how these "Old Testament historical books" functioned within a Persian-period setting.[30] I agree that many scholars, on the basis of the additions in 2 Kgs 25:22-26 and 27-30, falsely date this historical work to the early Babylonian period. Additions to it probably continued into the Hellenistic period, when composition and collection of texts really began to flourish in Judah.[31] Yet if the work is primarily concerned with the postexilic questions "[w]ho are the Yehudites" (p. 6) and "where [do] the Yehudites fit into an imperial culture dominated by Persia[?]" (p. 6) then Berquist faces the problem of explaining why Persian presence is not more palpable in this work.

More problematic is Berquist's critique of the conventional interpretations that "place a priority" on the land and the institutions of the monarchy and temple. He traces these readings to a radical break from the original, intended function of the work. According to Berquist, the Deuteronomistic History was written by imperially sponsored scribes in the Persian period, and their objective in writing this work was to show that Judeans, due to a long history of political failures and poor self-governance, "should not be allowed self-governance, perhaps even for their own protection and self-interest" (p. 7). They are "better off without self-control" (p. 8). "The Deuteronomistic History does not end in longing for restoration, and there remains no sense that a renewed monarchy could do any better" (p. 8). The imperially sponsored scribes and other Judeans who read this work were to "see themselves as parts of the empire rather than as members of a separate people" (p. 8).

In the course of time, the work came to be misinterpreted by the inhabitants of "colonial Yehud" who discovered in this literature "a history that they claim as their own" (p. 9). "This claiming-as-their-own is not necessarily a historical reality or an ethnic reality; it is a matter of identity" (p. 9). The post-colonial readers who resist empire now find in the text "heroes of the past" such as David, Solomon, and Josiah "who resisted empire or ran their own politics" (p. 9). The text now functions in a new genre that is neither historiography nor historical fiction but rather "fantasy." By adopting such a reading strategy, these readers and later scholars can resist empire, but they can also become imperial themselves. How? "Repeatedly through the history of interpretation, the Deuteronomistic History has become legitimation for the rise of new monarchies" (p. 10). The theory of the Deuteronomistic History fuses Joshua-Judges-Samuel-Kings with a prior agenda: Deuteronomy. Yet it fails to do justice to the anti-monarchic

---

30   It seems that Berquist could have used a less anachronistic term than "Old Testament books" when describing biblical literature from the Persian period.

31   Berquist's argument against the Babylonian provenance of the work would have benefited from engagement with the extensive defense of this position in Schniedewind, *How the Bible Became a Book*, pp. 139–94.

statements in this book. In short, the Deuteronomistic History "concerns itself [. . .] with the impossibility of human governance" (p. 11).[32]

These conclusions go beyond anything that has yet been written on the Deuteronomistic History. I would agree with the point that past readings of the Deuteronomistic History overlook the real weight of the work on the pre-monarchic period. But instead of interpreting the books of Joshua-Kings as an attempt to show that Judeans should give up any attempt of self-governance, I would argue, as alluded to in my discussion of Brett's paper, that the authors endeavor to *contextualize historically* a period of territorial sovereignty: Israel existed as a people long before it possessed its land; it is more than its land and its monarchic houses; the land is a divine gift that can be revoked; but once it is lost, Israel can continue to exist as a people as it did before the conquest of the land and construction of the temple.

In the books of Kings, which is most important for Berquist's argument, the temple represents territorial sovereignty inasmuch as it is built at the height of power. I find it difficult to accept Berquist's suggestion that the authors of Kings aimed to show how the gradual denudation and ultimate destruction of the temple was inevitable and imperial conquest was positive. The story in Kings is one of defeat. However, the fact that it concludes with conquest does not mean that the authors set forth foreign subjugation as the ideal. To the contrary, the ideal in this story is the beginning, where Solomon reigns in peace and prosperity, albeit not without problems. Solomon is presented as a great and opulent host who entertains at his table guests from far and wide. The book shows how in the end the tables are literally turned, with a Judean king now sitting not in the seat of the host but rather in the seat of the hosted (2 Kgs 25:27-30). The account, as Gerhard von Rad and many after him have noted, contains a glimmer of hope: Jehoiachin enjoys favor despite the circumstances. But the hope is not a life in perpetuity as a guest at someone else's table but rather the possibility of one day performing again the role of host. For the authors of Kings (in sharp contrast to those of the Esther scroll), these commensal arrangements required a form of territorial sovereignty similar to that granted to Solomon.[33]

There are other points that deserve at least a brief comment. First, scholarship on the Deuteronomistic History is increasingly turning its attention to the

---

32 What then is the alternative to *human* governance? Berquist offers "faith" as an answer in a similar article; see his "Resistance and Accommodation in the Persian Empire," in *In the Shadow of Empire: Reclaiming the Bible as a History of Faithful Resistance* (ed. R. A. Horsley; Louisville: Westminster John Knox, 2008), pp. 41–58.

33 See J. L. Wright, "Commensal Politics in Ancient Western Asia Part I," to appear in *ZAW* 122/2 (2010), and idem, "Commensal Politics in Ancient Western Asia Part II," to appear in *ZAW* 122/3 (2010).

formation of the Enneateuch or Primary History (Genesis-Kings) and the precursors to this extensive work.[34] Many would now agree that it is very unlikely that Joshua 1 represents the introduction of a large history (Joshua-Kings). In addition to Genesis, which at one time was probably transmitted independently, Exodus-Joshua and Samuel-Kings seem to have once existed as separate (and perhaps originally competing) histories. Berquist's criticism of scholars for not confining their attention to Joshua-Kings is accordingly problematic and does not speak to current research directions. Given this state of scholarly discussion, any treatment of the Deuteronomistic History must begin with the context of the larger Enneateuch.

Second, Berquist implies that Deuteronomy is opposed to native government by stating that scholars have failed to account fully for the book's anti-monarchic statements. Not only is "anti-monarchic" not the same thing as being opposed to native government, but I maintain that the book cannot even be designated "anti-monarchic." It seriously confines the jurisdiction of the monarchy so that a native Judahite king would likely not have looked kindly on the book, but it does not proscribe the institution completely.

Third, Berquist tries to eliminate positive attitudes toward "human governance" (p. 11) in Joshua-Kings by critiquing scholars who allow Deuteronomy to set the agenda for the reading of these books. But he inexplicably does not address the array of texts remaining in these books that present both the negative and positive side of government and territorial sovereignty.

Fourth, one is not sure what Berquist is referring to with his statement that readers and later scholars become "imperial" themselves when they have historically used the Deuteronomistic History as justification for establishing new "monarchies." Whatever the intention of this statement may be, it conflates imperialism with a much more moderate form of territorial sovereignty such as monarchies.

Finally, the choice to describe Yehud as a Persian "colony" is bewildering. By definition, colonies are established by non-natives. Aside from lending weight to the politicization of Second Temple studies, the point is simply historically false: Our oldest sources, such as the Nehemiah Memoir, know nothing about large scale Aliyot of Judeans back to their land and instead refer to the Judean survivors of the Babylonian captivity as the inhabitants of the province.[35]

Related to this discussion of the Deuteronomistic History, Klaas Spronk

---

34 See above all much of the recent work of Reinhard Kratz, Konrad Schmid, Eckart Otto, Jan Gertz, and Menachem Haran, as well many of the essays in M. Beck and U. Schorn (eds.), *Auf dem Weg zur Endgestalt von Genesis bis II Regum. FS Hans-Christoph Schmitt* (Berlin: De Gruyter, 2006).

35 See the discussion of Nehemiah 1 and 7 in Wright, *Rebuilding Identity*.

presents an interesting thesis: the book of Judges represents a late insertion between Joshua and Samuel, and was completed after the Greek translation of Joshua.

While Spronk's essay contains little in the way of defense of the first part of the thesis, he has a lot to say about the second part. This position — Judges as late insertion between Joshua and Samuel — is, however, not new. For many years now scholars have taken issue with traditional formulations of the Deuteronomistic History thesis by focusing their attention on the book of Judges.[36] Ernst Würthwein suggested that the earliest Deuteronomistic redaction, which created an extensive historical account, should be sought in the books of Samuel and Kings.[37] Similarly Reinhard G. Kratz has argued persuasively that the book of Judges represents a late literary bridge joining two earlier historical accounts: one recording the origins of the people of Israel in its land (comprising an early continuous layer that is isolated in Exodus 2–Joshua 11/12), the other narrating the origins of the kingdoms of Israel and Judah (comprising a redaction in Samuel-Kings), and both beginning with birth narratives (Exodus 2 and 1 Samuel 1). The lateness of the book of Judges is defended by appeal to various clues. For example, the expression "did evil in the eyes of Yhwh" is expanded in its horizon from Samuel-Kings to the later book of Judges: In the former, the subject of this action is Israel's kings; in Judges the identity of the culpable is "democratized" to include the people of Israel as a whole. Although Spronk refers at the outset to Kratz's book, he does not seem to be aware that it already presents a sophisticated version of the thesis he presents, or that this thesis builds on discussions conducted for many years in German scholarship.[38]

The way Spronk argues this thesis is, moreover, problematic. Although he makes many good observations on the connections between Judges 1 and Joshua 14–19, many scholars — indeed those who do diachronic analyses of Judges and thus who are most likely to be interested in his paper — consider Judges 1, the so-called "negatives Besitzverzeichnis" (Wellhausen), to be a *secondarily appended* pro-Judahite introduction to the book. Given this state of research, Spronk's insightful observations on Judges 1 will have no probative value for those scholars, like Thomas Römer and Christoph Levin, who remained convinced, *pace* Kratz's arguments, that the core of the book of Judges represents

---

36 See U. Becker, *Richterzeit und Königtum: Redaktionsgeschichtliche Studien zum Richterbuch* (BZAW 192; Berlin: De Gruyter, 1990).

37 E. Würthwein, "Erwägungen zum sog. deuteronomistischen Geschichtswerk. Eine Skizze," in idem, *Studien zum deuteronomistischen Geschichtswerk* (BZAW 227; Berlin: De Gruyter, 1994), pp. 1–11.

38 See the treatment of the book of Judges in relation to Samuel in Wright, "Military Valor and Kingship."

a constitutive narrative block in the framework of the Deuteronomistic History. For these scholars and others, Spronk's analysis will nevertheless be of value for the questions (dating and historiographical function) of Judges 1 itself. The same applies to Spronk's treatment of the relationship between Judges and the subsequent books traditionally attributed to the Deuteronomistic History. He focuses on the final chapters of the book that most people who do diachronic analyses agree were attached later to the core of the book.[39] It is not clear why, of all the texts he could have chosen, Spronk turned to these chapters to demonstrate that the book of Judges represents a late insertion between Joshua and Samuel.[40]

Spronk's discussion of the Samson story has the most evidentiary potential since it belongs to an older part of the book. With respect to the relationship between the Samson and Samuel birth stories in Judges 13 and 1 Samuel 1, I too am inclined to see 1 Samuel 1 as the older account. Yet Spronk does not present any new compelling argument in defense of this view. The clearest case for Samson (and Jephthah) beginning the wars against the Philistines and Ammonites ("begin to deliver") was made five years ago by the careful analyses in the award-winning book of Reinhard Müller, which Spronk does not cite.[41] Moreover, the new connections that he mentions are extremely tenuous.[42] Finally, the use of parallels to Greek literature as a basis for dating Judges should be balanced by an acknowledgment of the presence of many Greek literary motifs *also in the book of Samuel.*[43] Despite these problems with the essay, one must appreciate Spronk's important (independent) recognition that the book of Judges appears to have been inserted at a late point between Joshua and Samuel.

Finally Mark Leuchter has contributed an interesting paper that treats the figure of Ezra as a symbol in the book of Ezra-Nehemiah that transcends older sacerdotal divisions, comparable with earlier syntheses in such works as Deuteronomy or the entire Pentateuch.

---

39 Although I agree these chapters are later than the texts in Samuel he discusses, the correspondences he notes between them and the Samuel texts are not enough to convince anyone of his position. It is not enough to note a number of correspondences; one must develop some criteria for establishing a direction of dependency.

40 That some scholars have recently departed from this consensus regarding the lateness of Judges 1 and 17–21 does not provide Spronk a sufficient basis for attempting to make his case on these chapters.

41 R. Müller, *Königtum und Gottesherschaft* (FAT II, 3; Tübingen: Mohr-Siebeck, 2004).

42 They are: "Samson being driven by the spirit of YHWH like King Saul; Samson inventing a riddle and in this way showing himself to be wise like Solomon; Samson getting involved with foreign women, which recalls the risky marriage policy of King Solomon and of King Ahab; Samson bound and blinded like the last king of Judah, Zedekiah" (p. 24).

43 See, e.g., S. Isser, *The Sword of Goliath: David in Heroic Literature* (Studies in Biblical Literature 6; Atlanta: SBL, 2003).

Leuchter begins by drawing attention to the deliberate move on the part of Ezra-Nehemiah's authors to "obscure any clear view of Ezra at every turn" (p. 42). Yet this claim is questionable. I suggest that the elusiveness Leuchter observes in the depiction of Ezra has much more to do with the questions plaguing Leuchter than with the depiction itself: If the text presents an unclear image of Ezra with respect to his Zadokite versus Levitical allegiances, then perhaps the authors did not operate with these categories. In any case, I think one should proceed on the working assumption that the ancient authors (in contrast to the modern use of the "unreliable narrator") attempted to make their message as clear as possible rather than to obfuscate it.

It is not so patently obvious, despite Leuchter's assumption, that the authors highlight Ezra's Zadokite pedigree. The passing reference to Zadok (Ezra 7:1b-5) in the selective list of names leading back to Aaron, the first priest, cannot bear the significance Leuchter attributes to it. Accepting earlier suggestions that the whole passage represents a secondary accretion, he suggests that a later hand may have interpolated it as a response to challenges that local Zadokite authorities posed for Ezra's "mission." The text identifies Ezra as "one of their own" (p. 45). The suggestion is problematic given the absence of much explicit "Zadokite" material elsewhere in the book (see, however, Neh. 11:11). Instead of Zadok, the figure who stands prominently behind priests (over against Levites) in late editions of Ezra-Nehemiah is *Aaron* (in addition to this passage see also Neh. 10:39 and 12:47). This is in keeping with the move, consistent with the Priestly writing (P) and Chronicles, to identify all legitimate כהנים as *sons of Aaron*. In its focus on the Zadokites, Leuchter's paper proceeds as if this Aaronide polemic, which pervades so much of Second Temple literature, were not an issue.[44] Thus Leuchter argues that 7:1-5 traces Ezra's lineage primarily back to Zadok but "also opens the door to its extension back to Aaron, the purpose of which is related to the ritual re-enactment of the Exodus and Wilderness wandering" (p. 46).

As for the most important evidence in Leuchter's argument, the interpretation of Nehemiah 8, much rests on hypotheses that are themselves highly speculative. For example: "The H[oliness Code] authors, living and working in exile in Babylon, appropriated the methods of lemmatic exegesis earlier employed by the Deuteronomists as a way of superseding them as the undisputed theological-intellectual elite of their time and place" (p. 55).

That "the Deuteronomistic Levite tradition had blossomed in the eastern Diaspora as a distinct theological/intellectual institution" (p. 51) is possible,

---

44 This question becomes all the more acute given that the Aaronides seem to have been in tension with the Zadokites in Ezekiel 40–48 and much of late Second Temple literature. On Ezekiel 40–48, see T. Rudnig, *Heilig und profan: redaktionskritische Studien zu Ez 40–48* (BZAW 287; Berlin: De Gruyter, 2000).

but the one bit of evidence Leuchter produces cannot sustain this broad claim: "Considering the paucity of Levites in Ezra's delegation to Yehud (Ezra 8:15), it would seem likely that many Levites enjoyed a high degree of authority and influence in the eastern Diaspora and were reluctant to leave that behind . . ." (p. 51). This interpretation of Ezra 8 represents, I maintain, a misreading of the textual evidence. By allowing Ezra to tell how he discovered that Levites were missing from his entourage, the authors of this insertion in 8:15b-20 did not aim to say that Levites were reluctant to return to the Land, but rather that Ezra, a hero of the Restoration, recognized the importance of the Levites and would not budge before they joined his Aliyah. This is an example of sophisticated fiction with a polemic message. It may be compared with the emphasis on the contribution of the Levites in a number of late insertions in Ezra-Nehemiah and Chronicles affirming the superiority and indispensability of the Levites; it is especially similar to Neh. 12:27, 13:10-14 (cf. 2 Chron. 31:4-5), and 22. Moreover, the identification of Casiphia as "the place" (המקום) is not "identified in Deuteronomistic terms" (p. 52) but is indeed in opposition to it: in Deuteronomy "the place" represents the one and only cultic center in the Land.[45]

In general, Leuchter's paper assents to the wide array of interpretational possibilities and probabilities noted by prior scholarship, and it is exemplary in the secondary literature it cites. Yet one wishes for more sustained engagement with the competing claims and methodological disparities in this literature. Just like this essay sees the authors behind the portrayal of Ezra as great synthesizers of conflicting traditions, so is the essay itself synthetic in its approach to previous work. Such creative synthesis needs to be balanced with more focused analysis, yet one welcomes Leuchter's willingness to build bridges across interpretational divides.

In conclusion, I would like to thank the authors of these papers for their provocative contributions. I hope I have not misunderstood or misrepresented their views. And above all, I look forward to continuing these worthwhile conversations in other times and places.

---

45 That the emphasis on rebuilding gates in Nehemiah's account has anything to do with the gates as Levitical locales of jurisdiction in Deuteronomy is highly unlikely. One should, however, consult Leuchter's article, "Ezra's Mission and the Levites of Casiphia," in *Community Identity in Judean Historiography: Biblical and Comparative Perspectives* (eds. G. N. Knoppers and K. A. Ristau; Winona Lake: Eisenbrauns, 2009), pp. 173–96, which the author kindly forwarded to me. In it, he argues at length for the view defended here (viz., המקום as Deuteronomistic term).

Index of Biblical References

Genesis
15:13–14 135
15:18–21 135
39:2 23

Exodus
2 164
6:16–19 76
21–23 43

Leviticus
16 34
16:29 34
16:29–30 34
17–26 43
19 34
21:14 35
23 55
23:26–44 34
23:34–43 55, 56

Numbers
3:17–39 76
8:14 77
16–18 55
16:9 77
16:21 77
29:7–38 34

Deuteronomy
7:6 33
7:12 135
10:8 77
16:18–20 54, 56, 57
17:8–13 56
17:13 56
23:3–4 33
23:7–8 33
31:9–13 56, 57

31:12 159
31:25–26 57

Joshua
1 163
4:19–20 21
10 20
11–12 164
14–19 20, 164
14–24 20
15:13–14 19
15:15–19 19
15:63 20
16:10 19
17:11–13 19
19:19 20
24 19, 21, 24
24:24 21
24:28–31 21
24:31 21

Judges
1 19, 20, 22, 164, 165
1:1 23
1:1–3:6 21
1:2 20, 21
1:3 20
1:5–8 20
1:6 24
1:8 20
1:11–15 19
1:18–19 20
1:20 19
1:21 20
1:27–28 19
1:27–2:5 20
1:29 19
2 21, 24
2:1 21

2:1–10 21
2:2 21
2:7 21
2:7–9 19
3:12 18
4:19 25
7:6 25
9:8–15 25
11 26
11:29–40 26
13 23, 24, 165
13:2 23
13:5 23
13:7 24
16:3 24
17:1 23
17:6 21
18:1 21
18:5–6 22
18:30 46
18:31 22
19:1 21, 23
19 22
19:10–12 22
19:13 22
19:29 22
20–21 21
20:1 22
20:3 22
20:18 23
21 26
21:1 22
21:5 22
21:8 22
21:12 22
21:19 22
21:21 22

1 Samuel
1 22, 23, 164, 165
1:1 23, 47
1:11 23
1:19 22
2:11 22
7:5–14 22
9:1 23, 47
11:7 22
12 18
12:8–11 17
12:11 18
22:10 22
22:13 22
28:6 22
28:16 22

2 Samuel
2:1 22
2:3–4 24
5:6–12 20
11:22 18
21:20 23

1 Kings
12:31 44
15:3 102

2 Kings
10:29 102
12:3 102
12:19 102
14 107
23:1–3 54, 56
23:26–25:26 8
24:9 8, 116
25:22–26 161
25:27–30 8, 116, 161,
   162

Jeremiah
11:18–23 50
26–45 57
29:7 51
36:1–4 51
36:17–18 51
45 57

Ezekiel
2:8–3:3 53
40–48 33, 166
44:10–13 55

Zephaniah
1:1 47

Qohelet
4:13 28
10:17 28

Ezra
1–3 58
4–6 58, 129
4:1–5 102
6:19–21 35
7 57
7–8 42
7–10 43, 49, 53, 58
7:1–5 44, 45, 47, 52, 160, 166
7:1–6 54
7:2 46
7:6 52
7:10 160
7:16–17 48
7:21 59
7:25 48, 53
8 167
8:15 51, 167
8:15–19 33
8:15b–20 167
8:24–30 33
9 34, 54, 56
9–10 130, 160
9:1 33
9:1–2 33
10:8 77
10:16 77

Nehemiah
1 163
1:3 53
2:3 53
2:8 53
2:13 53
2:17 53
5 33
5:1–13 160
6:1 53
6:17–19 160
6:14 159
7 163
7:3 53
8 34, 43, 49, 54, 55, 56, 159,
   166
8:1–12 55
8:2 54
8:4 54
8:13 56
8:13–14 42
8:13–18 55, 56
8:15 55
8:17 56

8–9 159
8–10 49, 54, 56
9 54, 56
10 56, 62, 159, 160
10:29 160
10:39 166
11:11 166
11:19 53
12:25 53
12:27 167
12:28 35
12:30 53
12:47 166
13 54, 130
13:4–9 102
13:4–31 160
13:10–14 167
13:19 53
13:22 53, 167
13:24 158

1 Chronicles
1 103, 105, 106
1:35–54 105, 137
1:43 105
1:51 106
4 20, 28
6:1–33 76
13 106
13–16 106
13:5 75
15 106
15:3 75
16 106
18:11–13 106
20:6 23
22 72
23 80
23–27 67, 68, 69, 70, 71,
   72–83, 84, 88, 90, 118, 119,
   124, 142, 153
23:1 72, 74, 75
23:2 72, 73, 74, 75
23:3–5 77, 82, 83
23:3–6 73
23:4 73
23:5 73
23:6 75, 76, 80
23:6–13 73
23:6–24 82
23:6–27 76
23:13 77, 80, 82
23:13–14 73
23:15–24 73
23:15–32 73
23:24 77

23:25 77, 81
23:25–26 75, 77, 80, 82, 89
23:26 77, 80
23:27 77, 82
23:28–32 75, 77, 78, 80, 82
23:28 78, 81
23:30–31 78
23:32 77, 81
24:1–19 73, 79, 80, 81, 82
24:3 75, 82
24:4 74
24:5 74, 75
24:6 75, 81, 82
24:19 80, 82, 89
24:20 81, 82
24:20–31 73, 83
24:30 81
24:31 81, 82
25:1 74, 75, 76
25:1–6 73

25:7–31 73
26 106
26:1–3 73
26:1–19 77, 83
26:4–8 73
26:9–11 73
26:12–18 73
26:19 73
26:20–27:34 83
26:20–32 73
26:26 74
26:32 75
27:1 74
27:1–32 73
27:3 74
27:5 74
27:8 74
27:22 74, 75
27:23 75, 88
27:31 74, 75

27:34 74
28–29 72
28:1 72, 73, 74, 75
28:5–21 72

2 Chronicles
8:17 106
12:13 105
20 106
21 107
21:8–10 106
22:2 105
25 107
25:24 107
28:17 107
31:4–5 167

2 Maccabees
3:12 36

INDEX OF AUTHORS

Abrams, D. 68
Alonso-Núñez, J. M. 98
Altmann, R. 152
Anderson, B. 29, 31, 125, 155
Andersson, G. 16
Assis, E. 105–6
Auld, A. G. 4, 17, 117–8

Barnard, F. M. 158
Bartelmus, R. 23
Barth, F. 124–5
Baumgartner, W. 26
Beck, M. 163
Becker, U. 164
Becking, B. 4, 26
Bedford, P. R. 45, 62
Ben Zvi, E. 103–4
Berman, J. 156
Berquist, J. L. 6–9, 11, 68–9, 114–6, 125–130, 133–4, 136, 138, 139, 143–4, 152, 160–3
Blenkinsopp, J. 41–2, 84
Blum, E. 18, 117
Boccaccini, G. 42, 46, 52
Boda, M. 54
Boer, R. 10
Boroujerdi, M. 37
Bosman, J. P. 68
Brett, M. 29, 34–6, 40, 120, 125–6, 130, 134–6, 147, 154, 158–9, 162
Brettler, M. Z. 17, 100–1, 108, 123
Brewer, M. B. 70
Briffard, C. 25
Brown, J. P. 25
Burchell, B. 68

Campbell, A. F. 4
Carr, D. 94, 114, 156
Chapman, C. 96, 99, 103
Clines, D. J. A. 30

Cody, A. 84
Conversi, D. 37
Cross, F. M. 156
Cruesemann, F. 32

Davidson, N. 156
Davies, P. R. 31, 124
De Fina, A. 69
De Vos, J. C. 20
Diebner, B.-J. 25
Dimock, W.-C. 109
Dirksen, P. B. 68, 72, 77–8, 81
Doty, L. T. 153
Dozeman, T. B. 59
Duggan, M. 54, 56
Dutcher-Walls, P. 62
Dyck, J. E. 67, 104

Ehrensvaard, M. 114
Eskenazi, T. C. 32–4, 60, 135, 159
Esler, P. F. 103

Finkelstein, I. 156
Fishbane, M. 55–6, 61
Fowler, R. 98
Frankenberg, R. 139, 145
Fraser, C. 68
Frazer, J. G. 26
Fried, L 41, 43, 48, 58–9
Frolov, S. 19
Frow, J. 101, 108–9, 152
Fox, R. L. 99
Fuchs, A. 150
Fuhs, H.-F. 22

Gallagher, W. R. 95–6
Gaster, T. H. 25
Geertz, C. 40
Gergen, K. J. 68

Gerstenberger, E. 84
Gertz, J. 163
Giliomee, H. 65, 91
Glassner, J.-J. 94, 96
Glatt-Gilad, D. A. 47
Gnuse, R. 26
Goodblatt, D. 29–31, 36, 125, 154
Goswami, M. 37
Grabbe, L. L. 48, 83–87, 95, 153
Graham, M. P. 152
Gray, P. 157
Grayson, A. K. 94–5
Greenfeld, L. 32
Grosby, S. 29
Grundlingh, A. 66
Guillaume, P. 16, 116
Gunkel, H. 123
Gunneweg, A. H. J. 84

Hagedorn, A. C. 48, 61
Hall, J. M. 40
Halpern, B. 20–1, 32, 46
Hamilton, M. W. 95
Hanson, P. D. 50
Haran, M. 163
Hardt, M. 145
Harrison, T. 97
Hartog, F. 97–9, 150
Hastings, A. 29, 154, 155
Havel, B. 144, 147
Hayes, C. 35
Hens-Piazza, G. 4
Hirsch, S. W. 99
Hogg, M. A. 68–70
Holloway, S. W. 95
Hornsey, M. J. 70
Hudson, W. S. 32
Hunt, A. 42, 84, 85

Isser, S. 165

Jameson, F. 30
Jamieson Drake, D. W. 140
Janzen, D. 129
Japhet, S. 45, 58, 66, 68, 72–3, 102–3, 107–9,
    118, 151
Jonker, L. C. 67, 68, 76, 118–21, 124–5, 134,
    136, 141–3, 153–4
Joosten, J. 35

Kelso, J. 104
Kessler, J. 37, 89, 125
Klein, R. W. 68, 72–3, 77–9, 81, 119
Knohl, I. 34
Knoppers, G. N. 44, 59, 66, 68, 71–83, 103–7,
    118

Koch, K. 46, 48
Kraemer, D. 49, 54, 57
Kratz, R. G. 5, 15, 163–4
Kraus, H. J. 15
Kroeze, J. 78, 81

Laato, A. 95
Lake, M. 36
Lentin, R. 157
Leuchter, M. 23, 32, 42–3, 45–60, 62–3,
    119–20, 125, 129–31, 134, 138, 146, 165–7
Levin, C. 164
Levin, Y. 45
Levine, D. G. 99
Levinson, B. M. 32, 43, 50, 60
Lincoln, B. 97
Linville, J. 102
Liverani, M. 150
Luce, T. J. 98
Luckenbill, D. D. 95

Mandel, P. 43
Mantel, H. 62
Mbenga, B. 65, 91
McEwan, G. J. P. 153
McKenzie, S. L. 4, 68, 72
Meier, S. A. 15
Mendels, D. 29
Middlemas, J. 50
Milgrom, R. J. L. 34–5, 55
Miller, J. C. 31
Mitchell, C. 94, 101, 108–9, 118–9, 121,
    127–30, 133–4, 137, 141, 149, 151–3
Maldonado-Torres, N. 145
Momigliano, A. 97–9
Moore, G. F. 25
Morrison, T. 136
Mullen, E. T. 31, 101–2
Müller, R. 165

Naudé, J. 78, 81
Nauerth, C. 26
Negri, A. 145
Nelson, R. D. 4
Niditch, S. 114
Noort, E. 19
Noth, M. 4, 15–6, 117
Nurmela, R. 71, 84

O'Brien, M. A. 4
Oliver, K. 157
Olyan, S. 35, 41, 102
Otto, E. 32, 37, 163

Pakkala, J. 42, 44–6, 49, 52
Peltonen, K. 119

Perdue, L. 117
Perlitt, L. 154
Person, R. F. 4, 113–4, 116–7
Polaski, D. C. 8
Priest, J. F. 25
Prior, M. 135–6

Rake, M. 19
Renan, E. 155
Rendsburg, G. A. 54
Rezetko, R. 114
Ricoeur, P. 144
Rigsby, K. 36
Roediger, D. 145
Römer, T. 4, 6, 8, 26, 28, 114, 164
Rooke, D. 41
Rösel, H. N. 19
Rousseau, J. J. 155–6
Roshwald, A. 29
Rudnig, T. 166

Sancisi-Weerdenburg, H. 99
Schaper, J. 41, 50, 53, 71, 80–1, 84–7, 153
Scherer, A. 16, 126
Schiller, F. 155–6
Schivelbusch, W. 155
Schmid, K. 163
Schniedewind, W. M. 43, 53, 156, 161
Schorn, U. 163
Schüssler-Fiorenza, E. 133
Schwartz, B. J. 47, 53
Scott, J. 142
Shanske, D. 98–9
Shils, E. 40
Shotter, J. 68
Siedlecki, A. 104–8
Silberman, N. A. 156
Sivertsev, A. 62
Smith, A. D. 154
Smith, M. S. 51, 129
Smith-Christopher, D. 37, 125
Snyman, G. 136
Soggin, J. A. 27
Sourvionou-Inwood, C. 98–9
Sparks, K. 35
Spronk, K. 116–7, 126–7, 130, 134, 140–1,
   144, 163–165
Stackert, J. R. 43, 57

Stager, L. 46
Stainton Rogers, R. 68
Steiner, R. C. 41, 58
Stott, K. M. 151
Sweeney, M. A. 47, 50, 156

Tambiah, S. 38
Tan, N. 106
Taylor, C. 30, 33, 37–40, 126, 160
Tebes, J. M. 105
Thompson, T. L. 101
Tollefson, D. 35
Tuell, S. S. 72
Turner, J. C. 68

Vanderhooft, D. S. 44, 51
VanderKam, J. C. 49, 58
Van der Kooij, A. 21
Van der Merwe, C. H. J. 78, 81
Van der Toorn, K. 17, 27, 50, 52, 114
Van Midden, P. J. 17
Van Seters, J. 100–1
Verbrugghe, G. P. 100

Wan, S.-K. 146
Washington, H. C. 103
Watts, J. W. 42, 52
Weeks, J. 136, 138–9
Weine, S. M. 157
Weinfeld, M. 52, 61
Weitzmann, S. 36
Wellhausen, J. 164
Wells, B. 43
Whitebrook, M. 68
Wickersham, J. M. 100
Wiesehöfer, J. 99
Wiggermann, F. A. 150
Willi, T. 71, 84
Williamson, H. G. M. 35, 42–3, 53–5, 58–60,
   73, 83, 103, 118
Wilson, S 38
Wong, G. 16
Wright, J. W. 71–75
Wright, J. L. 42, 48, 58–9, 149, 159–60, 162–4
Würthwein, E. 164

Young, I. 114, 140
Younger, L. 101